	DATE DUE	
NOV 1 9 1999		
DISCARDED		

THE BRITISH MONARCHY AND THE FRENCH REVOLUTION

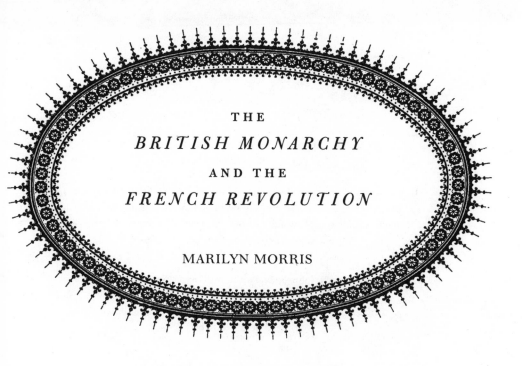

THE
BRITISH MONARCHY
AND THE
FRENCH REVOLUTION

MARILYN MORRIS

YALE UNIVERSITY PRESS   NEW HAVEN AND LONDON

Published with assistance from the Annie Burr Lewis Fund.

Designed by James J. Johnson and set in Monotype Bell and Bulmer types
by The Composing Room of Michigan, Inc.
Printed in the United States of America by Vail-Ballou Press,
Binghamton, New York.

Library of Congress Cataloging-in-Publication Data

Morris, Marilyn, 1957–
    The British monarchy and the French Revolution / Marilyn Morris.
        p.   cm.
    Includes bibliographical references and index.
    ISBN 0-300-07144-2 (cloth : alk. paper)

    1. Great Britain—Politics and government—1789–1820.   2. France—History—
Revolution, 1789–1799—Influence.   3. Great Britain—Civilization—French
influences.   4. George III, King of Great Britain, 1738–1820.   5. Monarchy—
Great Britain—History—18th century.   6. Monarchy—Great Britain—History—
19th century.   I. Title.
DA520.M67   1998
320.441′09′033—dc21   97–16330

A catalogue record for this book is available from the British Library.

1   3   5   7   9   10   8   6   4   2

Contents

Acknowledgments

Researching and writing this book has extended over three chapters of my own history—London, England; New Haven, Connecticut; and Denton, Texas—and I have incurred many intellectual, personal, and professional debts along the way. John Dinwiddy, my supervisor at the University of London, put me on to studying the monarchy. Most of the archival research on which this book is based came out of my doctoral dissertation, "The Monarchy as an Issue in English Political Argument During the French Revolutionary Era" (1988). I wish Dr. D. were here to see the result of this endeavor. My Ph.D. examiners, H. T. Dickinson and Alice Prochaska, offered useful suggestions for turning the dissertation into a monograph. At Yale University, Linda Colley's critique and encouragement inspired me to widen the scope of my study.

At the University of North Texas, as the manuscript pages rolled off the printer, Alex Pettit read them, circumvented many stylistic and organizational atrocities, set me straight about Bolingbroke, and rekindled my interest in eighteenth-century studies. D. Harland Hagler, who must be credited with keeping me sane throughout this process, then went beyond the call of duty by extending his editing skills on short notice. Paul Monod evaluated the manuscript at the request of Yale University Press. He provided a most thorough appraisal of the manuscript's strengths and weaknesses that ultimately gave me the courage to undertake major structural changes and to clarify my argument in places where I'd hedged. Denis Paz read the result and caught new errors I'd introduced during the course of my revisions. Any remaining defects are due to my own cussedness or inattention.

In the course of working on this project, I have tested out my ideas in seminar and conference papers at meetings organized by the Institute of Historical Research, American Historical Association, Southern Historical Association, Consortium on Revolutionary Europe, Hofstra University, and various branches of the North American Conference on British Studies. I have benefited from the advice of Bill Kuhn, Anna Clark, Rachel Weil, Jim Sack, Ian Fletcher, Penny Carson, Carole Taylor, Claire Daunton, Julie Flavell, Phil Schofield, John Styles, Michael Harris, and Jeffrey Merrick. David Kerr of Hampshire College inspired me to study history in the first place—thanks Dave. I am also grateful for the assistance I received from the librarians and archivists at the British Library; Institute of Historical Research; Public Record Offices at Chancery Lane, Kew, and Norwich; National Library of Scotland; Yale Center for British Art and Sterling Memorial Library at Yale University; and Willis Library at the University of North Texas, especially the Inter-Library Loan Office.

I am greatly indebted to my parents, Stephanie and Charles Morris, for their unfailing encouragement and financial backing of my education. My sister, Stephanie Choma, and her family have been instrumental to the preservation of my sense of humor and perspective. Nick Midgley provided support and companionship during the London years, and his family, Cynthia and John Midgley and Clare Midgley, opened up their homes to me, as did Henk van Kerkwijk, who presided over that haven of sustenance, entertainment, and creativity that was 83 Farleigh Road.

The personnel of various institutions also extended practical assistance for which I am grateful. I appreciate the efforts of Royal Holloway College's staff in helping me cope with the stress and expense of being a resident alien. The University of London and the Bentham Project at University College braved the wrath of the Home Office and obtained work visas for me. The Institute of Historical Research also furnished me with gainful employment and dispensed moral support. The Bentham Project introduced me to word processing and allowed me to use its computers after hours. I would also like to thank the Papers of Benjamin Franklin for giving me employment as well as access to the incredible facilities at Yale. The University of North Texas granted summer research funds and its history department offered essential patronage of this project. I appreciate the judicious teaching-load reduction, as well as Betty Burch's help in sorting out computer glitches, calming frazzled nerves, and dispensing chocolate as needed.

Finally, I would like to thank the many friends who continued to call me in spite of the dramatics and antisocial behavior that attended the writing of this book.

Introduction:
The Meaning of Monarchy

I N 1791 Thomas Paine inquired, "But, after all, what is this metaphor called a crown, or rather what is monarchy? Is it a thing, or is it a name, or is it a fraud? Is it a 'contrivance of human wisdom,' or human craft to obtain money from a nation? If it is, in what does that necessity consist, what services does it perform, what is its business, and what are its merits? Doth the virtue consist in the metaphor, or in the man? Doth the goldsmith that makes the crown, make the virtue also? Doth it operate like Fortunatus's wishing cap, or Harlequin's wooden sword? Doth it make a man a conjurer? In fine, what is it?" Paine posed these questions rhetorically in order to expose the monarchy as "all a bubble, a mere court artifice to procure money" and "the master fraud which shelters all others." He went on to observe: "It appears to be a something going much out of fashion, falling into ridicule, and rejected in some countries both as unnecessary and expensive."[1] Paine's prediction proved to be wildly inaccurate with regard to the British monarchy, at least. In fact, the key to understanding the reasons for the British monarchy's remarkable longevity lies in the events of the decade following Paine's premature reading of the last rites over the institution.

This book is an investigation into the ways the political exigencies and public discourse generated by the French Revolution helped lay the foundations for the modern British monarchy's character and ideology of justification. Paine's detection of a certain incoherence in royal rule was not completely off base; however, he failed to recognize the institution's capacity for resolving its inner contradictions as well as its ability to evolve when economic, political, and social changes threaten it with obsolescence.

After the Revolution of 1688 rendered the idea of divine right untenable, British kingship underwent what can be described as an identity crisis. The rise in the power of Parliament turned monarchs into political players and jeopardized their sanctity. After the succession shifted to the Hanoverian line in 1714, kings appeared to be even more dependent on their ministers. Moreover, the preoccupation of the first two Georges with Continental affairs, as well as their neglect of both royal ceremonial and patronage of native artists, helped beget a nationalism that was independent of the monarchy. The British-born George III reversed these trends.

Owing to a peculiar mix of forces and circumstances, the later years of George III's reign mark a major turning point in the history of the British monarchy. No longer politically absolute after the events of 1688–89, the monarch found a new social ascendancy. No longer a representative of God, the monarch became a cultural icon: the embodiment of a British heritage. George III's stolid patriotism, his dedication to the duties of kingship, and his paternal disposition helped shape the outcome of the debate on the French Revolution's implications for Britain. The dialectic between democratic reformers and supporters of the political status quo produced a species of kingship that melded patriarchalism with egalitarian republican ideals. In exploring the process by which the monarchy's image formed, I hope to enhance our comprehension of what monarchy represents in a democratic age, the functions it performs, and why it perseveres.

My goal in this book is to refine the theories presented by scholars from a number of disciplines who have attempted to pin down both the reason for the British monarchy's longevity and the source of its powers. Many who have examined the monarchy recognize a quality of duality at the root of the institution's charisma, yet they vary in what they conceive this duality to consist of. This line of investigation was launched by Walter Bagehot, who, on the eve of the Reform Bill of 1867, informed Queen Victoria's subjects that their monarchy was really a republic. In his exposition on the English constitution, Bagehot relegates the queen and the Lords to the "dignified" part of the government in contrast to the "efficient" Commons. The monarchy participates in another sort of duality within its lofty sphere; its splendor and pageantry preserve a link with the heroic past that stirs the patriotism of "the vacant many," while its complex constitutional role satisfies "the inquiring few."[2] Most scholars find this model untenable, yet Bagehot's perceptions of the

British monarchy's republican aspect, the importance of its historical resonances, and its multifaceted appeal reappear in subsequent studies.

John Cannon's longer historical view of the monarchy presents the institution's duality as a function of its ability to adapt to Britain's changing social, economic, and political conditions, a flexibility that he sees as the key to
its survival. Starting with the execution of Charles I and the subsequent le-
gitimizing ideology, which allowed for the survival of the monarchy in spite
of the death of the monarch, Cannon traces the process by which the institution came to terms with the aristocratic challenge of the seventeenth century, the reform movement of the eighteenth, nineteenth-century liberalism,
and the democratization of the state. The British monarchy preserved enough
of its forms and traditions to reassure supporters of the status quo while at
the same time adapting sufficiently to social and political change to satisfy
proponents of reform. For Cannon, the monarchy's duality goes beyond its
mixture of continuity and modification. He rejects Bagehot's bifurcation of
government and instead reinforces Ernest Kantorowicz's model of the king's
two bodies, the corporeal and the divine, which, Cannon argues, endows
monarchy with the combination of human and spiritual elements that subjects desire of their rulers.[3]

Kantorowicz's study of the symbolism attached to medieval kingship
shows that the sovereign's self-contained duality gained acceptance because
it emulated the Christian construct of the body and spirit of Christ. Legal fic-
tions impart divinity: the king never dies; the king can do no wrong; and the
king is always present, although invisible, in the courts of law. Sovereigns possess simultaneously the sympathetic frailties of their humanness and the awe-
inspiring omnipotence of their office. Their ability to switch back and forth
between their personal and public identities produces a divinity that is independent of any ideology purporting a divine right to rule.[4]

Tom Nairn also relies upon Kantorowicz's model in his critique of the
twentieth-century monarchical regime that, he maintains, has retarded British
social, political, and intellectual progress with its mind-numbing mystique. At
the root of this mystique is the twofold duality of the monarch: the human
frailty of the person and the strength and immortality of the office, as well as
the affecting juxtaposition of ordinariness and glamour. Royal personages
achieve their charisma by being "ordinary in appearance but quite super-or-
dinary in significance. . . . an interface between two worlds, the mundane one
and some vaster national-spiritual sphere associated with mass adulation, the
past, the State and familial morality." The mystery does not have to rely on a

sanctity derived from the monarch's association with an established church. Nairn perceptively suggests that by the end of the eighteenth century, history had replaced God. The collapse of the divine-right monarchy of the Stuarts left a void that was eventually filled by kings who embodied a "synthetic past [that] had turned into a version of national identity." The British monarchy's continued popularity is in a large part due to the flexibility of its image. As in the major religions, there is a version for everyone. "Men, women, children and different social classes all have their own Monarchy: 'Our own dear Queen,' in Piers Brendon's phrase. And yet this varying spectrum of emphases can also be *one*—reconciled at some deeper level by one enchanted glass."[5]

Nairn dismisses Bagehot's model as a "bit of self-congratulatory twaddle" and laments its mythogenesis in support of the idea that the working part of the government is democratic and that Britain is in fact a "disguised Republic." In actuality, the British government has preserved a monarchical framework in which the prime minister assumes the authority of an absolute ruler. Nairn likewise turns Cannon's thesis on its head by arguing that the monarchy had not in fact adapted to aristocracy, liberalism, and democracy; rather, the forces of modernity had been forced to accommodate the British monarchy and its "glamour of backwardness." He explains that the British have long deceived themselves by seeing their national identity in their monarchy, their "enchanted glass": "A gilded image is reflected back, made up of sonorous past achievement, enviable stability, and the painted folklore of their Parliament and Monarchy." Obsession with monarchy has become "a surrogate nationalism."[6] Bagehot's "inquiring few" are as deluded as his "vacant many."

The point at which these analyses converge is in their sense that the British monarchy achieved some mystical power by uniting antithetical qualities. The sovereign is kingly but republican, preeminent yet vulnerable, perfect yet flawed, strong but weak, permanent and ephemeral, sacred and mortal. Where investigations into monarchy's mystique tend to disagree is in its meaning: Is royal charisma a function of its long association with Christian divinity or of mythologizing and propagandistic manipulation? Or is monarchy somehow inherently sacred?

Some scholars think so. In a study of Queen Elizabeth's coronation in 1953, two sociologists, Edward Shils and Michael Young, observe that the monarchy acts as a repository for society's sacred beliefs. The ceremony provided an opportunity for subjects both to be touched by monarchy's spiritual power and to demonstrate their commitment to the shared moral values that the queen personifies: the values that give society peace and coherence. Shils and

Young conclude that the rationalist, intellectualist bias of the modern era discourages proper recognition of human spiritual needs. Contact with sacred institutions offers a rejuvenating transcendence from everyday existence.[7] Similarly, a team of political scientists from the University of Leeds interviewed spectators at the investiture of the Prince of Wales in 1969 and found that a majority displayed a deep emotional commitment to monarchy that went beyond the sort of idolatry associated with pop stars. The degree of moral excellence that the public expects from the royal family heightens the esteem in which subjects hold royalty. The Leeds study suggests that in the modern era Kantorowicz's model of medieval kingship obtains. The sovereign must be sacrosanct; a distant, dispassionate figure is necessary in order to appeal to the disparate groups that make up society, while the sacred figure of the monarch must have a personal side in order to captivate the emotions of individual subjects.[8]

Other scholars are dubious about royal sanctity; they look at the same images and rituals and come up with completely different interpretations. In response to Shils and Young, Norman Birnbaum observes that one should not make too much of the appearance of universal participation in the coronation because it had been a mandatory holiday. And as a holiday it had little connection with normal social relations and attitudes. One could as easily argue that the ceremony was less an affirmation of unity and support than an occasion for smoothing over and providing temporary relief from the usual dissension between the various classes in British society. Moreover, members of the royal family seem more like movie stars than sacred figures; they simply become the focus of their admirers' fantasies and self-identification.[9] Similarly unimpressed by the monarchy's mystique, Richard Rose and Dennis Kavanagh relegate the monarchy to the decorative role delineated by Bagehot. They maintain that monarchy survives as long as the royal family refrains from involvement in politics and instead presents itself as the guardian of order, unity, and moral excellence. Royalty does not enchant, it simply entertains. Rose and Kavanagh compare the queen to a picture on a box of chocolates— some people enjoy the picture while others ignore it; only a small minority refuse to eat the chocolates because of the picture on the box.[10]

Although these authors deny royal sanctity in a religious or spiritual sense, they do acknowledge that some sort of idolatry inhabits the way a significant proportion of the population regards royalty. Here Nairn's analysis becomes most useful. Because subjects each have their own vision of the monarch, different levels of meaning become attached to the monarchy. As Britain becomes an increasingly pluralistic society, the notion of sanctity itself has evolved and expanded. No longer dependent on Christian doctrine, the monarchy is sacred in that it is capable of affecting people in ways that extend beyond rational understanding, and, in turn, it receives protection from attempts to undermine this power.

One can see a species of secular sanctity in Freudian analyses of kingship, for example, that speak in terms of the psychological rather than spiritual needs that monarchs fulfill. Richard Gretton's definition of kingship encompasses all heads of state, including the presidents of republics, who satisfy the human desire for a sense of unity. Gretton explains that a monarchical regime acts upon a people in the same way that a personality functions in an individual: by smoothing over inner conflicts, contradictions, and inconsistencies to achieve a solid identity. Both processes involve shaping all the facets of a complex existence into a unified whole. Much as a personality imparts an individual's sense of self, kingship assures the existence of a nation as an entity. Gretton rejects the notion that heads of state are necessarily formal and ornamental. The strength of kingship does not consist merely in the ability to bestow an appearance of continuity. Indeed, monarchies that adapt to the changing characters of their people survive the longest. These regimes preserve their existence by providing orderliness: a fixed point of nationhood around which contradictory elements in the state can be organized. Kingship transcends contradictions and provides a shared truth, a focus for the common desire of disparate individuals for belonging and purpose.[11]

Ernest Jones, a pupil of Freud's, saw the psychology of monarchy's attraction operating on an even more fundamental level. According to Jones, most individuals long for a strong leader who will take responsibility for their impulses, while at the same time they harbor the conflicting desire to resist the oppressive nature of authority. Jones's analysis links the ambivalent attitude of the individual toward government with the working out of the Oedipus complex. The child perceives the father as more powerful, more beneficent, or more cruel than he actually is, and endows him with magical qualities. These irrational perceptions in the childhood unconscious carry over into the adult relationship with authority figures. Subjects have these same opposing impulses toward dependence and independence, affection and destruction. A constitutional monarchy that has a hereditary king as the symbolic ruler and an elected prime minister as the functional ruler allows a bloodless resolution of the patricidal impulse of the Oedipus complex. The ruler is in effect two persons: "one untouchable, irremovable and sacrosanct, above even criticism, let alone attack; the other vulnerable in such a degree that sooner or later he will surely be destroyed, i.e., expelled from his position of power." By presenting an idealized picture of statecraft, the monarch renders the banalities of governing magical; he lifts people out of "the inevitable sordidness and harassing exigencies of mundane existence."[12]

Some academicians are unwilling to accept explanations for monarchy's ability to beguile that leave us in the realm of the spiritual, the unconscious, the magical, or the irrational. Cannon, for instance, begins his case for adaptability being the key to the monarchy's survival by disputing the sociological and psychological explanations of monarchy's mystique. The psychological advantage of having an inviolable monarch and vulnerable prime minister does not satisfactorily explain the institution's longevity given that few of the surviving monarchies in the world are so constituted. The notion of shared values advanced by Shils and Young likewise defies positive proof. The supposition that an ingrained attitude of deference lies deep in subjects' psyche in monarchical states appears ridiculous after the "bon-bon" theory of Rose and Kavanagh, as well as the disrespectful actions of, say, the Russians, a supposedly deferential people who effectively did away with their own monarchy. Cannon asserts that it is simply the perpetuity and historical weight of the office that renders the monarch sacrosanct, while a willingness to adapt to change keeps the monarchy relevant.[13] Be this as it may, Cannon's explanation does not account for the emotional reaction that royalty is capable of generating.

Cannon does show some respect for the treacherous waters that he and his co-author, Ralph Griffiths, were entering as they embarked upon a popular history of Britain's royal regimes: "It is not always easy for the historian to recognize the realities of the situation when set against such lofty ideals and concepts." Their solution of striking a balance "between cynicism and sentimentality," however, further suggests the near impossibility of scholars being able come up with a rational explanation for monarchical power. Nairn warns that moving in close enough to observe royalty makes it difficult to maintain sufficient scholarly distance. "Both the personality of the Monarchs ('What they're really like,' etc.) and how they appear to their subjects have grown over-significant for deeply-rooted reasons. Before she knows what's happening, any scholar of these phenomena can find herself as 'obsessed' by them as the most befuddled onlooker at a Royal parade." As William Kuhn's research intimates, even critics of monarchy, including Bagehot himself, have a deep ambivalence regarding its sanctity. Kuhn demonstrates that managers of Victoria's court rituals, the ostensible controllers of public opinion and "inventors of tradition," were not immune from emotional reactions during royal ceremonial occasions.[14]

Nairn sees the tongue-tied befuddlement to which even the most august intellectual can be reduced in the royal presence as the effect of centuries of indoctrination. Manipulation of royal dualities allows the Crown to transcend class tensions and to deflect criticism. The institution is shielded by its personification, while its personnel are protected by the ideals attached to the institution. The monarchy's combination of the magical and the mundane persuades the working class to disassociate the royal family from the detested privileged orders—although its members undoubtedly belong to "a class where people are unduly well cared-for." The "symbolic cult-idea of Royal niceness" renders criticism of the royal family carping, churlish, ungallant, and, most important in a country imbued with the gentlemanly ethos of good sportsmanship, unfair. To attack royalty is to attack civilization itself. Looking too far askance at individual royal misbehavior is unfair because the royal family traditionally does not stoop to answer criticism or take recourse in the libel laws. Scandals not only place the arduous duties attached to royal birth into sharper relief; royal misbehavior feeds the public obsession for personal details that will answer the unanswerable question, "What are they *really* like?" In essence, royal culture's "weird mixture of cheap fun, exalted moments and great spectacles" is more positive and energizing than anything republicans have been able to offer.[15]

Organized religions provide the same kinds of universalities, mysteries, and taboo structures. Clifford Geertz's anthropological investigations point out universal qualities shared by gods and kings, particularly in the similar ceremonies and imagery used to express their powers. Geertz, however, sees a king's divinity as a function of his centrality rather than a duality. A sanctified majesty provides a center from which a society can construct and legitimize a framework of political authority. Hence, the charisma of royalty arises out of monarchy's position as the central symbol of power: the monarch stands proxy to God as well as to the essential values that support the social order.[16]

Inspired by Geertz's findings, some scholars have focused on the ceremonial side of monarchy in an effort to understand monarchy's otherworldly aspect. David Cannadine and Simon Price have organized a collection of case studies that examine the function of royal ritual in traditional societies ranging from ancient Babylon to contemporary Ghana. Although these studies show that the reasons for ceremonial display vary—to give a show of stead-fastness during strife, to reinforce the social hierarchy in times of stability, to offer an invocation of divine support and consensus to shore up an unstable regime—the source of its power consistently lies in the fusing of the sacred and the commonplace. These diverse royal rituals all involve the infusion of elements from everyday existence with new meanings through their combi-nation with pomp and circumstance, as in the king's sacred public bathing ritual in nineteenth-century Madagascar, for example. Many of these cere-monies involve the granting or reinforcing of political power; again, the cer-emonial part of government cannot be disconnected from and rendered sub-ordinate to the practical part. Power and pomp coexist in too interdependent and complex a relation. Ritual does not merely act as a camouflage for force; it can be a force in itself. As Nairn's analysis implies, the monarchy cannot be so easily dismissed as the "dignified" part of the government. We must be aware of the effects that its forms, traditions, and ideology have upon the "ef-ficient" aspects of rule. In the same vein, Kuhn's research reveals a high de-gree of ministerial involvement in the planning and execution of royal cere-monies during Bagehot's time; disassociating monarchy from politics proves impossible.[17]

Cynthia Herrup criticizes the tendency of English historians to produce compartmentalized studies of monarchy and cautions against focusing on iso-lated elements of kingship, such as its ceremonial function: "Because power in our world is always divided, we have implicitly denied the defining char-acteristic of early modern kingship, its holism. A sitting king was the center of the English structure of power—the center of politics, of culture, of law, and of religion."[18] Her observation also applies to modern regimes. Perhaps this is not readily recognizable because we also tend to associate real power with political systems and to consider cultural influences their handmaidens.

Antonio Gramsci's theory of hegemony tells us that a ruling class does not dominate only by force. Rather, it achieves a spirit of consensus by em-ploying the ideology and cultural institutions of civil society as instruments of coercion. The interdependencies between political and social forces make cultural hegemony crucial to the exercise of power. Yet Gramsci's model is weakened by his assumption that the dominant class always has hegemonic forces under its control. The ruling class "might not enjoy any intellectual or moral prestige, i.e. might be incapable of establishing its hegemony, hence of founding a State. Hence the function of monarchies, even in the modern era."[19] So, for Gramsci, monarchy's cultural influence becomes a tool of a dominant group. He does not entertain the possibility that institutional instruments of hegemony might become powers unto themselves. The essays assembled by Cannadine and Price show this to be the case with royal ritual, while Nairn suggests that the monarchical framework has imprisoned the ruling class.

Opponents of monarchy like Paine and Nairn would argue that the British have created a Frankenstein's monster. We are the monarchy and the monarchy is us. Others accept kingship, in whatever form, as a necessary component of human existence. Analysis of the meaning of monarchy is difficult because we all adhere to different systems of faith and vary in our ability to suspend disbelief. The monarchy has the capacity to touch us all on some level, be it producing goosebumps at a royal wedding or disgust at yet another tabloid revelation. Judging by the terms and tenor of the debate, monarchy arouses a variety of strong emotions in all kinds of people, including those attempting dispassionate analysis. Although it has the entertainment value of a soap opera, unlike daytime drama, the monarchy cannot be easily dismissed or even tuned out. Those who disapprove of the royal pageant or profess to consider it trivial can still participate by donning the disguise of academic investigation. The source of monarchy's power, then, is its ability to support multifarious meanings and simultaneously maintain its own sense of identity. The monarchy may be locked into a historical process; the monarch's character preserves autonomy.

The number of popular books and magazine articles that persist in probing into and attempting to explain the lives of the current British royal family indicates that the monarchy has managed to retain a tiny grain of ineffableness: this, I believe, is the source of its fascination. Popular writers even feel the need to take recourse in scholarly theory. In anticipation of Queen Elizabeth's visit in 1991, an American journalist regaled his readers with an account of the British tabloids' irreverent treatment of the royal family. He concluded, however, with an analysis of the meaning of that attitude. "The palace tends to regard the press with upper-class disdain. But the royals also recognize that the monarchy must be accessible and seen to be serving the public or it could be dissolved. So with a carefully calculated blend of mystery and accessibility, the royal family poses, performs and keeps the soap opera going."[20] The mystery is under scrutiny, and the idea of the duality of monarchy has entered common parlance, but the institution maintains its allure as it continues to defy understanding.

Bagehot recognized all the essential elements of modern kingship back in 1867. Having a family on the throne provides a point of unity with which subjects can identify personally. As an institution steeped in mysteries and traditions, monarchy endows the workings of government with an aura of sanctity. The royal family's position as head of society gives its members much latitude in influencing social mores. Unsullied by competition for office, and secure in preeminence, the monarch is in the perfect position to set a high moral example. Monarchical government gives the impression of continuity; it disguises political changes and thus allows transitions to take place with minimal upset and upheaval.[21] Bagehot identifies the whats but does not attempt the whys and hows.

Although the British monarchy no longer has significant direct political power, its cultural influence has permeated so many aspects of public and private life, both at home and abroad, that it is difficult to extract ourselves from the web of rhetoric, principles, structures, and assumptions it has generated. Heeding Herrup's plea to produce studies of kingship that acknowledge its holism, I shall leave the tangled web intact while tracing its strands back to their sources: the political and religious struggles of the seventeenth and eighteenth centuries; the monarchy's connection to other institutions, particularly the family, the church, and the law; the manner in which the monarchy has been used to support rival political ideologies; and the development of the royal family's role as leader of society and moral exemplar.

The construction of the modern British monarchy involved the redefinition of sanctity. This process began in the eighteenth century with the demise of divine-right ideology. Tracing its early stages will bring us closer to the source of the British monarchy's mystique. We shall see the notion of sanctity being reinvented in political discourse, legal argument, and theological expositions, then sustained in court rituals and visual representation. Key to this reinvention is a characteristic of monarchy stressed by Geertz as well as Nairn: its centrality. In the decade of the French Revolution, the monarchy regained its place as a focal point in political argument, but, no longer politically absolute, the monarch's place at the head of the social hierarchy took on new importance.

Edmund Burke would not have approved of this enterprise. In 1790 he saw the French monarchy coming under the prying eyes of the vulgar and feared the consequences:

All the pleasing illusions, which make power gentle, and obedience liberal, which harmonized the different shades of life, and which, by a bland assimilation, incorporated into politics the sentiments which beautify and soften private society, are to be dissolved by this new conquering empire of light and reason. All the decent drapery of life is to be rudely torn off. All the super-added ideas, furnished from the wardrobe of a moral imagination, which the heart owns, and the understanding ratifies, as necessary to cover the defects of our naked shivering nature, and to raise it to dignity in our own estimation, are to be exploded as a ridiculous, absurd, and antiquated fashion.[22]

Ironically, in reaction to his *Reflections on the Revolution in France,* the British monarchy came under increased vulgar scrutiny, most notably by Thomas Paine. But far from bringing the end to civilization, tearing off "the decent drapery" actually served to humanize the British monarch and to pave the way for the social role it has come to play in modern culture. Indeed, during the 1790s, the crown became a powerful metaphor.

History and Legitimacy

To understand the construction of the modern British monarchy, we must first consider its history. When the monarchy began to acquire its modern characteristics during the late eighteenth century, figures, events, and ideas from the seventeenth century in particular retained a strong presence in political argument. Advocates of parliamentary reform and their opponents each professed a concern for the king's welfare as they formulated their positions. This rhetorical strategy required that partisans on both sides of the reform debate clarify their positions on the monarchy's place in the government and in society. The resulting argument on kingship shows that the monarchy had developed a sanctity based upon tradition; the lessons of history underpinned monarchical authority. Because every event in history can be interpreted in many ways, the possession of a historical basis of legitimacy endowed kingship with adaptability, a characteristic that continues to be the key to its survival. Moreover, the monarchy not only was the product of its history; the institution's sanctity became based on its symbolization of the nation's past struggles and achievements.

After the seventeenth-century assault on monarchical sanctity, the basis of the institution's legitimacy became more complex. Indeed, both the right by which British monarchs rule and the precise range of their powers remain obscure. Paul Kléber Monod sees divine-right ideology as having been the British monarchy's last viable ideological foundation. He asserts: "The cult of monarchy that developed under George III was intoxicating but theoretically empty; to this day, monarchy in Britain has no clear basis, except tradition."[1] A survey of the rhetoric of royal entitlement, however, suggests that the ideology of divine right provided no more—in fact, perhaps less—of a stable framework for rule than the precedent-based rights enjoyed by George III and his successors.

On the face of it, divine right seems a stunningly straightforward ideology: monarchy is God's government; succession to the throne is based upon primogeniture, an indefeasible hereditary right; the king's power is indivisible; monarchs are subject only to God; and rebellion against the sovereign is a sin against God. Its simplicity in principle, however, belies its ambiguities in practice. This ideology of obedience originated, paradoxically, in opposition to authority, and it engendered a set of contentious postulates and practices.

Divine-right monarchy developed in the later Middle Ages as a strategy against papal encroachments upon the sovereignty of secular rulers. The Roman Catholic view of the state held that all power came from God and that the pope was his representative on earth. In order to meet the exigencies of ruling the Holy Roman Empire, this view evolved into an arrangement whereby both pope and emperor considered themselves God's vicegerents. This power-sharing predictably bred struggle, and emperors began to argue that a God-given authority should not be subject to the approval of the pope or any other earthly ruler. English monarchs found this argument useful in the clashes with the papacy that eventually brought about Henry VIII's break with Rome. The ideology of divine right also helped English monarchs consolidate their power against feudal lords and establish a hereditary succession.[2]

The idea that monarchs reigned by God's behest coexisted with various theories concerning whether subjects ought to—or could—resist bad rulers. Although the early Christians tended to favor passive obedience, a relationship between subject and sovereign based on martyrdom lacked practical appeal. In the fourth century, Christians began to reason that the biblical injunctions compelling monarchs to follow God's laws meant that a bad king was also a heretic who should be resisted. The old Germanic tribes that overran Europe between the fifth and ninth centuries had a similar view. The Visigoths, Ostrogoths, Lombards, Anglo-Saxons, and other tribes simply stopped obeying any king who proved to be bad or incompetent and elected another. The relationship between subject and sovereign was not based on obedience but on fealty, with reciprocal obligations set down by law. In England, the Magna Carta of 1215 gave constitutional legitimacy to this arrangement by formalizing the legal limits of royal power and, in theory, giving subjects an official procedure for asserting their right to resist a monarch who had broken the law. Theories of justified resistance, however, met a formidable foe in the doctrine of divine right. These two conceptions of monarchical power met head-on during the reign of the Stuarts.[3]

When James VI of Scotland become James I of England in 1603, divine-right monarchy was well-entrenched in practice. For most of Elizabeth's reign, the domestic religious divisions and foreign conflicts generated by the Protestant Reformation had allowed strong monarchical rule to be justified by necessity. Theories that justified resistance to rulers, however, gained currency in both countries. In England, the monarchy headed toward trouble. The Spanish Antichrist, weakened by the defeat of the Armada, remained a threat; but Elizabeth's parliaments became increasingly reluctant to grant money for these less glorious military purposes. By the end of Elizabeth's reign, the warrior virgin queen seemed more like an imperious old woman who was using her prerogative to bypass parliamentary control of the government's purse strings.[4]

In Scotland, meanwhile, James developed his own version of divine-right theory as part of a lifelong rebellion against his tutor, George Buchanan. Buchanan espoused the theories of the late sixteenth-century French Huguenot writer Philippe Duplessis-Mornay. Mornay maintained that political authority originated in a contract whereby a people gave up liberty for security by conferring authority on their rulers. The people's elected representatives were the ones who determined the propriety of resistance when rulers broke the terms of the contract. Going further, Buchanan extended the right of resistance to the people as a whole and viewed rulers not as real leaders or authorities but as guardians, who lost their position if they betrayed their trust. In 1584 James had the Scottish Parliament formally denounce Buchanan's ideas and set to work establishing what he considered the proper relationship between subject and sovereign.[5]

The Trew Law of Free Monarchies: Or the Reciprock and Mutuall Dutie Betwixt a Free King, and His Naturall Subjects appeared pseudonymously in 1598. James wrote this tract in response to Puritan and Catholic controversialists in Scotland and probably did not intend it to be read by his future subjects; the work presented the English character as having been marred by the depredations of the Norman Conquest. Nevertheless, the treatise did find its way to London in 1603, where, predictably, it caused a stir. *Basilikon Doron, or His Majesties Instructions to His Dearest Sonne Henry the Prince* (1599) followed. Intellectual historians note that James's version of divine-right kingship contained only one new twist: the notion that monarchs inherited their godly qualities through the royal line.[6] James's glorification of the principle of heredity is understandable after Henry VIII's determination to exclude the Stuarts from the throne and the uncertainties the Tudor king's multiple marriages had introduced into the succession.[7] Once installed in England, however, James demonstrated a willingness to debate. He even began drawing upon arguments from the English common-law tradition, particularly the myth of the ancient constitution, the idea that the English state was founded on Saxon liberties. Although his writings contained few original ideas, the specter of a British king engaged in theoretical discourse had not been seen since the glorious Alfred, and to some it was a rather disquieting sight. What really alarmed the English, however, was not James's theoretical innovation but rather the similarities between his writings and those of Continental absolutist theorists. The English feared foreign influence as much as the high degree of power and authority James seemed to claim for kings.[8]

In keeping with the ambiguities already visible between the principles and practice of divine-right monarchy, however, James's attempt to make a strong assertion of kingly power in *The Trew Law* featured back-pedalling and prevarication. Throughout the work James intertwined, or perhaps muddled, the notions of power, right, and necessity. Good kings naturally followed the law. Yet kings made the laws on earth, which technically placed them above the law. James pointed to the history of the British Isles to prove that laws came after kings and that subjects craved laws. He acknowledged that early societies chose their kings on the basis of strength and ability, but argued that a monarch's right to rule did not differ in this case from that of a conqueror; all kings ruled by force of divine will. Yet he also stated that the coronation oath set down the duties by which kings would "maintaine the whole countrey and every state therein, in all their ancient Priviledges and Liberties." This was not to say that the oath constituted a contract, the breaking of which justified resistance. Subjects were incapable of judging their own cause. Only God had the wisdom and authority to determine whether a king had done wrong and to punish him accordingly. Monarchy was divine, James reasoned, as the "forme of government, as resembling the Divinitie, approacheth nearest to perfection." James also saw monarchy's naturalness in its reflection of humanity's most common and natural association, the family: "By the Law of Nature the King becomes a naturall Father to all his Lieges at his Coronation." It was unnatural, James asserted, for children to rise up against their father.[9]

The English showed themselves capable of behaving both unnaturally and unfilially when they committed regicide and patricide in the following reign. James had been spared this shattering of his assumptions about filial affections by the fact that his application of divine right had more to do with style than substantive constitutional practice. The king continued to insist that his powers came directly from God. But God was not providing him with the money to run the government. Members of Parliament took up the cry of their Elizabethan forebears against fundraising techniques that involved going over their heads by the use of the royal prerogative. James's attachment to divine right caused them to view these royal prerogatives with increased suspicion, and James to guard them all the more defensively. The fierce debates over constitutional issues as well as the royal temper tantrums before Parliament left the impression that James was moving toward a complete rejection of Parliament.[10] Yet John Kenyon argues that these altercations did not signify a continually worsening relationship between Crown and Parliament but rather "a fluctuating but persistent degree of low-key contestation" that featured give and take on both sides.[11]

James's pronouncements on divine-right kingship stimulated the development of opposing ideologies. The common lawyers, most notably Edward Coke, questioned James's assumptions and, essentially, gave common or customary law the status that James had bestowed upon monarchs. This law, they claimed, bore the greatest resemblance to God's in heaven, it dated back to time immemorial, and it encompassed the wisdom and reason of generations. The common law predated and was independent of any particular king or legislator. Free from foreign influence, it peculiarly suited England. Judgments handed down in the kings' courts from the twelfth century onward had drawn upon this ancient custom, clarifying its tenets and expressing them in such a way as to keep the law relevant to society's needs. Thus, the common law maintained a high degree of excellence that could not be matched by any written law. Where did this leave the king? He was still the most powerful person in the realm, but ancient law precisely defined and limited his prerogatives.[12]

The discordant visions of kingly power held by James, members of Parliament, and common lawyers never precipitated a serious confrontation because the king's actual policies tended to steer a middle course between contending political and religious factions.[13] Charles I, in contrast, combined his father's sense of divine mission with policymaking as aggressive as it was unpopular, and consequently increased the national anxiety about the connection between divine-right monarchy and arbitrary rule. The reintroduction of an active Catholicism into the court with Charles's marriage to Henrietta Maria of France, and the Arminianism of Archbishop Laud, moreover, further tainted Charles's views of divine right with popish associations.

Charles's confrontations with Parliament were more dramatic than those of his father. In 1626 and 1629 he ordered recalcitrant M.P.s arrested on charges of sedition; this only increased parliamentarian resolve. Charles dissolved Parliament in March 1629 with the claim that a faction therein disrupted the business of government. He blamed England's military losses on Parliament's refusal to grant him sufficient supplies. Charles then made peace with his foreign enemies and ruled without a parliament for eleven years. As Kevin Sharpe's study of this phenomenon demonstrates, during the period of personal rule, Charles achieved relative peace and prosperity as well as reforms in the areas of religion, finance, commerce, trade, land management, and the military, particularly the navy. Although these reforms did not please everybody all of the time, they did not divide the country into competing factions. In Kenyon's estimation, "though this 'experiment' was not a resounding success from the king's point of view it was certainly not a failure, and if he had been able to avoid a foreign war his regime might have continued indefinitely."[14] Perhaps the problem resided in the circumstance that the "foreigners" in this case were the Scots and the Irish.

Charles's attempt to reform the Church by imposing a new liturgy upon the Scots sparked a rebellion. Charles now had to reconvene Parliament in order to finance a military force to subdue the Scots. The king not only faced hostility from Parliament; the controversy over the Prayer Book confirmed wider English Protestant fears that the Church was being corrupted by papist ideas and customs.[15] Moreover, the king's continued reliance upon prerogative taxation during the 1630s had brought into the open the long-brewing dissension that lay beneath the surface calm of the realm. The combination of Arminianism and personal monarchy convinced many Englishmen that they were on the road to Continental despotism.

Ironically, in the ensuing struggle, the document that had the greatest impact upon divine-right ideology and the long-term constitutional history of the monarchy was written by two of Charles's councillors and issued in his name, signed but unread, in June 1642. King and Parliament had reached an impasse over the issue of who would control the army raised to quell the Irish rebellion that followed upon the disorder in Scotland. Charles took up a position at York, where the Long Parliament sent him nineteen propositions "as the most necessary effectual means, through God's blessing, of removing those jealousies and differences, which have unhappily fallen betwixt you and your people." Essentially, these proposals involved the king handing over his prerogatives to Parliament. The document stipulated that the appointment of the Privy Council, high offices of government, judges, and tutors for the royal children be approved by Parliament. The same went for royal marriages.[16] In response, the king sent *His Majesties Answer to the XIX. Propositions of Both Houses of Parliament.*

This document, in citing the reasons why the king's particular prerogatives were necessary for the good of the state, inadvertently undermined the ideology of divine right. It described king, Lords, and Commons as three estates that needed to hang in even balance and "run joyntly on in their proper Chanell" to prevent the tyranny, faction, and anarchy found respectively in monarchy, aristocracy, and democracy, as practiced in their pure forms.[17] As J. G. A. Pocock observes, the *Answer*'s use of the doctrine of a mixed constitution went beyond the common-law tradition; it "imported the possibility of a republican alternative into English political thinking."[18]

This royal use of the opposition's rhetoric would change the way people thought about the monarchy. Pocock asserts: "We must see June 1642 as marking the moment when 'the ancient constitution' became authoritatively identified with the 'mixed' or 'balanced' constitution."[19] Michael Mendle argues that the document's great impact did not come from its novelty or the king's signature but rather "from its equivocation and confusion": "A republican language had been used to argue the case against a republic." He points out that Charles's councillors had conflated the old notion of the three estates of the realm—those who pray, those who fight, and those who work (clergy, Lords, and Commons)—with the classical notion of the three forms of government by the one, the few, and the many (monarchy, aristocracy, and democracy). Scottish Presbyterians had done this in the 1580s in order to deny the place of bishops in the government, a move that also had the effect of bringing the king down to the level of the Lords and Commons. James VI had declared this doctrine treasonable; Elizabeth I's Privy Council later treated it as seditious. Hence, discussion of the mixed constitution, an idea imported from Italy during the mid-Tudor period, faded out during the reign of the early Stuarts.[20] With *His Majesties Answer,* however, a balanced constitution and mixed monarchy became central themes in English political discourse, especially after their glorification in Montesquieu's *Spirit of the Laws* (1748). Because endless arrangements were possible for sharing power among the three parts of the constitution to achieve balance, the notion of mixed monarchy furnished much fuel for debate.[21]

Ostensibly, the Civil War and Interregnum destroyed divine-right monarchy, but in actuality, monarchical sanctity simply evolved, and many divine-right tenets survived the process. Events proved the strength of these principles. To justify their trial and execution of the king, the Rump Parliament drew upon the ideas of government by consent, accountability to the people, and the sanctity of the ancient, balanced constitution. Nonetheless, the Parliament also had to navigate its way around divine-right tenets. It needed to prove that Charles had violated the laws of God and nature.

Logistical problems abounded. Legally, the king could do no wrong; he was not capable of a criminal act. In the beginning of the conflict, some took refuge in "evil counselors behind the king" rhetoric by blaming the king's behavior on papist conspirators at court. In addition to his legal inviolability, opponents of the king also had to contend with the concept of the body politic. Because the king was the embodiment of the state, a king's treason could only be against himself, an unlikely prospect. It *was* possible for a king to be a tyrant, however, by subverting the fundamental laws of the land. A king could also be a sinner, by flouting God's law. This was the angle the prosecutors pursued. They pointed out that Charles, rather than protecting his people, waged war against them. Michael Walzer describes what developed as "the new sense of opposition rectitude which the English Puritans seem first to have introduced into political life."[22] The regicides had to persuade themselves that the king's death was a matter of absolute necessity. Carrying out the deed thus became a moral duty.

The rebels placed the king on trial not only to establish his guilt before the world but also to undermine monarchy's mystique. The execution of Charles in 1649 in his public character destroyed a central tenet of divine right: that the king (meaning the office) never dies. Nonetheless, visible aspects of royal divinity made up for the loss. Charles's deportment in his final days, coupled with the disappointments the new regimes engendered, helped endow the dead monarch with the aura of sainthood. On the scaffold Charles conducted himself with striking fortitude, even shaking off the stammer that usually dogged his public speeches, and proclaimed himself a martyr to the cause of his people. A secret royalist cult developed around the idea of royal martyrdom that elevated Charles into a Christlike figure. After the Restoration, the anniversary of the royal beheading, 30 January, became a day of public fasting and humiliation that remained on the church calendar until 1859.[23]

Oliver Cromwell's leadership had its own divine component. Once he become convinced that the king had to die, Cromwell began to view himself and the army as the instruments of providence, and the death as an act of divine vengeance. Overturning the monarchy became incorporated into his vision of England's godly reformation. Yet, although he spurned the title, Cromwell acted the king, an absolutist one at that, whatever his republican intentions. Even Parliament, the rights of which he had long championed, became an obstacle in his quest to become one of the elect.[24]

With respect to the history of the British monarchy, the most significant aspect of the Interregnum was the failure to achieve a republic. The monarchy was so well-established as an institution that it could not be effaced. After the chaos of the Interregnum, particularly the breakdown of Richard Cromwell's authority, the prospect of a strong king held considerable attraction. There even may be some truth in the revisionist claim that the Parliamentarians had not objected to the royal prerogative, but rather to Charles's abuse of it. The Restoration Settlement abolished prerogative courts and taxation, the source of the worst abuses. Yet the Cavalier Parliament voted the restored king what was meant to be sufficient revenue for the administration of government, and it relinquished most of the demands tendered in the Nineteen Propositions of 1642.[25] The scars of the Civil War and the unsettling of divine-right authority left a dual legacy for monarchy. On the one hand, the rebellion served as a chilling reminder to kings who contemplated stretching their prerogative. On the other, memories of the Interregnum made people reluctant to risk popular agitation against the government.

Divine-right monarchy can best be described as having gone into a state of occultation under Charles II. Although this Stuart was better known for spreading his seed than spouting encomia on royal sanctity, he showed himself perfectly capable of interrupting his pursuit of pleasure to lay claim to monarchical divinity's remaining assets. He temporarily quelled fears of royal absolutism with the Declaration of Breda of 4 April 1660, which stressed his desire for harmony. Accordingly, he promised to pardon all but the regicides and to support religious toleration. He bid Parliament sort out the property losses that had occurred as well as make up the arrears in soldiers' pay.[26] Yet the declaration left unresolved the question of the balance of power between the executive and legislative parts of the constitution and that of the relation between church and state.[27] Barry Coward's blunt assessment is germane: "The 'Restoration Settlement' is a misnomer. The series of *ad hoc* decisions made in the early 1660s by the Convention and Cavalier Parliaments, which are traditionally called 'the Restoration Settlement,' settled very little."[28] The wild celebrations up and down the country that greeted Charles's entrance into London on 29 May 1660 make it easy for us to forget the long, tortuous negotiations that preceded it, as well as how deeply divided England still was along a number of religious and political lines.[29] The English needed a monarch who would work with Parliament to clarify their respective constitutional roles. The complexity of competing interests in the nation coupled with the personality of the king produced a reign of muddling through rather than one of decisive purpose.

Charles II pursued the politics of appeasement. He distributed places among Cavaliers and former Parliamentarians alike, which generated resentments among some royalists who did not receive the rewards they expected. Charles kept his promise about making up arrears in army pay and indemnities, then disbanded the army. The Anglican Church, having survived its banishment during the Interregnum and reestablished itself with new militancy, scuttled Charles's plans for legislating religious toleration. His refusal to give full support to hardline Anglicans brought charges of crypto-Catholicism. Fears of popery intensified as Charles pursued an alliance with the hated French. But Charles had no intention of declaring himself a Catholic and forcing the issue of toleration (as he had promised Louis XIV he would do in the secret Treaty of Dover of 1670). He did, in fact, harbor Catholic sympathies, but he was not about to convert to the faith before he was safely on his deathbed; in the meantime, he adhered to the creed of political expediency.[30]

Charles's successor was not as savvy (or as hypocritical, depending on how you look at it) as his older brother. Under James II's reign, divine right resurfaced, firmly associated with Catholic oppression. James was neither willing to practice dissimulation nor able to engage in the sort of political maneuvering that Charles had undertaken to preserve the succession. During the Exclusion Crisis (1679–81), Charles had used his power to prorogue Parliament as a potent weapon against politicians determined to prevent the openly Catholic James from ascending the throne. Although Charles withstood the Exclusionist siege, the audacity and persistence of the earl of Shaftesbury and his party did much to formalize the complaints against the English monarchy, as well as the religious antagonisms that divided the nation. The terms of derision that became affixed to James's opponents and supporters had telling historical resonances. Supporters of James dubbed the Exclusionists "Whigs," a name originally applied to the Scottish Presbyterians who helped seal Charles I's fate, while Shaftesbury and his party called the supporters of what they saw as royal tyranny "Tories," an appellation for Irish thieves bestowed upon the rebels of 1641.[31] These pejorative designations endured as party labels and, like the monarchy itself, continued to garner new meanings.

The residual debate between supporters of divine right and theorists of contract and consent now became attached to party politics, and the theorists who came to epitomize the Tory and Whig positions emerged. The man whose name would become synonymous with the doctrines of passive obedience and nonresistance surfaced posthumously at the height of the Exclusion Crisis. Robert Filmer had written *Patriarcha,* his most famous exposition on divine-right monarchy, sometime before 1642, but it did not get into print until 1680. And it was not until the 1680s that the works he composed between 1642 and his death in 1653 received real attention.

Filmer's writings sought to institutionalize the patriarchal species of monarchy that James I had tried to practice. Although Filmer's ideas resembled those of the sixteenth-century French absolutist thinker Jean Bodin, among other opponents of theories justifying resistance to authority, Filmer took patriarchalism farther by giving it a foundation in sacred and secular history. He argued that all governments originated with Adam, whom God had fashioned as father and king combined. Filmer called the claims of contract theorists that people were free in a state of nature absurd; we are all obligated from birth to obey our parents. Any attempt to subvert this natural order would result in anarchy: "We do but flatter ourselves, if we hope ever to be governed without an arbitrary power. No, we mistake."[32] To Filmer, the idea of a limited monarch was oxymoronic. To be a king meant possessing absolute power. Kings' councils and parliaments advised and acted at the king's pleasure.

Filmer's work goaded opponents of absolutism into producing systematic defenses of their position. As in the case of *Patriarcha,* however, circumstances did not allow these works to be published at the time they were written. The Whigs were routed by their actual or alleged involvement in a number of real or imagined conspiracies that came to be known collectively as the Rye House Plot. After being outmaneuvered by Charles in Parliament in 1681, some Exclusionists still desired to place the duke of Monmouth, Charles's illegitimate son, on the throne. In the atmosphere of suspicion and alarm, meetings and loose talk suggested a grand design to assassinate Charles and James as they journeyed back to London after the Newmarket Races. In November 1682 Shaftesbury, who had continued to scheme against James's succession, learned that the government had issued a warrant for his arrest; he escaped to Holland, where he died soon afterward. His followers either went into exile or were apprehended and tried.[33] Taking on Filmer had to wait until after the Revolution of 1688.

The most noteworthy reply to *Patriarcha* was John Locke's *Two Treatises of Government.* Locke's influence on later generations of reformers remains controversial, and for the purpose of this study it is sufficient to note that the reformers of the 1790s certainly presented variations on his ideas, from whatever source. Direct references to him were rare, but striking.[34] In the first treatise, Locke presented a point-by-point refutation of *Patriarcha;* in the second he laid down what he saw as the true principles of government. Making a firm distinction between political and paternal authority, Locke argued that human beings enjoyed freedom in a state of nature. Individuals united to form civil society and *consented* to live under a government in order to protect their property, by which Locke meant "their lives, liberty, and estates" (bk. 2, chap. 9). Hence, government consisted in a trust and retained its legitimacy only as long as it fulfilled the function initially designated by its subjects. Subjects thus had the right to resist for the purpose of self-defense: when government failed to provide protection. To Locke this constituted a basic law of nature. A member of the Exclusionist party, Locke found it prudent to leave England in 1683 when the hysteria mounted over the Rye House affair. He returned in 1689 on the ship that was ferrying William's consort, Mary, back to the land of her birth. Although probably written in the 1680s, the *Treatises* did not see print until 1690, and did so anonymously. As John Dunn and others show, interpretations and reactions to the work varied.[35] Given the confused series of events that inspired the *Treatises,* this is not surprising.

For so precedent-setting a proceeding, the Revolution of 1688 lacked clarity and decisiveness from beginning to end. When Charles died in 1685, he left James II in such a strong position that the new king became overconfident in his pursuit of unpopular policies. Paul Seaward argues that James neither believed he was acting illegally nor intended to establish an absolute monarchy. Nevertheless, many subjects associated his wholesale promotion of Catholicism with the sort of despotism practiced by Louis XIV, including the persecution of Protestants. Kenyon notes that the English may have found James's sincere profession of faith refreshing after his brother's duplicity, but placing fellow Catholics in positions of power took religious devotion too far.[36]

Yet the revolutionaries would probably not have been sufficiently agitated by James's policies to rebel had not his wife, Mary of Modena, produced a Catholic heir to the throne. The birth, with its accompanying rumors that Mary had feigned pregnancy and a Jesuit priest had smuggled James Francis Edward Stuart into the birthing chamber by way of a warming-pan, gave William of Orange a pretext to invade England: protecting his wife Mary's claim to the throne against a spurious heir. James's troops outnumbered

William's invasionary force and might have repelled it had not James suffered an apparent mental collapse and fled. The events of 1688 and the changes they precipitated did not result from adherence to a well-thought-out ideological crusade but rather from pragmatic reactions to developments as they occurred.[37]

The ambiguity of its proceedings and the sheer bulk of the rhetoric expended to give them legitimacy left the revolution open to divergent interpretations. The protracted negotiations between the Convention—the parliamentary assembly that took charge in the absence of a monarch—and William deradicalized many of the revolution's elements. The Declaration of Rights that William and Mary swore to uphold when they were offered the joint crown, as Lois Schwoerer observes, "was a much-watered-down version of the Heads of Grievances." On the other hand, many of the so-called ancient and undoubted rights that the declaration purported to restore were clearly innovations, and the radical arguments that had been discarded in previous drafts became enduring elements of British political debate.[38]

In order to smooth over the extraordinary nature of and confer legitimacy upon the proceedings, traditional rituals and celebrations heralded the Revolution Settlement.[39] Yet William's legitimacy as king would never be secure because of the circumstances of James II's departure. Intercepted in flight, James returned to London, where he received a hero's welcome from the populace. His presence was awkward, to say the least, so William indirectly encouraged him to escape. James, however, buoyed up by the popular reception, was not about to skulk away. Before he left England, he issued a manifesto asserting that he departed reluctantly, out of fear for his life. No longer faced with a straightforward abdication, the Convention had to justify William's claim. The assembly settled on the argument that James had deserted his post. This still left the question of whether William ruled by conquest, heredity, or election. Smarting from the ambiguity and the resulting weakness of his position, William threatened to leave the country. Although the eventual decision to institute a joint monarchy gave William rights independent of Mary's, it was plain, after his consort's premature death at the end of 1694, that some the political nation still considered him a usurper. As Jennifer Carter's examination of the constitutional consequences of the revolution demonstrates, the most revolutionary aspect of these events lay neither in any direct limitations on royal power nor in the ban of Catholics from the throne but rather in the act of altering the succession. The hereditary principle, which had become intrinsic to divine-right monarchy, had been compromised.[40]

The textbook version of the Revolution of 1688 as the triumph of Parliament over the monarchy has been called into question by J. C. D. Clark. His revisionist model of eighteenth-century Britain as an ancien régime partially rests upon the assertion that the Crown did not lose power after 1688. He rejects the traditional view that events of the seventeenth century were revolutionary in character and paved the way for the rise of parliamentary government in the eighteenth. Clark points to a continuing exercise of the royal prerogative in the areas of legislation, foreign affairs, and war, as well as to the undiminished importance of the court.[41] Clark's observations are cogent. Nonetheless, he overlooks the obvious: the changing image of kingship.

The British viewed their monarchy in a different light after 1688, a perceptual change that significantly altered the manner in which monarchs exercised their power. The revolution may not have eradicated divine right, but it gave respectability to an array of contentious ideas about responsible government and constitutional balance. Eighteenth-century political discourse featured conflicting views of the English past and its precedents. Moreover, the expansion of print culture in the eighteenth century made the exercise of power and the conflicts between monarchs and politicians more public. Politicians, philosophers, and lawyers debated the relative powers of the different parts of government and how these powers should be exercised. It took a whole century for the monarchy to develop a coherent philosophy of rule along with a self-confident identity.

Clark is correct in exploding the old teleological model of the decline of monarchy and the rise of democracy, but he overstates his case for monarchical continuity. The official dictates of the Revolution Settlement made less difference to royal power than mundane elements of chance and circumstances. The monarchy did not undergo a steady evolution; it cut a zig-zag course, reviving particular traditions and practices or implementing innovations as conditions demanded. Although the doctrines associated with divine right continued to appear in different formulations throughout the eighteenth century, the revolts against monarchical authority of the seventeenth century served to limit the opportunities for personal rule and elevated the authority of Parliament. Historians seem to agree that Parliament's attainment of leverage against kingly power was not so much a dictate of the Revolution Settlement as a consequence of William's crusade against Louis XIV: raising funds for war necessitated frequent parliaments. Yet at the same time, the pressing concerns of war demanded strong, decisive executive leadership. John Brewer notes the paradox of the fiscal-military state to which the revolution gave birth. On the one hand, the revolution curbed a powerful executive government. On the other, the critics of strong, centralized government who supported the revolution realized that that same government now protected England's liberties against the threat of Catholic absolutism issuing from Europe.[42]

Historians continue to debate whether patronage-wielding monarchs or party-politicking parliaments had the upper hand after 1688.[43] Considering the evidence in support of each side of the argument, it seems that the answer depends on the day in question. England still had a strong monarch; the significant change came in the rules of the game. The Civil War had been the first step in the process of dismantling divine right. No longer God's vicegerent, the king had become a mere mortal: another political player open to criticism. As Vincent Carretta demonstrates, graphic royal satire proliferated under Charles II; treating the king with such levity would have been considered sacrilegious in previous reigns. Without divine right the sovereign became responsible for his or her actions. After 1688 the adage "the king can do no wrong" still existed as a legal fiction, yet it did so alongside memories of the error-prone Charles I and James II. The limitations on the power of the Crown remained vague in theory and had to be worked out in practice.[44] A revolution featuring compromise and improvisation produced a monarchy of the same character.

The politics of party confronted the monarchy with new challenges. Taking up a position on the moral higher ground, William III indulged his authoritarian tendencies, played politicians against one another, and sought to steer a middle course by constructing ministries composed of both Tories and Whigs. William could barely conceal his disdain for English politicians, whom he considered lazy and ignorant. He fought the Whigs' attempts to reduce his authority by enlisting political managers who would place the king's will before party concerns. Yet William took care not to allow individual politicians too much power. As long as the war against France went well and William seemed an essential instrument of English liberties, his parliaments provided him with funds. After bad campaigns and during peacetime, however, politicians could not wait to challenge his authority. His defeat in Parliament over the issue of disbanding the army in 1698–99 is probably the most striking example of the changes the revolution had wrought. Although legally William could have dissolved Parliament, leaned on the Lords, or used his veto to defeat the bill, he could not afford to alienate the Commons. The general populace was unstinting in displays of loyalty whenever William appeared in public, but the political nation was always ready to forget any favors William had done them.[45]

The reign of Queen Anne, who succeeded her brother-in-law in 1702, served as a transitional period between the personal, court-centered monarchy of the Stuarts and the public, supervisory role of the institution in its modern form. Unlike William, Anne had the hereditary cachet of being the native-born daughter of James II. Moreover, Anne worked to restore monarchy to its proper dignity, although she adhered to the revolutionary dictum that she was Queen-in-Parliament (she was, however, capable of becoming quite testy if a politician presumed to remind her of this). Anne inadvertently contributed to the appearance of personal monarchy by giving the impression that her favorites controlled her: first Sarah Churchill, duchess of Marlborough, then Abigail Masham. True, the court remained the center of power, and Anne's personal disfavor could break a career, but bedchamber politics did not predominate. Even more than William, Anne relied on political managers, or "undertakers," and unlike William, she allowed the development of a prime ministerial position, which was first held by the Marlborough-Godolphin duumvirate and subsequently by Robert Harley. Accordingly, these men managed the queen's ministries as her servants, not as party leaders. That Anne used the royal veto only once, in 1708, attests to the efficiency of this arrangement and to her position as Queen-in-Parliament.[46]

Anne pleased the Whigs with her steady support of mainstream Anglicanism, while she subdued the Jacobites with her apparent sympathy to their cause. Her comforting Stuart presence, however, masked an ideological disquietude still present in the nation that would erupt during the trial of Dr. Henry Sacheverell in 1710. Historians usually treat the Sacheverell affair as the product of high church–Tory hysteria and Whig idiocy.[47] In an exquisite show of cheek, Sacheverell chose 5 November, the anniversary of the Gunpowder Plot, to preach his sermon, *The Perils of False Brethren both in Church and State,* in front of the City of London Corporation at St. Paul's. To ensure that his message got across, Sacheverell subsequently published it. *False Brethren* sounded the tocsin against the religious nonconformity that Sacheverell saw unleashed by the Toleration Act of 1689. In the process of calling the rectitude of the Revolution Settlement into question, the sermon presented Godolphin as one of the many false brethren who conspired against the Church of England. Finding themselves unable to ignore such a deliberate challenge to their authority, the Whigs started impeachment proceedings against Sacheverell that only served to provoke mob action and impugn the government.

The Sacheverell trial exposed weaknesses in Whig and Tory precepts alike. The Whigs had the delicate task of defending the right of resistance to the government when they themselves were the ones who were being resisted. The prosecutors focused on the impropriety of any discussion of the topic when such a beloved queen reigned. Although they kept returning to the principle of necessity, the Whigs could never define the precise conditions that justified resistance. Whig argument also displayed inconsistencies regarding when and how a compact between governed and governors was formed and how subjects' consent to their government could be ascertained. The Tories, on the other hand, had the thankless chore of defending Sacheverell's bizarre assertion that William's invasion in 1688 did not constitute resistance against what the preacher called the Supreme Power. Taking advantage of the ambiguity of this expression, Sacheverell's defenders claimed that the Supreme Power meant the Crown-in-Parliament, which was certainly not the authority William supplanted. When confronted with the practicalities of rule, Whig and Tory positions sounded remarkably similar; they would intertwine in even stranger ways during the next two reigns.

The Hanoverian succession brought the implications of the Revolution of 1688 into sharp relief. The reigns of the first two Georges tested the Revolution Settlement as well as the monarchical tradition in Britain. Maintaining the Protestant ascendancy in 1714 meant bringing in a member of the Stuart family so far removed from Anne that it risked stretching the hereditary principle to the breaking point. George I was descended from James I's daughter Elizabeth, who had left England to marry Prince Frederick of the Palatinate, better known as Bohemia's Winter King for his part in the Thirty Years' War. Elizabeth and Frederick's twelfth child, Sophia, the mother of George I, spent her youth in the Netherlands in exile, then fled to her elder brother's court in Heidelberg, when she learned that her mother planned to marry her to her cousin, the future Charles II. Her brother later arranged a marriage for her with Ernst August of Brunswick-Luneburg.[48] Hence, George's right to the British throne was purely matrilineal, his family thoroughly Germanized, and his ties to England distant.

Many Britons questioned whether the fifty-four-year-old Elector of Hanover could set aside his absolutist heritage and Continental interests. Nicholas Rogers notes: "One of the most remarkable features of early Hanoverian politics was the persistent and deep-rooted hostility of Londoners to the new regime."[49] Although George's succession at first stood unchallenged, his coronation day inspired mob action in twenty-six towns in England and Wales.

Over the next five years, opponents of the Hanoverian regime and its defenders clashed in an additional thirty-one cities and towns. In Rogers's view,
popular anti-Hanoverian feeling did not indicate devotion to the deposed Stuarts but rather a perception of economic threat. He notes that Londoners
were not moved to violent protest until they saw George I supporting a Whig
oligarchy. The mercantile community believed that the Whigs' Eurocentric
policies would bolster the position of the new economic class of financiers at
their expense. Monod, on the other hand, asserts that historians underesti-
mate Jacobitism's strength and resilience. The new regime failed to develop
a feasible ideology of legitimacy; instead, the Hanoverians relied on anti-
Catholicism to maintain support. As symptomatic of the ideological muddle,
Colin Haydon points out that opponents of the new dynasty sometimes assailed George with anti-papist slogans.[50]

Monod observes that although George I tarnished the luster of kingship,
the young James Francis Edward Stuart, son of James II and Mary of Modena, dwelt untested and untainted in exile. Jacobite newspapers, verse, songs,
artwork, and speech not only ridiculed and vilified George I but also canon-
ized "James III." The family misfortunes of this usurped heir lent themselves
to portrayals of a Christlike figure, a tragic hero, a chivalric prince, an unre-
quited lover. Handsome, remote, and mysterious, James attracted romanti-
cization.[51] The image of idealized kingship built around him provided an outlet for those who revered monarchy but disliked the current regime. The
memory of Charles I as a royal martyr served the same purpose for those who
did not want to be implicated in the treason of supporting the Pretender during George I's reign, or his son, Charles Edward ("Bonnie Prince Charlie"),
during George II's. As a phenomenon, Jacobitism revealed immense variations and a multiplicity of facets; and its adherents had different degrees of
commitment to a Stuart restoration. The failed rebellions of 1715 and 1745
demonstrated that a coup could be brought about only with the assistance of
foreign troops and that such help was not forthcoming. The military defeats
also showed that many who idealized the deposed dynasty were unwilling to
risk the horrors of civil war. A good number of Tories became uncomfortable
with the Stuarts' unshakable connections to Catholic France and the potential threat this posed to the Anglican Church. Most Catholics avoided the rebellion of 1745, fearing a new wave of persecution should it fail.[52]

George I took his kingly duties seriously, gradually reduced the number
of his Hanoverian servants, and made efforts to balance the interests of Britain
and Hanover in his foreign policy. Notwithstanding these efforts, people saw

the worst in George's use of British resources as he continued his involvement in the Great Northern War. His frequent trips to Hanover further eroded confidence. George's family and his German courtiers drew blame for the shortfalls of the Civil List, although its inadequacy was due to factors unrelated to royal extravagance. Nonetheless, an image persisted of wanton, rapacious Hanoverians bleeding Britain dry.[53]

During the first half of the eighteenth century the British monarchy was eclipsed not only by a glamorized rival dynasty but also by the phenomenon of the Whig ascendancy and the twenty-year domination of Robert Walpole. Walpole shaped the role of political manager, which laid the foundation for the office of prime minister, after he secured a joint appointment as First Lord of the Treasury and Chancellor of the Exchequer in 1721. This political development led to misleading appearances. Studies suggest that the first two Georges, far from being ineffectual dullards at the mercy of Whig and Tory machinations, were well-informed and argumentative, particularly with respect to foreign affairs. Moreover, to continue in power Walpole had to stay in favor at court while making sure that the Commons supported his policies. He achieved this not only through cleverly formed policy but also by using Crown patronage to secure votes and maintain political loyalty. Additionally, he engaged in a ruthless smear campaign to represent all Tories as secretly plotting to restore the Pretender.[54] In the context of the apparent blandness of the first two Georges, Walpole's strong public persona and obvious love of power give the impression of a monarchy in decline.

As in the previous reign, the king's lack of charisma and his conspicuous absences from the political scene whenever he returned to Hanover allowed partisan rumor and speculation to shape popular conceptions of the monarchy. Public expression in general expanded in scope through the growing number of newspapers, sermons, pamphlets, broadsides, and caricature prints published during the eighteenth century. Walpole's neglect of artists and literati and his patronage of newspaper editors and hack writers brought an unprecedented degree of public discussion regarding the character and policies of the court. Carretta notes that between the reigns of George I and George II political satires increased both in frequency and in their direct criticisms of the monarchy. Propaganda portrayed George II variously as a decent king misled by corrupt ministers, a potential tyrant, a dolt, or a nonentity, depending on whatever was useful to the particular political issue at stake. Much of the rhetoric concerning the monarchy was full of inconsistencies. This absence of a firm ideological basis led to misinterpretations and trouble, as Alexander Pettit demonstrates in his study of Francis Hare, a progovernment bishop vilified at the hands of his own party when he dared to make unconventional comparisons between the Hanoverian and Caroline monarchs' positions on religious dissent.[55] Anti-Jacobite hysteria, ambiguities in the Revolution Settlement, political stratagem, and shadowy figures on the throne all worked against the ability of the early eighteenth-century monarchy to develop meaning and identity.

Notwithstanding the propagandizing, a dialectic emerged that helped formulate the idea of modern British kingship. Walpole's position on monarchy consisted of a self-serving defense of his use of Crown patronage to control the House of Commons. Because people were naturally rapacious and irretrievably corrupt, his argument went, effective government required a strong executive power with sufficient means to exploit this greed for honors and emoluments. Patronage was the best means available to regulate conflicting interests in society, protect individual liberties, and maintain tranquility.[56] When opposition politicians attacked patronage positions and pensions, Walpole's proponents represented them as enemies of the royal prerogative and hence, the Crown. This out-Torying of the Tories typified the rhetoric of the era. Old party distinctions blurred, allowing new ideological alliances and the reconciliation of previously incompatible positions.

Walpole's nemesis, Henry St. John, viscount Bolingbroke, had long labored to form a coherent Country party, which would unite Tories, dissident Whigs, and the independent country gentlemen who filled the back benches of the Commons. At the end of the 1730s he made a desperate attempt to achieve party identity and cohesion by constructing an alternative model of the monarchy. *The Idea of a Patriot King,* which circulated privately in the 1730s but was not published until 1749, incorporated Filmeresque paternalism, an anti-Lockean account of the origins of government, and ersatz contract theory.

The continuing debate on the meaning and significance (or lack thereof) of Bolingbroke's pamphlet attests to the period's confusion over monarchy. Bolingbroke's patriot king epitomized virtue; he would rise above party strife to regenerate, by his meritorious example, a constitution that was suffering inevitable decay, owing to the vices of corrupt politicians. This idea was taken up by the "patriots," the coterie of young opposition writers and politicians who gathered around Frederick, Prince of Wales, at Leicester House. The work gained notoriety after Frederick's premature death in 1751 as the instrument that allegedly imbued the young George III with absolutist notions.

Simon Varey's close reading of the work, however, shows that Bolingbroke's intentions were far from clear. It could even be argued that his patriot king was the Young Pretender. Modeled after Machiavelli's *The Prince, Patriot King* could well have been nothing more than an audacious satire of the current regime. As H. T. Dickinson notes, the piece was rather simplistic and vague as political theory, and certainly not Bolingbroke's best work.[57]

Dickinson's wider analysis of Court and Country ideas suggests that they coexisted in a "symbiotic relationship," which helped the Whig government achieve its "unique balance between authority and liberty." The Court and Country parties both accepted the post-1688 imperative of maintaining a balanced constitution but differed in their perceptions of how this was to be achieved.[58] The development of this debate produced a monarchy composed of historical and ideological elements that appealed to a wide range of political stances. The dispute between Walpole and Bolingbroke regarding the relative power of the Crown and the Commons demonstrates the growing importance of historical precedent as well as the extent of ideological reshuffling that took place after 1688. Bolingbroke appropriated the Whiggish common-law myth of the ancient constitution to support his view of English history as a continual struggle for liberty against corrupt leaders like Walpole. The original contract between governed and governors, however, was not seen in the Lockean sense as a universal agreement among the people but rather as an arrangement between family heads and a prince. Walpole, in response, resuscitated the view that had been propounded in support of the Tories during the Exclusion Crisis by Dr. Robert Brady, Cambridge professor of physic turned historian: that Parliament originated in a grant from the Crown during feudal times. This implied that the government, and thus the people, had not been free until Parliament triumphed over James II in 1688; it also allowed Walpole to be represented as a great instrument of political liberty.[59]

Brady's version, after shedding its Walpolean boosterism, ultimately endured: the Hanoverians triumphed over the Jacobites, and the realities of corrupt commercial society prevailed over the mythologized Country squirearchy. Frank McLynn aptly describes the overall struggle as "the divine right of kings versus the divine right of property." A connection existed between the monarchy's ideological crisis and the tensions introduced by the rise of capitalism and its challenge to traditional society. Linda Colley observes that in terms of charisma and appeal, the Hanoverians compared unfavorably to the Stuarts, but the former scored important points in the propaganda war by offering a more practical economic solution. The Hanoverians compensated for their want of glamour by providing domestic peace and security. Adherents to divine-right monarchy could console themselves for the loss of the Stuarts by interpreting British prosperity and security as a sign of divine approval of the new succession.[60]

As Dickinson intimates, the vanquished groups and ideologies did not simply lie down and die. The foreignness of the early Hanoverians, the cosmopolitanism of the burgeoning commercial society, the growing wealth and ostentation of the elite, and their neglect of native artists and writers paved the way for the growth of English nationalism outside of court society. In his account of the cultural protest that took place during the reign of George II, Gerald Newman contends that it forged a mythic English character that was xenophobic, middle-class, moralistic, provincial, and stultifyingly sincere. Farther down the social scale, as Rogers shows, the decline of royal ceremonial (discussed in chapter 7) increased the importance of the London civic calendar and allowed a vital plebeian political culture to develop. The calendar commemorated anniversaries that bore partisan party meanings, both Whig and Jacobite, such as Elizabeth's accession, the Gunpowder Plot, Charles I's martyrdom, the Restoration, and William's landing at Torbay. Although the aristocracy tried to use these occasions to reinforce the social hierarchy, the laboring classes acquired a political life of their own and demanded a freedom of expression bordering on licentiousness. This element added a sense of underlying menace to political controversy but did not become a serious ideological threat until the outbreak of the French Revolution.[61]

When George III ascended the throne in 1760, many of his new subjects had visions of a patriot king who would reconcile their society's conflicting interests. Twenty-two, English-born, and glowing with virtue and optimism, George's words to his first Parliament became legend: "Born and educated in this country, I glory in the name of Britain."[62] Country politicians interpreted the purge of the cabinet in 1761, an event colorfully known to history as the Slaughter of the Pelhamite Innocents, as the act of a patriot king, ridding the country of corrupt Walpolean party influence. Whigs, on the other hand, saw the change as a resurgence of Tory absolutism. This view gained credence when young George defied prevailing political opinion and insisted upon placing his beloved tutor, John Stuart, earl of Bute, in the cabinet. Bute's Scottishness also played into the xenophobia of the Country politicians and the belletristic community. George's political behavior rapidly undermined the optimistic reception his new regime had enjoyed.[63]

Throughout his reign, politicians and extraparliamentary reformers accused George III of introducing a new species of monarchy. His methods of purging politicians who were personally distasteful to him—such as his ousting of Charles James Fox from office and forcing the Commons to accept William Pitt the Younger as chief minister in 1783—raised constitutional issues that remain a source of historical controversy. Was George III recovering the monarchical power usurped by aristocratic cabals, or was he using corrupt means to undermine the balance of the constitution? Ian Christie concludes that George simply used the only means of governing available to post-1688 monarchs. Christie reinforces John Owen's observation that George II and George III were remarkably similar in their methods of influencing politicians, as well as in the degree of success they had in doing so.[64] The difference now was that confrontations between king and ministers were amplified by the ever-expanding press coverage of politics. The press grew alongside party conflict in the first half of the eighteenth century. During George III's reign, newspaper publishers fought for and won the right to report parliamentary debates.[65] The public's growing familiarity with the personalities involved in politics increased the appearance of accessibility to government, a development that eventually worked in monarchy's favor.

The ugly political conflicts of the 1760s and 1770s, the humiliating loss of the American colonies, and the rise of extraparliamentary political agitation (discussed in the next chapter) all made for a troubled monarchy. George III's despair was so great by the end of the American war that he contemplated abdication. The political impotency he felt in the war's aftermath also brought thoughts of retiring to Hanover. Yet the king's dogged patriotism and his obsession with fulfilling the terms of his coronation oath prevailed. Colley's studies of George III and the inception of British nationalism demonstrate that by the mid-1780s, the king's attention to royal ritual and patronage finally paid off: the cult of monarchy became a vehicle for the development of a national identity.[66] In addition, the political crisis generated by events in France forced the resolution of the contentious ideas about kingship produced by the upheavals of the seventeenth century.

By the eve of the French Revolution, the politically astute sensed that the monarchy had changed, but they viewed the action at too close a range to comprehend the nature and implications of this change. Nonetheless, as B. W. Hill asserts, most realized that their institutions were relatively amorphous, and they considered this quality a source of strength. The flexibility and evolutionary nature of political and social structures allowed "such apparently irreconcilable elements as parliamentary supremacy and a royal executive to exist together in balanced harmony."[67] Tradition, the first cousin of custom and the basis of common law, was as solid a doctrine as divine right. Judging by the controversies that surrounded Filmer's scriptural interpretations, "God's plan" offered no more certitude than "ancestral wisdom" when it came to the precise title by which monarchs ruled. As the common law drew upon centuries of judges' rulings, so monarchical tradition encompassed the lessons imparted by a long line of rulers. In the same way that English jurists could argue that the common law contained more wisdom than statute law, eighteenth-century Britons could claim that tradition-based monarchy was superior to a rigidly constituted government.[68]

TWO

The Burke-Paine Controversy

ALTHOUGH the political changes following the Revolution of 1688 and the ideological weakness of the Hanoverian regimes left the meaning of monarchy up for grabs, eighteenth-century theorists happily meandered around the issue until the French Revolution gave a new sense of urgency to the debate. The positions of Dr. Richard Price, a Unitarian divine, Edmund Burke, M.P., and Thomas Paine, international revolutionary and self-proclaimed "citizen of the world" framed the terms of debate for the rest of the decade. As subsequent chapters will show, the resulting dialectic, when combined with strong new directives from the throne, laid the foundation for a flexible, tradition-based, modern British monarchy.

It is customary to think of the French revolutionary era as a time of intense political polarity in Britain. It is true that party animosity ran high, but the clash of ideas brought some reconciliation over the monarchy. Linda Colley sees the shift in attitude toward George III as having occurred a decade earlier. By 1786 the British had shaken off the indignity of colonial defeat, and the Crown was firmly in the forefront of a new, defiant, patriotic fervor. The improvement of the king's reputation was manifest in the outpouring of public affection toward him that year after the deranged Margaret Nicholson tried to stab him. The short-lived optimism of his early reign seemed to be reviving, while George displayed a new self-confidence after he triumphed over his nemesis, Charles James Fox, and secured the services of his faithful workhorse William Pitt the Younger in 1783. Opposition politicians, who traditionally gained strength and bolstered party cohesion by gathering at the residence of the Prince of Wales, were now poorly served by the association. By the mid-1780s, the perennial conflict between Hanoverian kings and their heirs apparent, usually a liability for the Crown, favored the king because the prince was such a reprobate. The great turning point in George III's popularity came in 1788, when he became ill and deranged, prompting Fox to push for a regency that would have made him head of government, replacing Pitt. The Regency Crisis made the bulk of Britons aware of what they would be losing should the king die—or perhaps, what they would be gaining should the dissolute prince and the disreputable Fox take over.[1]

Although the Crown had strengthened its place in the polity by the mid-1780s, its ideological underpinnings remained shaky until the mid-1790s. The positions of Price, Burke, and Paine illustrate the disparate strands of thought on the monarchy that were present in Britain on the eve of the French Revolution. The viciousness of political partisanship had somewhat abated with the taming of John Wilkes, the radical M.P. for Middlesex, and the resolution of the American crisis, but the reform movement was on the upswing in the 1780s. Although political reformers did not achieve their goals during the 1790s, their arguments played an instrumental role in the process of redefining the post-1688 monarchy. Agitation for reform, after all, had its roots in the conflicts between monarchy and Parliament during the seventeenth century. Charles II had enacted the Corporation Act in 1661 to purge local government of potential Puritan rebels, and Parliament had passed the Test Acts of 1673 and 1678 to halt the creeping Catholicism of the future James II. These statutes had long-term repercussions for Dissenters; even those who supported the Revolution of 1688 continued to be barred from enjoying full political rights. The crusade for the repeal of the Test and Corporation Acts became conjoined with the agitation for equal representation that developed at the time of the War of American Independence. Competing political and religious groups developed rival ideologies of kingship to promote partisan interests.

The Burke-Paine controversy issued from the morass of diffuse but interconnected political, social, and religious tensions that had been building since the demise of the Stuart monarchy. Appropriately, the debate on the French Revolution and its implications for Britain was launched by a sermon preached on 4 November 1789 by Price (1723–91), who was coming to the end of a long career of fighting for religious liberty and political rights for Dissenters. Price delivered this sermon to a meeting of the London Revolution Society, whose membership included prominent Dissenters, churchmen, and politicians—a move that signified the union of politics and religion outside the confines of the church-and-state establishment. This was a development that profoundly alarmed Burke. Moreover, Price's interpretation of events in France as being in accordance with the principles of 1688 showcased the ambiguities of the Revolution Settlement.

The Revolution of 1688 had shaken the constitution of the established church as well as the constitution of the state. Staunch Anglicans saw the two as sacredly allied. The collapse of divine-right monarchy left theologians as well as politicians scrambling for new ideologies of justification for their altered polity. Anglican bishops skirted the abyss of divine-right ideology as they explored new theoretical formulations that would preserve the place of religion in government. They embraced a wide range of positions on the origins of government, the terms of obedience to authority, and the conditions justifying rebellion. At one extreme, some churchmen maintained a stolid insistence that monarchy was the form of government preferred by God. At the other end of the spectrum, some flirted with notion of popular sovereignty. A large middle range constructed different models of mutual obligation between ruler and ruled without directly endorsing contract theory, tainted as it was with republicanism. As Robert Hole demonstrates, Filmeresque patriarchalism and Lockean contractarian ideas were equally important to the eighteenth-century debates on the relation between church and state and the nature of government and society.[2]

The Church of England also needed to build a case against the claims of Nonconformists. The Revolution of 1688 allowed Parliament to develop its power and capacity; simultaneously, it opened the door for Protestant Dissenters to play an enhanced role in national life. The Toleration Act of 1689 had rewarded trinitarian Dissenters for their loyalty by granting them freedom of worship. Yet Unitarians were still anathema, and Catholics beyond the pale. Although various relief measures increased opportunities for Nonconformists, the Test and Corporation Acts continued to limit their participation in politics. George I was committed to toleration, but during George II's reign, Walpole's political machinations slowed down progress to a frustrating degree. Many Dissenters lost their stomach for politics and turned to the commercial world, where they quietly built fortunes. Barred from taking degrees at Oxford and Cambridge, they founded their own educational academies—Daventry, Warrington, Hoxton, Hackney, Northampton—which turned out a good proportion of eighteenth-century Britain's preeminent scholars, scientists, and inventors.[3]

During the reign of George III, the campaign for repeal of the Test and

Corporation Acts revived, as Dissenters became involved in the various branches of extraparliamentary agitation for political reform. Many Dissenters found that they shared interests with metropolitan radicals, manufacturers of the middle ranks who were disgruntled over the new class of wealthy financiers reaping the benefits of government contracts. Others numbered among the international coterie of Enlightenment intellectuals who were striving to break free from old superstitions and build new systems of knowledge based on rational thought. Their friendship with Benjamin Franklin eventually drew these British intellectuals into the cause of American independence and into the drawing rooms of English opposition politicians. Eminently clubbable, the Rational Dissenters filled the ranks of the Society of Supporters of the Bill of Rights and the Society of Honest Whigs, associations that grew out of support for Wilkes's stand in the 1760s against the government's use of general warrants and its interference in elections. Arguments for parliamentary reform and for American independence were thus linked and strengthened when their proponents appropriated the Dissenters' ideological justification for religious liberty: a plea for natural rights and natural justice.[4] These speculative, rights-based principles became the object of Burke's strongest attack, for they forged a bond between religion and politics beyond the jurisdiction of, and thus posing a rival model to, established institutions.

In spite of persistent campaigning and the efforts of sympathetic politicians, Dissenters had failed to win legal recognition of what they considered their rightful place in civil society. The Dissenters' Relief Act of 1779 made it easier for ministers and teachers to fall within the auspices of the Toleration Act, but it did not lift the ban that the Test and Corporation Acts had imposed against Nonconformists holding government office. Granted, repeal of the Occasional Conformity and Schism Acts in 1718 and the Acts of Indemnity of 1727—legislation that had been designed to close loopholes in the Test and Corporation Acts—did give some latitude to the spiritually less scrupulous, and enforcement of the acts was sporadic; nonetheless, these statutes remained a potential weapon in the hands of anyone who chose to use them. They stood as a constant reminder to Dissenters of their second-class status in the polity.[5]

Price's sermon to the Revolution Society coincided with a renewed assault upon the Test and Corporation Acts by the Foxite Whigs in Parliament. The arguments presented in 1790 differed little from those of the 1730s. Fox pointed out that times had changed; no pope or pretender threatened, and Dissenters had proven loyal, responsible subjects. Religious tests instituted to exclude anti-monarchical men from office now penalized the staunchest friends of the Crown. The real danger, he added, came from the high-church party's hypocritically raising false alarms against their theological opponents. Pitt's counterarguments stressed the continuity of the British state. Pitt cautioned against throwing away ancestral wisdom: having no test was "contrary to the genius and spirit of monarchy." An established church was essential "to meliorate the morals of the people," and for this service it deserved protection. Lest he be accused of High Toryism, he made the resplendently Whiggish point that the Test Laws acted as a salutary check on the king's power, for they limited his choice of officers to those who had a proven attachment to the government. Hence, they continued to work for the purpose for which they had been enacted, namely, to defend and preserve the constitution.[6]

The ultimate wall that Protestant Dissenters and Catholics repeatedly ran up against in their quest for complete integration into the state came in the form of the nominal head of the Church himself. From the beginning of his reign, George III had been concerned about the growing impiety and licentiousness that he saw in his country. During the 1770s he described the Dissenters' noisy petitions against the Test and Corporation Acts as indicative of "a general disinclination to every restraint."[7] George's piety and sense of duty manifested themselves in his obsession with upholding the terms of the coronation oath. Although he did not believe himself personally infallible, he had the utmost faith in the constitution of church and state. Moreover, having endured increasingly disrespectful challenges from the radical camp, beginning with the "Wilkes and Liberty" agitation of 1764, George III stubbornly supported to the letter all legislation discouraging any sort of nonconformity. His reaction to a bill for Catholic emancipation proposed in 1795 reveals the assumptions underlying his position. After noting that such legislation would subvert the statutes set down by the Revolution Settlement, the king reasoned:

It seems also that an inviolable observation of all these Statutes is made obligatory upon every King and Queen of the Realm by the Coronation Oath. Is it not advisable to put an end at once to a claim that is inconsistent and incompatible with the terms of the original contract between the King and the People, and subversive of that part of the Constitution formed for the preservation of the Protestant Religion established by law? The same great fundamental statutes which secure the *Rights and Liberties of the People,* secure also the *Protestant Reformed Religion* as by law established, and if that part of them which secures our religion is to be repealed now, what security remains for the preservation of our civil rights and liberties?[8]

What could Dissenters do with such a monarch?

Price's solution was to construct a model of monarchy that he conceived to be consistent with the Revolution Settlement even as it incorporated the intellectual, social, and economic advances made since 1689. He employed the well-worn oppositional device of "Majesty misled" to criticize monarchical policy without impugning the monarch. In his sermon commemorating the Glorious Revolution, *A Discourse on the Love of Our Country,* Price lamented that the civil and religious rights gained since 1689 had been subverted by government corruption. The adulatory style of address toward royalty that was currently in common usage indicated that the British people had sunk to a pitiful state of servility. In the messages to the king upon his recovery from illness in February 1789, for example, the people "appeared more like a herd crawling at the feet of a master, than the enlightened and manly citizens rejoicing with a beloved sovereign, but at the same time conscious that he derives all his consequence from themselves." He admitted that these addresses could be considered formulaic or merely the expressions of good-natured warmth; nonetheless, they embodied a dangerous tendency. Adulation always corrupted men in power by giving them an improper idea of their status. Rulers acquired a sense of inherent superiority, which they then believed gave them license to treat their subjects proprietorially. At the same time, employing an adulatory style of address fostered an abjectness in subjects that debased them.[9]

Price told the Revolution Society that the old divine-right doctrines of passive obedience and nonresistance to monarchs still had currency in England. The society had a duty to promote a proper understanding of the principles of 1689 so the British people could bury these slavish ideas once and for all. Price expressed firm convictions regarding the proper relationship between subject and sovereign:

> Civil governments are properly the servants of the public; and a King is no more than the first servant of the public, created by it, maintained by it, and responsible to it: and all the homage paid him, is due to him on no other account than his relation to the public. His sacredness is the sacredness of the community: and the term MAJESTY which it is usual to apply to him, is by no means *his own* majesty, but the MAJESTY OF THE PEOPLE. For this reason, whatever he may be in his private capacity; and though, in respect of personal qualities, not equal to, or even far below many among ourselves— For this reason I say (that is, as representing the community and its first magistrate), he is entitled to our reverence and obedience. The words MOST

EXCELLENT MAJESTY are rightly applied to him; and there is a respect which it would be criminal to withhold from him.[10]

The respectful tone Price employed when discussing the king's status is striking. In a study of the minister's career and writings as a whole, D. O. Thomas concludes that although Price disavowed divine-right monarchy, he believed government in general to be divine in that it was part of God's plan. At the same time, Price considered the people's continued participation in government essential; the monarchy should be under constant surveillance and popular control.[11]

Price's interpretation of revolutionary principles threatened those of a conservative bent because he did not shrink from discussing the right of resistance to the abuse of power. Price claimed that in 1688 the English people had reconfirmed their right to choose their own governors, "cashier them for misconduct," and frame their own government. These were the points that would be debated endlessly during the 1790s. Price saw the revolution across the Channel as operating on the same principles and hoped that it would serve as a catalyst for the English people to reform the abuses that had crept into their own government. He took an immoderate delight in having lived to see "a king led in triumph, and an arbitrary monarch surrendering himself to his subjects." By this point in the French Revolution, the market women had marched to Versailles for bread and brought Louis XVI back to Paris, where he was proclaimed "King of the French" by the National Assembly. Price confidently predicted that liberty would spread; events in France heralded "a general amendment beginning in human affairs; the dominion of kings changed for the dominion of laws, and the dominion of priests giving way to the dominion of reason and conscience." As Price warmed to his subject, his language became more punchy: "Tremble all ye oppressors of the world! Take warning all ye supporters of slavish governments and slavish hierarchies!" His parting line to these unnamed oppressors conveyed an air of menace: these abuses should be corrected "before they and you are destroyed together."[12]

To Burke, this threatening and, perhaps worse, disrespectful language was symptomatic of a dangerous turn that British society had taken as a result of Dissenters' involvement in politics and of extraparliamentary agitation in general. Burke had supported American independence in the 1770s and played an active role in the campaign for economic reform during the 1780s; hence, contemporaries saw Burke's negative response to the French Revolution as apostatic. When the progression of his thought is viewed in retrospect, however, his response does not seem so surprising. Nevertheless, scholars who take on the task of mapping a coherent philosophy throughout Burke's writing find themselves on a slippery path. As Frank O'Gorman points out, Burke was first and foremost a politician; he formed his positions in response to circumstances. This gave his thought a little-appreciated originality. When he no longer found the Whiggism of the seventeenth century relevant, Burke reformulated its doctrines to recover party dynamism and give Whig politics a new direction. In the process he picked and chose among the ideas of Harrington and Bolingbroke, as well as of Locke, to come up with what O'Gorman describes as a position so idiosyncratic as to defy labels. Frederick Dreyer believes that O'Gorman is too dogmatic in his conception of a systematic ideology. He insists that Burke, although he drew upon a number of political traditions in forming his philosophy, never contradicted Locke. Yet in order to trace the main principles that imparted consistency to Burke's thought, Dreyer discounts certain arguments on the grounds that they were insincerely offered in the course of political maneuvering.[13]

These assessments are useful to an understanding of Burke's position on monarchy. During the 1760s, Burke did not bother to conceal his dislike of George III, whom he believed to be introducing a new species of absolutism. He took up the old Bolingbrokean rhetoric of government corruption but with a significant twist. Instead of a patriot king, he looked to the great Whig magnates as the natural aristocracy: the true leaders of the country, who had a permanent stake in its welfare. Nonetheless, as Michael Freeman points out, Burke consistently supported a strong monarchy in the context of a balanced constitution. Bad kings were one thing; the institution of kingship quite another.[14] In the early part of George III's reign, Burke saw the overweening influence of the Crown as the most serious threat to the sacred balance; but by the late 1780s, extraparliamentary agitation threatened to tip the scales too far toward the popular branch of the constitution. According to R. R. Fennessy, Burke's shift from intemperate outbursts against George III to a heightened appreciation of the hereditary principle took place during the Regency Crisis, as he and the Foxite Whigs parried with Pitt.[15]

In *Reflections on the Revolution in France* (1790), Burke took a reverential attitude toward monarchy and dwelt on the violence and disorder that had accompanied the French royal family's removal to Paris the previous October. He acknowledged that Price had correctly condemned gross adulation but argued that calling the king a servant was "flippant vain discourse." The language revealed a dangerous tendency in light of Price's ideas on "cashiering kings for misconduct." In one sense, wrote Burke, kings could be considered servants, in that their power had no other purpose than to provide for the general good of the nation. But unlike servants, kings did not obey any other person, nor were they removable at anyone's pleasure. When the British people obeyed their king, they were obeying the law he embodied. The law referred to him as *our sovereign Lord the King.* Furthermore, he achieved this status by a fixed rule of succession. A monarch's removal rarely occurred without force, and it usually involved civil war.[16]

The most striking change in Burke's thought was his vilification of Dissenters as conspirators against monarchical establishments. His hostility had developed gradually as he perceived a shift in the threat to the constitutional balance. Burke's position in 1790, however, seemed a violent turn-around, blown out of proportion by his alarmed reaction to the spectacle of rampaging *menu peuple* across the Channel.[17] His former ally, Fox (with whom a weeping Burke split over the issue of the French Revolution in a histrionic scene on the floor of the Commons), presented a "motion for the repeal of certain penal statutes respecting religious opinions" in 1792 and touched the nerve that Dissenting agitation had exposed: "In this country we were governed by King, Lords and Commons. No man would contend, that any of these powers was infallible? for so they did, if they claimed exclusive privileges, and enforced penalties on those who differed from them."[18] Fox perhaps went too far in his use of the word *infallible* but the issue at stake was indeed the slipping authority of the state.

Burke, in an attempt to shore up this erosion, went beyond the old Warburtonian alliance of church and state the 1730s in his response to Fox's motion. He pronounced the alliance a misnomer because it implied a relation between two distinct and independent bodies. In a Christian commonwealth, church and state were one and the same, being integral parts of the same whole. Burke's model revived the importance of the monarch as head of the Church of England:

> Religion is so far, in my opinion, from being out of the province or the duty of a Christian magistrate, that it is, and ought to be, not only in his care; but the principal thing in his care; because it is one of the great bonds of human society; and its object the supreme good, the ultimate end and object of man himself. The magistrate, who is a man, and charged with the concerns of men, and to whom very specially, nothing human is remote and indifferent, has a right and a duty to watch over it with an unceasing vigilance, to protect, to promote, to forward it by every rational, just, and pru-

dent means. It is principally his duty to prevent the abuses, which grow out of every strong and efficient principle, that actuates the human mind. As religion is one of the bonds of society, he ought not to suffer it to be made the pretext of destroying its peace, order, liberty, and its security. Above all, he ought strictly to look to it when men begin to form new combinations, to be distinguished by new names, and especially, when they mingle a political system with their religious opinions, true or false, plausible or implausible.[19]

Burke strayed dangerously close to the abyss of divine right. Ursula Henriques argues that he avoided falling in by presenting the ecclesiastical constitution as the responsibility of the state in its corporate capacity, not of the monarch personally.[20] Indeed, although in this Commons speech Burke appeared to be advocating some form of personal monarchy, he avoided implications of absolutism by stressing the social rather than the political role of the monarch. Here, Burke not only seemed clairvoyant in his prediction of the French Revolution's outcome; he also anticipated the British monarchy's modern incarnation.

In the *Reflections,* Burke presented the subject's relationship with the sovereign as something natural—indeed, as a vital component of the human condition. His deservedly oft-quoted apostrophe to Marie Antoinette, which lies at the center of the work, is rich in its emotional resonances:

It is now sixteen or seventeen years since I saw the queen of France, then the dauphiness, at Versailles; and surely never lighted on this orb, which she hardly seemed to touch, a more delightful vision. I saw her just above the horizon, decorating and cheering the elevated sphere she just began to move in,—glittering like the morning-star, full of life, and splendour, and joy. Oh! what a revolution! and what a heart must I have, to contemplate without emotion that elevation and that fall! Little did I dream when she added titles of veneration to those of enthusiastic, distant, respectful love, that she should ever be obliged to carry the sharp antidote against disgrace concealed in that bosom; little did I dream that I should see such disasters fallen upon her in a nation of gallant men, in a nation of men of honour and of cavaliers. I thought ten thousand swords must have leaped from their scabbards to avenge even a look that threatened her with insult.—But the age of chivalry is gone.—That of sophisters, oeconomists, and calculators, has succeeded; and the glory of Europe is extinguished for ever. Never, never more, shall we behold that generous loyalty to rank and sex, that proud submission, that dignified obedience, that subordination of the heart, which kept alive, even in servitude itself, the spirit of an exalted freedom.

The unbought grace of life, the cheap defence of nations, the nurse of manly sentiment and heroic enterprize is gone! It is gone, that sensibility of principle, that chastity of honour, which felt a stain like a wound, which inspired courage whilst it mitigated ferocity, which ennobled whatever it touched, and under which vice itself lost half its evil, by losing all its grossness.[21]

Burke began by luxuriating in the radiance of royal splendor, sharing with his readers the magical effect of being in the queenly presence. He then grabbed his entranced audience by the lapels and dragged them down into a crepuscular antipodes, where they could only shake their heads in despair over the spectacle of exalted femininity degraded. In this passage Burke implied that veneration of royalty was tightly woven into the whole moral fabric of society: what he elsewhere referred to as "the decent drapery of life." As James Boulton notes, the natural grace, beauty, and order embodied by Marie Antoinette stood in sharp contrast to the monstrous depravity and blood-thirstiness of the revolutionaries whom Burke described so vividly in the pages leading up to the apostrophe. Burke drew upon familiar images—nature, family, and the noble house—as well as biblical allusion to build a cozy image of the established order so that his readers would be inspired to protect it against the evil and anarchy emanating from France.[22]

Burke's conception of nature was complex, caught up as it was in the wider debate started by Locke on the relation of natural and civil rights.[23] In Burke's writings the "nature of things" intersected with tradition and experience. Burke based natural law on prescription, or usage immemorial. He treated the precise origins of human institutions as immaterial; they were all ultimately the product of divine wisdom and will. In Burke's model, the progress of mankind followed God's predetermined plan.[24] Hence, Burke argued that the Revolution of 1688 occurred for the sole purpose of recovering ancestral wisdom by preserving the hereditary Protestant succession: "No experience has taught us, that in any other course or method than that of an *hereditary crown,* our liberty can be regularly perpetuated and preserved sacred as our *hereditary right.*"[25]

Burke insisted that the accession of William involved only a temporary deviation from the strict order of succession in response to "a grave and overruling necessity." Burke saw the beginnings of a nefarious plot in Price's interpretation of the events of 1688 as "cashiering for misconduct," as well as in his characterization of George III as virtually the only lawful monarch in the world because he owed his crown to the choice of the people. Burke accused Price and the Revolution Society of attempting to plant the doctrine of elec-

tive monarchy in the minds of the people in order to set up their own elec-
toral college. He discoursed ad nauseam upon the impropriety of the word
misconduct. James II had broken the original contract between the king and
people by endeavoring to subvert law, liberty, and the established church.
Moreover, the Convention Parliament had made provisions against the events
of 1688 ever serving as precedent for future revolutions by preserving the doctrine "the king can do no wrong" and by placing all responsibility for misrule
on his ministers.

Burke disputed Price's claim that the French Revolution followed the
same principles as the Glorious Revolution. While the latter had reestablished
the sacred balance among the three parts of the British constitution, the
French were replacing the despotism of absolute monarchy with the license
of democracy. Burke inquired: "Have they never heard of a monarchy directed
by laws, controlled and balanced by the great hereditary wealth and hereditary dignity of a nation, and both again controlled by a judicious check from
the reason and feeling of the people at large acting by a suitable and permanent organ?"[26] The revolutionaries had chosen to have "a degraded king . . .
without any sort of deliberative discretion in any one act of his function."
Louis XVI no longer stood as the fount of justice since he did not choose
judges but only authenticated the choices of others; moreover, he executed
sentences in which he had no say. In this capacity he was little better than the
common hangman and would grow to be as despised, Burke predicted. Nor
was the king any longer the source of honor. The National Assembly dispensed all rewards, leaving the king without the means of granting favor; he
had to exact obedience by using fear of punishment or force of arms. This
contravened the first principle of effective executive government: subjects
ought to be encouraged to love and venerate the one to whom they owed obedience. Authority based on fear and mistrust would not be obeyed cordially
or endured for long. A king with powers as circumscribed as Louis's could
be concerned only with self-preservation; this rendered him unfit for an office that required confidence, vigor, and the desire for glory. Taking away his
power to declare war and peace was equally impolitic. How could foreign powers take a ruler seriously when they knew that he could not make his own decisions? Burke believed that the French had undermined the royal prerogative in order to bring monarchy into contempt and to prepare the way for its
abolition, not to correct its vices.[27]

Burke's interpretations of events in France appalled Thomas Paine, although they hardly could have surprised him. After all, when Paine had returned to England in 1788, after fourteen years in America, he witnessed the sordid political maneuverings of the Regency Crisis. He had been dismayed by the Whig party's subversion of democratic principles when they tried to place the Prince of Wales on the throne without obtaining the consent of the people. Ever optimistic and convinced of the truth of his views, Paine still expected Burke to see the light when he wrote to him from Paris on 17 January 1790 describing what he saw as a well-organized revolution that had the potential to overcome centuries of animosity between England and France. Although Paine had become a committed republican in America, in 1788 he had been too preoccupied with making money to pursue serious political issues with Burke while he was a guest in the statesman's home. The French Revolution, however, rekindled Paine's interest in British politics. When he caught wind of the *Reflections* he badgered Burke's publisher for details and hastily prepared his rebuttal. The degree of anger and personal resentment expressed in *Rights of Man* is startling, according to Fennessy, considering that Burke and Paine continued to meet during this period with the understanding that neither would mention France in the other's presence.[28]

Paine came bursting into the stately mansion of Burke's established order and broke up all the furniture. He presented the British monarchy as a ruinously expensive, corrupt, and ineffective form of government, and the British constitution as a figment of Burke's imagination. At the center of Paine's argument was an assault upon the sanctity, wisdom, justice, and utility of the heredity principle. Hereditary rule could never come under Burke's definition of government as "a contrivance of human wisdom" because ability could not be inherited. A contrivance that allowed government to fall into the hands of an idiot or an infant hardly embodied wisdom. Moreover, the heredity principle degraded people by treating them like chattel. Paine spent an entire chapter in *Rights of Man* arguing that hereditary government would soon become obsolete, as people became aware of its inherent weaknesses. Kings succeeded one another regardless of their mental or moral characters. Such a system of a government could not maintain consistency, subject as it was to accidents and irrational passions. Hereditary succession was a "burlesque upon monarchy," requiring no special talents: "only the animal figure of a man—a sort of breathing automaton." In addition, contested hereditary claims occasioned longer, bloodier, and more frequent civil wars than elections. Hereditary regimes also had permanent family interests that dragged them into foreign wars. In short, the difference between government by election and representation and government by hereditary succession was the difference between reason and ignorance.[29]

Paine availed himself of the old radical claim that the "Norman yoke" had subjugated the British people, but did not invoke the customary vision of an earlier golden age of Anglo-Saxon liberty.[30] He argued that Burke's support of an unalterable succession implied that the British polity descended directly from the Norman oppression. He predicted that in a thousand years Americans would look back with pride at the origins of their government, while supporters of monarchy would shroud its foundations in the haze of antiquity, as Burke had done: "Hard as Mr. Burke laboured under the Regency Bill and Hereditary Succession two years ago, and much as he dived for precedents, he still had not boldness enough to bring up William of Normandy and say, *There is the head of the list! there is the fountain of honour!* the son of a prostitute, and the plunderer of the English nation." Like Price, Paine observed that Britain still bore the marks of conquest; for example, in the slavish way parliaments addressed the king. Even in 1688 Parliament had declared that it would submit itself and posterity to William and Mary. Paine called *submission* a term for vassals. Its language betrayed the fact that Parliament had been created by a grant or boon from the Crown instead of having being based on the people's right to representation. He contrasted this shameful heritage to the new French government: all sovereignty rested in the nation, the legislature preceded the executive, and the law came before the king.[31]

Paine parted company with Price, other Dissenting theorists, and the politicians who supported the French Revolution (Burke's misguided "New Whigs") with his interpretation of the so-called Glorious Revolution. As a conquered nation, Paine reasoned, Britain could not take advantage of the rights that Price claimed had been gained by the events of 1688–89. Britain's hereditary succession exhibited "as many instances of tyranny as could be acted within the limits to which the nation had restricted it." Paine explained that when the Stuarts tried to go beyond the limits of their "assumed rights," the other parts of the government conspired to divide their power. They placed William III on the throne by promulgating the falsehood that he descended from the same stock as James II. Paine called the Declaration of Rights, now called the Bill of Rights, "a bill of wrongs and of insult." Any rights won during the revolution had been violated as soon as they had been proclaimed. Parliament, for example, had assumed the right to bind posterity to a particular form of government. Paine argued that each generation ought to be free to act for itself.[32]

Although Paine presented himself as the champion of the rights of the living over the rights of the dead and reviled Burke's notion of government based on prescriptive rights, he was not above citing historical precedents. To vilify the monarchy as an institution he concocted a fanciful account of the state of nature. In the "early and solitary ages of the world," men had peacefully tended flocks and herds until a "banditti of ruffians" overran the world. They divided the world into dominions, and their chiefs changed their names from robber to monarch. Naturally, the chiefs quarreled with one another and thus perpetuated the customs of war and conquest that had always been a characteristic of monarchy. "What at first was plunder, assumed the softer name of revenue; and the power originally usurped, they affected to inherit." Wars, observed Paine, that once were fought to satisfy monarchical pride now served as an excuse for inflicting greater taxes.[33]

Expense and corruption become refrains running though *Rights of Man*. Paine compared Britain unfavorably to America, a country ten times the size governed at a fortieth of the expense. He declared that George Washington's sense of honor would never permit him to accept the seventy million pounds that Paine estimated had been soaked up by the present king of England. He bristled at the thought that the royal family even handed over their physician's bills for the state to pay. Individuals, claimed Paine, should be remunerated in accordance with the service they provided, and no office could be worth more than ten thousand pounds a year, especially when "thousands, who are forced to contribute thereto, are pining of want, and struggling with misery." Paine connected the "coming of the Hanoverians" with a "constant increase in the number and wretchedness of the poor and the amount of the poor rates" due to thirteen millions of new taxes collected annually on articles of consumption. Before this, he claimed, some equity had been achieved between taxes on land and consumer goods. Even worse, the million per annum commanded by the Civil List did not further the public good; rather, the funds perpetuated the abuses. The splendor of the throne supported the corruption of the state. The court consisted of "a band of parasites, living in luxurious indolence, out of the public taxes." Meanwhile, the only efficient parts of government were republican in form—from the office of constable through the various courts of law.[34]

Paine dismissed Burke's beloved mixed constitution as "ludicrously styled, a government of *this, that,* and *t'other.*" He explained why the system did not provide the checks against corruption that its supporters claimed:

> In mixed Governments there is no responsibility, the parts cover each other till responsibility is lost; and the corruption which moves the machine, contrives at the same time its own escape. When it is laid down as a maxim, that *a king can do no wrong,* it places him in a state of similar security with that of idiots and persons insane, and responsibility is out of the question with respect to himself. It then descends upon the Minister, who shelters himself under a majority in Parliament, which, by places, pensions, and corruption, he can always command; and that majority justifies itself by the same authority with which it protects the Minister. In this rotary motion, responsibility is thrown off from the parts, and from the whole.

Paine maintained that "universal peace, civilisation and commerce" were only to be achieved by "a revolution in the systems of governments."[35]

What did this mean for the monarchy? Paine's account of Louis XVI's role in the French Revolution reveals that even a committed republican had difficulty disentangling himself from monarchy's bonds. In the first part of *Rights of Man,* written before the royal family's unsuccessful flight to Varennes in June 1791, Paine presented Louis XVI as an unwitting agent of despotism. Notwithstanding the French king's personal virtues, centuries of despotic principles had become ingrained, "and the Augean stable of parasites and plunderers too abominably filthy to be cleansed, by anything short of a complete and universal revolution." By the time Paine produced the second volume of his work, Louis had not yet been imprisoned but obviously was in danger. Paine avoided any further enumeration of the sins of the French monarchy; instead he shifted his focus to the virtues of the American republic. The only reference to Louis occurred in the allegorical tale of the Berne bear: Citizens of Berne had been taught that their bear preserved their welfare. They therefore kept him at great expense. One day the bear died unexpectedly, and could not immediately be replaced. When life went on without any disasters befalling them, the people finally recognized the inconvenience of keeping a creature that not only had an insatiable appetite but also required declawing to prevent his injuring them.[36]

Ironically, Paine almost lost his life trying to save that of Louis XVI after his position placed him on the wrong side of the Jacobin revolution. As a member of the French National Convention, he argued that Louis should be tried in order to expose monarchical perfidy and then imprisoned for the duration of the war. Afterward, he should be exiled to America, where he would learn the true principles of free government. Paine took for his precedent the Catholic Stuarts; they had become so corrupted that their whole line was banished forever. He believed that Louis would have been a good man had he been born in obscurity, but all kings became robbers, whatever their personal virtues. The French ought not tarnish their newfound enlightenment and liberation by taking revenge against such a wretch. It was time for the country to make a decisive break from the sanguinary legacy of monarchy.[37]

Although decrying Paine's involvement with the French regicides, a British loyalist made an insightful observation regarding the uncomfortable position that Paine had placed himself in with his anti-monarchical rhetoric: "Even the voice of Mr. Paine, although he had long *declared war against the whole hell of monarchy*' was lifted up to deprecate the murder of Louis XVIth—the author of *Rights of Man* has no objection to stripping kings naked and turning them out as vagabonds upon the charity of the world; but his *gentle* nature *revolts at the idea* of covering himself with their blood:—which shows what many have denied, that there is *one crime* congenial with republicanism, which Thomas Paine is *not yet up to.*"[38]

Presumably, Paine envisioned the same sort of exile and reeducation for George III. His treatment of the king in the text of *Rights of Man* is curious. He insisted on ignoring the significant fact of George's native birth and persisted in referring to him as the Elector of Hanover. Paine indulged in strikingly indirect sniping, which mostly took the form of passing references to the absolutism found in the German states. He sneered at the idea of such a xenophobic nation as Britain importing a foreign family to govern it, particularly the incongruous "House of Brunswick, one of the petty tribes of Germany." He voiced doubts that a foreign king could feel the appropriate responsibility or respect for a nation entrusted to his care. Paine also revived the old anti-Hanoverian rhetoric of the previous two reigns: the king's inordinate involvement in foreign affairs drained the public revenue. These allusions reveal Paine to be more concerned with the preservation of the French Revolution than the British polity. With the rest of Europe undergoing revolution, instead of interfering in the domestic affairs of other countries, France would be safe, at peace, and no longer expending money and men on military defense.[39]

Price, Burke, and Paine each held a view of monarchy that promoted his particular interests. Price had a vision of a king who would possess sufficient self-confidence to accept his status as the servant of the people according to the dictates of the Revolution Settlement. This king would break away from the outmoded alliance between church and state and allow complete religious freedom. This would finally bury the persistent divine-right notions that kept the British people in a state of vassalage and that excluded from the polity a large body of loyal citizens. A monarch who felt secure enough to acknowledge the natural rights of the people and base his authority on the service he provided them would be guaranteed a body of devoted and dutiful subjects.

Paine, the product of a Quaker father and an Anglican mother, had broken away from organized religion and embraced Deism.[40] Distanced from the Dissenters' campaign for equal political rights, Paine did not have the same stake in moderate reform of the British polity. He could afford to reject Price's optimism about the potential for productive change through reform of the established system. For Paine, the institution of monarchy was fundamentally corrupt and beyond regeneration. The basis of government had evolved from priestcraft to conquest, and monarchs had moved from using superstition to applying force in order to maintain their position. In the process, the two had become interdependent:

> A race of conquerors arose, whose government, like that of William the Conqueror, was founded in power, and the sword assumed the name of a sceptre. Governments thus established, last as long as the power to support them lasts; but that they might avail themselves of every engine in their favor, they united fraud to force, and set up an idol which they called *Divine Right,* and which, in imitation of the Pope, who affects to be spiritual and temporal, and in contradiction to the Founder of the Christian religion, twisted itself afterwards into an idol of another shape, called *Church and State.* The key of St. Peter, and the key of the Treasury, became quartered on one another, and the wondering cheated multitude worshipped the invention.[41]

The final stage of this process, government by reason, could be achieved only by republican revolution.

From Burke's point of view as a professional politician, the framework of the British state acted as a sound protection against absolutism and demagoguery alike. Although by no means perfect, Britain's mixed monarchy had the means of reforming itself built into its structure, and it had been following a gradual, steady course of improvement. Any attempts to initiate innovations that deviated from this course were motivated by personal ambition or enmity. Burke saw attacks on the established church and the monarchy as the first steps in a plot to undermine the integrity of the state. The upheavals in France were proof of the connections between anarchy, atheism, and disrespect for royalty.

Burke has been credited with prophetic powers in light of his predictions regarding the outcome of the French Revolution.[42] Indeed, he also showed considerable clarity of vision regarding the importance of the social, cultural, and psychological roles of the modern British monarchy. Price's insight also deserves recognition. Although Burke realized the importance of personal aspects of rule, Price's view that monarchical sanctity is based on utility became an important aspect of political argument during the 1790s. The Burke-Paine controversy heralded a period of intense political contestation, with party animosity sometimes breaking out into physical violence. But in the debate on monarchy, a synthesis occurred between the Burkean and Painite extremes that scholars have not explored. The next two chapters will trace the course of this process in the rival camps engendered by the controversy: the loyalist association movement and the societies of newly politicized plebeians who wound up commandeering the campaign for parliamentary reform.

THREE

Recasting the Ideological Foundations of the British Monarchy

HOMAS PAINE'S assault upon monarchy in general and the British regime in particular provoked serious examination of the assumptions on which monarchical government rested. The arguments promulgated by Richard Price and Edmund Burke, as well, demonstrated that considerable dissension existed regarding the British monarchy's role, power, and source of legitimacy. Paine's republican challenge, the revolution in France, and the burgeoning reform movement at home gave new imperatives for supporters of the political and social status quo to clarify the ambiguities that had developed around kingship since 1688. The political discourse inspired by the Burke-Paine controversy involved recasting the British monarchy into an institution that was not rigid in its forms and imagery but rather had sufficient flexibility to satisfy partisans of many political stances.

In this chapter I examine the ideas about monarchy presented in the replies to Paine's *Rights of Man* and in the writings by members of the Association for Preserving Liberty and Property against Republicans and Levellers (APLP). Loyalist literature demonstrates that supporters of the British state had wide-ranging perceptions of its constitution. Loyalists characterized the basis of monarchical rule with formulations that extended from the democratic to the Filmeresque. More important, however, some writers began to meld patriarchal and republican ideologies, making the claim that the British monarchy encompassed the ideals of each.

Historians vary in their conceptions of the loyalist position. Donald Ginter argues that the movement contained a strong contingent of reformist sympathizers. Although he is correct in pointing out the wide spectrum of political positions one could embrace during the early stages of debate, he overlooks the aggressive conservatism that most loyalists espoused. In contrast, J. C. D. Clark and J. A. W. Gunn emphasize the survival of the High-Tory notions of order and submission to authority after 1688. As Joanna Innes points out, Clark's model of eighteenth-century England as an ancien régime ignores the significant fact that the English polity had been founded on a revolution, which had spawned a large middle ground of political thought. Gunn more convincingly presents the tenacity of divine-right doctrines as symptomatic of the ambiguities that riddled the Whigs' position after the revolution. The new regime had considerable difficulty in reconciling the arguments used to justify the removal of James II with the ideology of order and obedience that government practice required.[1]

Although H. T. Dickinson may be reading the last rites over High Toryism prematurely, as Gunn alleges, he presents the fullest picture of late eighteenth-century conservative thought. He demonstrates that as extreme as the conservative reaction to the French Revolution had been, loyalists continued to address the issue of liberty in their arguments supporting the political system and the social hierarchy. More important, Dickinson acknowledges the degree to which conservative ideology developed in reaction to radical thought. Nevertheless, he insists, the conservative position had more integrity than the radical, and it won overwhelming support within the political nation in consequence. David Eastwood and John Dinwiddy take issue with what the latter describes as the "new Dickinsonian consensus": the view that the conservatives won the decade's political debate by the power of their ideological position. Eastwood notes the degree to which conservatives appropriated radical language to make their ideas more palatable. Dinwiddy argues that Dickinson and others give short shrift to the enduring elements of the radical position, thus obscuring the dialogue that took place between the two camps.[2]

The eighteenth-century debate on the role and power of the monarchy certainly involved exchange and compromise; and early studies of the anti-Painites overemphasize polarization. In fact, R. R. Fennessy pronounces "Burke-Paine controversy" a misnomer: it did not consist of a debate but rather of "two appeals to English public opinion, from two entirely different and totally irreconcilable points of view." Fennessy does not see the political nation as having broken into rival Burkeite and Painite camps, however. He describes the subsequent pamphlet war as "a collection of answers to Burke by people who did not agree with Paine, and of answers to Paine by people who did not agree with Burke." Fennessy and others also note that the chronic misrepresentation of opposing viewpoints precluded any real exchange.[3] Robert Hole's survey of the loyalist propaganda produced throughout the decade offers a more sophisticated analysis. He observes that Paine's arguments dictated what issues remained key points of debate, while Burke's conceptions of British institutions helped form a loyalist sensibility.[4] A closer inspection of ideas on monarchy reinforces Hole's impressions. Paine's challenge forced supporters of the status quo to clarify issues they had previously glossed over or discounted; and when clarity proved elusive, they took refuge in Burkean appeals to sentiment, prejudice, and tradition.

These various treatments of loyalism suggest that, contrary to appearances at the time, the movement did not embody a unified, monolithic force. It acquired a corporate identity when John Reeves established the APLP on 20 November 1792. Historians are divided over the nature of loyalist organization, as well as its ideology. Although a fan of the loyalist movement, R. R. Dozier notes the smoke-and-mirrors quality of the APLP's founding. Reeves, who had held minor government posts and had friends at the Treasury and the Home Office, issued a report to the press of an APLP meeting having been held at the Crown and Anchor Tavern presided over by the fictitious John Moore. The imaginary meeting's press release inspired loyalists in the provinces to follow the model and organize more formally; many had already heeded the call for public vigilance embodied in the royal proclamation against seditious meetings and writings of 21 May 1792 by holding meetings to draw up petitions in its support and by going door to door to collect signatures. Although the London APLP and its branch associations varied in character, they all dispensed the same sort of propaganda.[5]

The degree of the Pitt administration's involvement in the APLP has been controversial because the question of whether the loyalist movement was a true expression of British public opinion hinges on this issue. Eugene Charlton Black states unequivocally that the APLP "was organized with government connivance and support to marshal public sentiment behind the ministry and to assist in the suppression of dissident opinion." Reeves, after all, was a government employee who received lucrative sinecures for his loyalist work. But M. J. Quinlan disputes Black's account and cites Reeves's public statement in denial of government sponsorship of the association. Henry R. Winkler finds Reeves's protestations suspiciously energetic and interprets the published declaration as a deliberate attempt to mask government machinations. He cites correspondence between ministers and APLP leaders that show collaboration. Austin Mitchell, on the other hand, is unconvinced by the idea of a government conspiracy. He notes Pitt's reluctance to encourage popular societies; the minister even considered legislation that would ban all political meetings. Yet others did not share Pitt's reservations. Dickinson concludes: "If [Reeves] was not directly encouraged by the government to set up the Association, at the very least he knew that the scheme would meet with ministerial approval. The government certainly welcomed the proposal and helped to publicize it." Dickinson considers the question of government involvement academic, however; the APLP's success demonstrated that it did not express mere government propaganda but reflected the views of the majority of Britons.[6]

It is hard to separate the activities of the government, the APLP, and independent supporters of the monarchy. Paine's challenge constituted a threat to the British government, designed as it was to stir up indignation in a plebeian audience. Moreover, *Rights of Man* was reaching this audience in a cheap edition, which, rather like the court's popularity as Paine described it, "sprung up like a mushroom in a night" in every corner of the country. Paine was convicted in absentia of seditious libel (he had gone to France to take a place in the new National Convention) by a special jury in the Court of the King's Bench in December 1792. But before resorting to legal prosecution, the Pitt administration launched a propaganda campaign to discredit Paine, first commissioning George Chalmers, a Scottish antiquarian and historian who had been clerking for one of the Privy Council committees since 1786, to dig up unsavory details from his past. The ensuing *Life of Pain,* which appeared under the pseudonym "Francis Oldys, A.M., of the University of Pennsylvania," went through numerous revisions in the course of ten editions published between 1791 and 1793. Chalmers gradually expanded the work to attach sinister implications to passages of Paine's writings as well as to episodes in his personal life.[7] Not all the respondents to Paine were sponsored by the government, however, and not all the replies were simple ad hominem attacks. The positions on monarchy that developed in loyalist literature must be viewed as a mixture of government directives and personal initiative and as having been inspired by a variety of motives.

The forty-six pamphlet replies to *Rights of Man* that I examine here provide a cross section of the sort of persons moved to take up active loyalism. A third of these dedicated their pamphlets to the APLP, had identifiable connections to the government, or were in positions to benefit from Crown preferment. In this last category, at least eight respondents were clergymen.

John St. John, Bolingbroke's nephew, sat in the Commons during the 1770s and 1780s, then was appointed surveyor general of the Crown land revenues. Frederick Hervey, earl of Bristol and ensign in the First Foot Guards, became M.P. for Bury St. Edmonds in 1796. Richard Hey, mathematician, jurist, and occasional essayist, was a fellow of Magdelene College, Cambridge. One of the pamphleteers, Tobias Molloy, a Dublin barrister, lashed out at the anonymous author of *Remarks on Mr. Paine's Pamphlet* (Dublin, 1792), whom he identified as "a gentleman (it is said) high at the revenue board." John Bowles and John Gifford both received disbursements from the Treasury for their loyalist writings.[8]

Some writers harbored other interests. William Cusac Smith, a young Irishman, wished to express his admiration of Burke. Isaac Hunt and Charles Harrington Elliot, American loyalists, still bore grudges against Paine. John Quincy Adams, a Federalist, published an anonymous reply to Paine that was attributed to his father, then vice president of the United States, and described by James Madison as "a mock defence of the Republican constitution."[9] Not all respondents can be characterized as conservatives, however. Sir Brook Boothby, seventh baronet, wrote poems, drama, fables, and satirical essays, frequented literary and scientific societies, and struck up a friendship with Rousseau in the course of his frequent sojourns to France. John King's published correspondence with Paine identified him as a reformer disillusioned by events in France.[10]

Regarding the question of these pamphlets' audience, Winkler's observation of 1952 still holds: "How widely and in what circles they were read is of course more easily asked than answered."[11] Loyalists handed out a substantial percentage of the APLP tracts gratis; whether the working poor actually read them or used them to light their pipes remains a matter of speculation. For the purposes of this study, it is sufficient to observe that the ideas worked out in the anti-Paine pamphlets appeared in, and thus had wider broadcast through, sermons, legal argument, and royalist rituals (which will be discussed in later chapters). These pamphlets provide a useful view into the historical assumptions and acrobatics of logic underlying the loyalist approach toward monarchy.

A survey of the pamphlets' contents shows the anti-Painites to have had different degrees of concern about the threat to the monarchy. Roughly a third gave more attention to monarchy than to other topics, another third devoted as many pages to monarchy as they did to other issues, and the rest gave little or no notice to Paine's critique of kingly government. Some of the pamphleteers in the last category shared the attitude articulated by St. John: "A treatise on the utility of monarchy in the year 1791 would come rather late after so many volumes have been written; and as I have nothing new to observe, I shall be satisfied with remarking, that Mr. Paine appears to be in the same predicament, and nothing being advanced by him, no answer is wanted."[12] Instead, these writers expended more effort in exposing what they considered the fallacy of Paine's claims for the superiority of republican government: "It shall be our business to assign to consequences their true causes; though the result may strip republicanism of her most alluring garments, with which indeed she ought never to have been clothed."[13]

These writers argued that Paine's beloved American republic had gradually adopted the British mixed constitution as the country became more prosperous and the people became corrupted by luxury. They predicted that the Americans would eventually find that the election of a supreme executive magistrate promoted political intrigue and tumult. Bowles, one of the writers remunerated by the Treasury, insisted that this was Paine's intention in recommending such a government for Britain: the ensuing chaos would give him the opportunity to satisfy his lust for power.[14]

Paine's adversaries produced some trenchant history lessons to counter the historical models that he had presented to illustrate the oppressive origins and continuing despotism of hereditary monarchy. More than half the pamphlets I consulted contained lurid descriptions of oppressive or weak republican and elective regimes, such as those of ancient Rome and contemporary Poland. Loyalists got a lot of mileage out of Cromwell's Protectorate, "that late and disgraceful period of national delirium" when "the sceptre was broken and a bloody sword appeared in its place."[15] An anonymous writer warned that republics harbored treachery, even those established with the best intentions. The Long Parliament had set out to preserve liberty but wound up destroying it by sacrificing the monarchy. The annihilation of monarchical power meant that the title by which rulers held their authority was gone, which had allowed Cromwell to usurp the government.[16] Several pamphleteers supported Burke's axiom that pure democracy inevitably degenerated into mob government. Charles Hawtrey, for example, declared: "The tyrannical and personal cruelty of a king can never reach beyond the extent of a very small circle and that must necessarily be of but a very short duration; but the tyranny of the people has no limits." Loyalists pointed out the potential for tumult and oppression that came with the rise of the demagogue—"democracy's giant offspring," in the estimation of William Cusac Smith, Burke's young Irish admirer.[17]

Paine's aggressive republicanism and the disorder in France promoted British nostalgia for absolutist certitudes. The ideas of Robert Filmer were still around at the end of the eighteenth century, and the Burke-Paine controversy gave them new relevance. Paine's contention that God had endowed Adam with certain inviolable rights that rendered all men equal brought out the patriarchalists. They countered that God had created patriarchal government with Adam, and given it further sanction by his covenant with Abraham. As an anonymous loyalist proclaimed: "The first government was Monarchy, not established by force or by compact, but by filial duty, which supersedes all human institutions, being the law of God and of Nature."[18] The political climate in Britain tolerated High Toryism. Although few had shared Burke's alarm regarding events in France in 1790, by the time *Rights of Man* appeared, many Britons had become aware that ancient institutions across the Channel were going the way of the Bastille.

Predictably, clergyman displayed the strongest inclination to employ the language of divine right. Such usages contained some equivocation, however. Citing Romans 13:1–2, John Riland suggested that the APLP should resist republican principles by defending the rights of God: "The *Kingly Government* in *England* is of GOD; not as particularly modified by him, but as, in general, proceeding from him, and according to him. The Scriptural Account of Governors is the Account of Government by *Kings*. They, therefore, who would overthrow our English Constitution must overthrow GOD's."[19] Both Riland and "Chaplain of the Navy" warned that rebellion against kings always brought on divine wrath.[20] Obedience, then, seemed more a practical imperative than a spiritual directive.

Gayle Trusdel Pendleton's wider assessment of conservative propaganda during this era reveals that a significant proportion, but by no means the majority, of the pamphleteers presented variations on Filmerism.[21] Answers to Paine contain variations reminiscent of the ideological scramble after 1688, with Tories trying to find some way to reconcile themselves to the new regime, and Whigs trying to justify the revolt against James II without risking the same treatment. William Lewelyn, a dissenting minister from Leominster, came the closest to describing kingly power as divine. Quoting from Proverbs, he named "Wisdom" as the source of the power by which kings reigned. The voice of Divine Wisdom proclaimed:

The best thing I can do is to make them love me; and the best thing to do to make them love me is to make them kings and grandees. Hereby I begin to glorify man with the glory of God; make him a partaker with the divine nature, in names of divinity; the honour and excellence of God are thus rendered visible among men: that the frequent pronunciation of his transcendent titles might endear him to them, and encourage them to raise their expectations high; and to inspire them with the ambition to be good and great. I say, therefore unto them, you are kings; you are princes; you are nobles; you are gods, that you may act like God. I wisdom put his highest names upon you, to make you imitate his excellences.[22]

By substituting the abstraction "Divine Wisdom" for God himself, Lewelyn gave a prudent veneer of utility to kingly divinity.

The tone of such pamphlets suggests that although monarchs could no longer claim to reign by divine right, some subjects still believed that they did. James Brown issued a mild disclaimer, as he noted the relevance of religious tenets to the terms of government: "So that without ascribing the sanction of divine right to any particular form of government in preference to another; we may in general affirm, that a regular government consisting in an established subjection to laws and lawful authority, to magistrates and rulers supreme and subordinate, is the natural means by which the Divine Providence ordained peace, prosperity, and happiness to be preserved in human society."[23] Similarly, Chalmers (alias Oldys), Paine's unauthorized biographer, cited scriptural passages in support of the notion that all earthly authority and rulership had its origin in an act of God, thus avoiding the supposedly exploded notion that kingly government in particular was divine.[24]

Other pamphleteers employed utilitarian arguments to justify submission to authority as a vital political precept. Gifford, the Treasury staff writer, presented obedience to the king as a matter of common sense and pointed to events in France as proof of the evil consequences of its absence. He hastened to underline the connection between practical virtue and Christian principles as he mocked the arrogance of reformers: "The humble spirit of Christianity and the morals it inculcates are seldom quoted by authors who contend for those aerial rights which are inconsistent with either, or one might argue, from those neglected writings, *The Scriptures,* that we are not thrown very far out of the line of our duty to God by doing honour to the king." He footnoted this passage: "'Fear God!—Honour the King'—says St. Peter."[25]

The Cambridge fellow, Hey, used the same sort of argument but couched his reply in the secular language of the philosophes. He stressed that one should be careful when dealing with the question of abstract rights and equality—ideas that Paine, in Hey's opinion, had treated superficially. True, excess subjugation enslaved, but submission to fair, constitutional practice begot a noble freedom: "Submission is essential to the maintenance of society. If there be any exception to this, it is only in a government absolutely despotic, and includes only one person in the whole kingdom. I am so happy as to live in a country where I can say without fear, that the Monarch himself is under Submission to the Laws. And I will add, that this is one instance, among others, in which the Monarch has an opportunity of displaying the Dignity of *Man*."[26] Hey appropriated the old common-law tradition of emphasizing the supremacy of the law. Yet he gave the idea an Enlightenment twist by stating that submission to law brought the possibility of achieving true dignity and happiness to all members of society. In this schema, the king stood at the same level as his subjects.

Hey's position represents a trend visible in a good portion of the replies to Paine: the assertion of traditional values while conceding points to egalitarian argument. Molloy, the Dublin barrister and probably the most libertarian of Paine's antagonists, agreed with Price that the French Revolution operated on the same principles as the Revolution of 1688. Molloy had a Lockean preference for a limited monarchy "reared on a solid base of an *express contract* originating from the *voluntary act* of the people, and considered by the *high contracting parties,* as the mutual covenant equally binding upon each." Yet he also felt compelled to answer Paine's attack on biblical justifications for hereditary monarchy, which he characterized as blasphemous. Molloy asserted that the first king, Nimrod, began a reign modeled on the government of heaven four hundred years after the deluge.[27] Other anti-Painites achieved a greater synthesis by expounding the idea of Britain's balanced constitution. Like Hey, they worked from the premise that everyone was equal under law in Britain. To convince potential followers of Paine that the British constitution already provided the liberties that Paine claimed existed only in a pure republic, these writers constructed a model of constitutional kingship that contained a significant republican component.

Paine's opponents insisted that he presented a distorted picture of monarchy by considering it only in its absolute form. St. John's description of the king's role in the British constitution made use of a classic metaphor: "A limited monarch, who is the supreme executive magistrate, and who constitutes a part of the legislature, and is subservient to the law of the land, is the keystone of the arch, which is, indeed, the most elevated, the most expensive, and the most weighty stone in the bridge, yet its weight and pressure serve to strengthen, bind, unite, and incorporate all the rest into one firm, compact, and solid mass."[28] Loyalists discoursed on the wondrous balance that enabled each part of the mixed constitution to work under restraint to provide a maximum of liberty for the subject while maintaining security for the government. Monarchy with its power unrestrained was tyranny, but excessive restraint rendered the Crown the bauble of the aristocracy and led to other abuses of power.[29] Some described the king as a mediator who prevented the natural jealousies between the Lords and the Commons from erupting into a war. Others argued that the royal prerogative acted as a particularly valuable check on the Commons, acknowledged to be the strongest branch of the constitution. One writer stated that kingly power "forms an independent control on the popular branch, in which the great power of the state resides, it concentrates its force, and directs it in the execution of the will of the whole."[30]

Although most writers dismissed Paine's condemnation of the corruption fostered by mixed government as ridiculous, some defended the Crown's influence. A couple of loyalists described places and pensions as acts of wisdom or generosity that the sovereign made to reward those of the highest ability and to prevent bribery of public servants.[31] As a politician in favor at court, St. John expended quite a few pages justifying his support of influence, and he did so in fine Walpolean fashion. Because purity could not be achieved in any human institution, each had to be modeled so as to work within the framework of men's passions, prejudices, and interests. This did not impair the morals of the English, "a high-spirited and gallant race, unenervated as yet by corruption." Influence exercised judiciously guaranteed that in times of controversy members of Parliament would defer to those who possessed superior ability, experience, information, and office. This, St. John argued, was much more conducive to wisdom than members voting according to conscience on every occasion.[32] (Uncle Henry—Bolingbroke—must have been rolling in his grave.) The alleged patrician at the Revenue Board argued testily that the very existence of complaints against the system of influence demonstrated that no veil of corruption had been drawn over the eyes of the English: "A late House of Commons voted, that '*The influence of the crown had encreased, is encreasing, and ought to be diminished,*' and by the very act of voting it, proved the falsity of the proposition."[33]

Loyalists also used constitutional balance to defend the royal prerogative of declaring war and peace. Paine alleged that wars served only as an excuse for raising taxes and generating opportunities for corruption through government contracts. The right of declaring war should lie where the expense fell: with the people. Paine's antagonists countered that in actuality such *was* the case in Britain. When the king exercised his royal prerogative, he represented the will of his people. When a good, constitutional king declared war, he did so confident that Parliament, representing the people, would vote him supplies. Similarly, he did not make peace or form alliances without Parliament's ratification. Operating under these constraints, yet situated at a height from which they could distinguish national from individual interests, the king and his ministers occupied the best position for conducting foreign affairs that required secrecy and dispatch. The constitution made them guardians of the nation's welfare.[34]

As numerous episodes in British history demonstrated, kings and their ministers did not always behave in such a public-spirited manner. To dissociate the present reign from past tyrannies, Paine's respondents presented the monarchy as a product of historical evolution. This involved updating the medieval idea of the king's two bodies: a king's public character was independent of his personal attributes. Charles Hawtrey pointed out that Paine was "confounding the pride and ambition of an unconnected individual with that of a public character of a king, with which a whole community is connected."[35] In his public character, the king symbolized the nation and embodied its unified will. John Jones, leader of the Canterbury APLP, defined kingly authority as resting on "the obedience of rational beings, towards a power they have created, or acknowledged, and whose support they deem essential to the welfare of the community. Englishmen discriminate between the office and the man who fills it; the kingly office, as the repository of their rights, has their steady and uniform veneration." Loyalists insisted that the law only gave the king the power to do good.[36] Although the monarch as a man possessed human flaws and frailties, the monarch in his public capacity achieved perfection according to the dictates of the constitution. The king's immortality by law ensured the uninterrupted function of the executive and judiciary. The dictum "The king can do no wrong," which Elliot pronounced "a prudent fiction," preserved the power and dignity of the Crown, and thus the nation. Furthermore, it was only right that ministers be held responsible for misgovernment because a constitutional king acted upon their counsel.[37]

Paine's respondents used their model of a historically constructed public character of monarchy to refute Paine's allegations that the nation still bore the marks of conquest. They explained that the king's speeches to Parliament and the manner of their delivery reflected the monarchy's preservation of

laws and customs that dated back to time immemorial. The high-sounding
language that might suggest that the king considered the Parliament his property was, in fact, formulaic. Parliament's submission to the king did not imply vassalage, only deference and esteem. Boothby asserted:

> Mr. Paine does not see that these marks of reverence and submission have
> been carefully preserved by our ancestors as necessary substitutes for the
> real prerogative which they took away, and when we say we most humbly
> and faithfully submit ourselves, heirs and posterities, for ever; this is the vol-
> untary submission of freemen to an institution which they have judged nec-
> essary to the preservation of a national permanent freedom. When they de-
> prived their kings of the power to do them harm, they very wisely and safely
> entrusted them with the power of doing good, because they considered the
> preservation of that constitution which from reason and experience they
> best approved. We therefore love and venerate our limited monarch, be-
> cause we believe that he preserves us from a ferocious venal democracy,
> from a cruel haughty aristocracy, and, from the unlimited tyranny of a
> master.[38]

Similarly, supporters of the status quo defended the expense of monarchy
by arguing that the splendor of the throne belonged to the nation. A king's
outward aspect had to reflect the dignity of his station for him to be an effective leader. An appearance of wealth, confidence, and strength aided him
in his dealings with foreign powers and ultimately had a direct bearing upon
the prosperity of his subjects. Properly exercised economy was a virtue, but
inappropriate retrenchments brought harm. A nation of Britain's promi-
nence needed an expensive court establishment to support its status. Paine's
cost comparison between Britain and an unpolished, rising young state like
America, therefore, was specious: republicans, the loyalists argued, "may estimate the value of pence and farthings, but they are utterly ignorant of the
nature of man. A proper dignity, and a becoming state, make more lasting impressions on mankind, than the most forcible precepts that can be delivered;
and unreasonable it may appear, but the fact is undoubted, that laws, however
excellent, will be poorly obeyed, if there is not a splendour and dignity in the
magistrate to enforce the observance."[39]

At the same time, the pamphleteers did not wish to represent the British
people as dolts, dazzled and demeaned by the chicanery of royal trappings, as
Rights of Man had portrayed them. These writers expropriated the examples
of monarchical tyranny that Paine had used to illustrate the institution's inherent despotism and applied them to the argument that liberty had made

steady progress in Britain. To the anti-Painites, the government possessed sufficient republican spirit. They offered Bolingbrokean renditions of brave Britons struggling for freedom against the overweening ambitions of their rulers. As Jones declared: "It is the only country in Europe, where despotism has not crushed the spirit of the people; the flame of freedom, although it has been smothered at different periods, has never been extinguished; and kings have successively been obliged to confer certain privileges to the people, which have reduced their own power to the standard of rationality. . . . These blessings, which are obtained with difficulty and by slow degrees, are enjoyed with moderation and preserved with fidelity."[40]

This was all very well in the abstract. When dealing with specific instances of confrontations between kings and people, however, loyalists were drawn into discussions of resistance in ways Burke hardly would have approved. Writing anonymously, David Rivers became somewhat carried away in expressing his conviction that the British people had proven themselves capable of dealing with monarchical tyranny: "When Charles I, that weak, that insincere prince, dared to trample upon the sacred liberties of the people, and infringe the laws of the constitution; the nation took the alarm; and the battle of Edge Hill shewed that the British nation were never to be enslaved." In another exposition on British history, in a pamphlet dedicated to the APLP, Thomas Hearn admitted that the king's right to the throne, although secured by law, could never be considered independent of the will of the people. He hastened to add, however, that Charles I's execution and James II's expulsion were unlawful and therefore did not establish any legal precedent; these actions came about only after the monarchs had subverted the constitution.[41]

Discussions of the right of resistance, filled with self-satisfied pronouncements of British pluck combined with grisly depictions of the resulting calamities, were at once resolute and noncommittal. An anonymous writer contended: "Sovereigns are entitled to allegiance, only in proportion as they grant protection," and professed a hope that the people would always be ready to resist arbitrary power. Yet the inevitable back-pedaling followed. Confrontations between sovereign and subject usually resulted from mutual offenses and misunderstandings; a ruler's injurious intent therefore had to be ascertained and the people fully apprised of the consequences of resistance. How these factors were to be determined and by whom was not spelled out. Similarly, Boothby stated that the "constitutional whigs" venerated monarchs who followed the law; however, "they will, if necessary, depose the monarch to preserve the monarchy."[42] Who were these people, and how were they to act? Such rhetoric suggests that loyalists invoked a revolutionary or republican spirit in order to tame it within the ideology of order.

Loyalists repeated Burke's account of the Revolution of 1688 to support their argument that proper constitutional channels provided sufficient recourse for dealing with a rogue monarch. As an anonymous pamphleteer's account of the progress of freedom in Britain explained: "The efforts that have been made to subjugate this country at various periods, have been subverted by the wise provisions of parliament, whose power is eminently conspicuous in the coronation oath, wherein the Prince in the most solemn manner, binds himself to govern according to the statutes of a parliament agreed on, and the laws and customs of the state."[43]

Some of the pamphleteers implied that the issue of resistance could never pertain to the present regime because the constitution had reached near-perfection. Along these lines, King, Paine's disillusioned friend, proclaimed: "Some reform is certainly wanted; but let it be fought for constitutionally—let it go to the King through the Representatives of the People; when was he ever yet known to refuse redress of grievances?" Graham Jepson confidently stated that nowadays subjects had no need to resist the king: should anyone feel that the king had done him injury, he could apply for recompense in the king's own court of law without any doubt of obtaining it.[44]

The right of resistance was by necessity indeterminate because the precise right by which kings reigned was itself obscure. One must remember the pedigree of the balanced constitution: a desperate attempt by two of Charles I's advisers to counter the parliamentary challenge to royal authority. As J. G. A. Pocock observes, at the time the idea was "both constitutionally incorrect and a disastrous tactical error in royalist polemic." The doctrine of balance gained constitutional sanction with the Revolution Settlement, but it remained riddled with ambiguity. Gunn thinks it no more than a convenient idea that "made it easy to endorse an image of the constitutional *status quo,* without thereby committing oneself to saying what exactly it entailed, let alone pronouncing on which theory best explained it."[45] Like Pocock's royalists of 1642, loyalists of 1792 took up this rhetoric in response to a threat (albeit of much lesser magnitude) to the established order. They drew upon the classical republican theory of Polybius, which defined the parts of government in terms of their respective virtues and their ability to check the vices of the others, rather than in terms of the specific function they performed. Like the moderate writers of the Interregnum, most anti-Painites presented the government as the product of men incorporating imperfect institutions into a smooth-running system, rather than the product of a compact or contract under God. Yet they were not above appealing to divine law when other arguments failed.

When it came to setting down the precise right by which kings reigned, loyalists found themselves on shaky ground. According to Burke, the Revolution of 1688 was a restoration of constitutional balance and a reinforcement of the hereditary succession. This meant that to define and justify the role and power of the monarch, one had to take into account the nature of the pre-1688 monarchy as well as the terms of the Revolution Settlement. Burke had wisely not tried to delve into the depths of antiquity to come up with some decisive account of the origins of monarchy in England. Paine had challenged him on that point and had accused him of wishing to hide monarchy's shameful heritage. Hunt, the American loyalist, saw this as yet another example of Paine's disingenuousness: "Wise men have laid it down as a maxim, which should be adopted in politics, not to be too inquisitive concerning the original title of the reigning powers. None of them will bear an exact scrutiny, no not even the new Sovereigns of his favourite States." Others deemed the notion of right immaterial compared to the security that a hereditary crown gave to the nation.[46]

Some writers countered Paine's spurious historical accounts with some inventive interpretations of their own. William the Conqueror, it seems, was not such a bad sort after all. He had conquered Harold, not the English nation, as he claimed his just right to the throne. He had taken the same coronation oath as any monarch. His son's accession was then ratified by election.[47] A few loyalists even toyed with the Lockean notion of consent to counter Paine's account of the despotic origins of monarchy. For instance, Elliot argued that the monarchy rested on consent because the early successions had been ratified by election. Similarly, Hearn explained that before hereditary descent became established by law it had taken root by usage; the system could not have continued without the consent of the people.[48]

The myth of the ancient constitution, a device usually employed by eighteenth-century reformers, was commandeered by loyalists who found the reign of Alfred the Great a serviceable starting point for the English state. According to this model, the Norman Conquest had not destroyed the liberties established by Alfred and Edward the Confessor but only temporarily retarded the growth of the constitution. Jepson expressed the hope that one mark of the Conquest would forever remain: the memory that the nation had been conquered and had emancipated itself. Again, we have the notion of monarchy as the product of historical evolution, molded and meliorated by its people. Bowles and Hervey acknowledged that some of the early kings had been despotic but argued that this was understandable considering that war had been their main occupation. The king had to hold the entire executive power in order to deliver immediate justice and succor. Once the threat of invasion and internal strife abated, nations had been able to modify the power of the Crown according to circumstances. Whether early kings had been tyrannical was irrelevant to the present advanced state of civilization.[49]

In addition to arguments based on scriptural authority and precedent, loyalists employed more personal precepts in justification of hereditary monarchy. They presented the terms by which the king reigned in Britain as fundamental principles interwoven into the whole fabric of society. A king inherited the throne in the same way that his subjects inherited private property. His rights and revenues were the lawful inheritance of his family. St. John and Hervey treated Paine's attack on the hereditary principle as a nefarious republican plot against property, designed to dissolve the bonds of society. In his anonymous pamphlet, Hervey suggested that inheritance was the principle underlying all matters of trust: "When hereditary honors and hereditary property die, the stockholder's existence hangs by a single thread. If we can tear from the true descendants, the titles and estates which their ancestors purchased with lives of toil and hardship; if we can dissolve the terms on which our fore-fathers have bequeathed their property, we cannot be bound by the condition of their debt."[50]

Invoking Paine's assertion that every nation had the right to choose its own form of government, others maintained that England had chosen hereditary monarchy and no individual or group had the right to dispute it. Boothby explained that the Crown remained hereditary in the same way that laws retained their force and, "as liable to fewer objections than any other mode," would continue so "till altered by the power of the legislature or the force of the nation, exactly in the same manner with every other law and institution whatever."[51] Loyalists constructed a monarchy that evolved as society's needs changed. Such a regime preserved the fundamental values that gave the nation continuity, coherence, and cohesion.

The peculiarities of George III's public persona and style of rule allowed juxtapositions of libertarian sentiments and authoritarian principles. On the one hand, loyalists praised George for securing the liberties that had been reinforced by the Revolution of 1688, bringing prosperity to his subjects, and promoting their intellectual improvement. They cited his attachment to the constitution and the law, his justice, clemency, benevolence, love for his people, piety, domestic virtues, and assiduous patronage of the arts and sciences. On the other hand, because he had thus demonstrated that he acted as the best of constitutional monarchs, he should be treated with reverence and obeyed accordingly. Gifford feistily derided adulation, then demurred, "But praise founded on truth is the tribute of justice: and he who performs, with exemplary virtue, the duties of a husband, a father, and a man, is justly entitled to the highest commendation whether he graces a cottage or a throne." He concluded by blending the personal and the public figures of the king: "When I contemplate the virtues of the man, I am led to *esteem* the king whom my religion teaches me to honour."[52]

George III's attributes provided support for Burke's view that the wisdom of government power was embodied in an individual. Hearn stated with assurance that "the right of kings, the inviolability of their persons etc. can never be called into question, whilst their government continues mild, just, and rational; the king who reigns in the hearts and affections of his people needs not the effect of such terms to support his authority, nor the influence of force, in order to procure permanency to his succession; the love and veneration of a happy and grateful nation is the principal security, which a wise and virtuous prince requires, or should depend on; this tie, the tie of justice, reason, and of nature, is superior to all law, and paramount to the otherwise unavailing authority of statutes." In reforming a tyrannical government, Hearn explained, it might be necessary to go back to the first principles of government, as the French had done. In that case, invoking the sovereignty of the people, challenging the hereditary succession, and promoting a spirit of inquiry might be appropriate. When the king possessed such qualities as George III, however, "the promulgation of such opinions . . . should be considered as wanton, inflammatory and seditious"; doing so could have "no other end than an intention of raising discontents, and fomenting discord in the minds of a giddy and unthinking multitude."[53]

Unlike most kings of the era, George III remained faithful to his consort and spent a lot of time with their thirteen children. These qualities encouraged the development of a patriarchalism relatively free from the taint of Filmerism. When loyalists of the 1790s invoked the old platitude that the king was the father of his people, they were able to efface its old association with absolutist regimes by conjuring images of George's tender attention to his immediate family. When it suited propagandists, they conflated the private and public life of the king, both to elicit sympathy and to represent personal attacks on George as libels on the national character. They pointed to the trials that rulers endured on behalf of their subjects: their position deprived them of the comforts and privacy that most people took for granted and exposed them to extraordinary worries, slander, and conspiracies. Hence the importance of loyalty, as Bowles asserted: "While the high and important office of King, for the sake of the public good, calls for such sacrifices from the Man, how unworthy and ungenerous must it be to delight in wounding his personal feelings, and in planting his Crown with additional thorns? How much more consistent with the duty as well as the interests of subjects, to alleviate his cares, and to smooth his rugged path by demonstrations of fidelity, loyalty, and affection!"[54] Paine's opponents stressed the maliciousness of representing Britain's ruling dynasty as a ruinously expensive parcel of foreigners. Elliot noted that only the wicked would attempt to "seduce us from the paternal wing of such a government."[55]

Discussions of the French monarchy reinforced the human dimension of royalty. The loyalists described Louis XVI's predicament in emotional tones reminiscent of Burke. The "Chaplain of the Navy," for instance, described Louis as "a worthy, legal patriotic King robbed of his throne by a sacrilegious *gang* of ungrateful wretches, who have not only deprived him of all his prerogative as a Monarch, but even all his Rights as a Husband, a Father, a Brother, and a Man!" Like Burke, the anti-Painites contrasted a saintly French king with the atheistical ruffians who had seized the government. Events in France provided poignant images. St. John declared: "Let them not shut the doors of our Houses of Parliament, and calling themselves a National Assembly, adjourn to the Tennis-courts. Let them not substitute the lamp-iron in the place of our Commissions of Oyer and Terminer and Gaol Delivery, and let them not imprison our King, and allow him to hunt only with the Captain of the Guard in St. James's Park." An associate of the "Butchers of the National Convention," as King characterized him, Paine had to share responsibility for the guillotining of Louis in January 1793. King noted sadly that Paine had broken his vow that the king's execution would be a signal for his own departure from France. Chalmers's biography of Paine presented "our *king-killer*" in the thick of a Jacobin plot to rid the world of all monarchs, starting with the assassination of the king of Sweden in 1792.[56]

The correspondence and publications of the APLP shared many of the anti-Painites' concerns and came up with similar solutions.[57] Many of the publications that were geared toward the lower echelons of society sought to cultivate a personal bond between George III and his subjects, a tie that should inspire feelings of protectiveness, even gallantry, toward the king. Mostly taking the form of ballads and homespun dialogues between rural characters, these pieces drew parallels between the subject-sovereign relationship and familial affiliations. A ballad that celebrated the prosperity and security George's reign had brought to all people made striking use of the family metaphor:

> John Bull at his Monarch may now and then grumble,
> But will never permit base Seducers to Mumble,
> Like man and wife, when they jar, 'tis but Peace to restore,
> And far better to love, than they e'er did before.

The didactic letters between John Bull and his brother Thomas contained an anecdote of a soldier menacing a man who proposed a toast to Paine. The soldier then raised his glass to the king, "a good husband, a good father, and a good man," with the vow, "Sooner than lift my hand against the man that feeds me, I would chop it off!"[58] The age of chivalry, it would appear, was not dead.

The letters that loyalists sent to the Home Office and to the London APLP provide a view of the motivations behind their propaganda campaign. Some stressed the importance of cultivating and preserving a strong, positive image of royalty. Grove Taylor of Southwark, jeweler and part-time spy, complained about shop windows that displayed caricature prints disrespectful to the royal family. Such representations, claimed Taylor, were "manifestly tending to alienate the Duty[,] obedience and affection which in well-regulated governments are so necessary on the part of the Subjects to their Sovereigns to be preserved inviolable." Along the same lines, a London man who had recently returned from a trip to the West Country was alarmed to find disaffected persons meeting the mail coach, securing a copy of the evening paper, and entertaining all assembled with heavily edited readings of the news. He voiced particular concern about their charges that the king was pocketing the £900,000 Civil List. He recommended that paragraphs be inserted in the newspapers explaining issues that might be open to rumor and speculation. Similarly, the rector of Wolsingham, Durham, warned the APLP that complaints about the Prince of Wales's debts and speculations on the extent of the king's wealth "engross the conversation of the vulgar." He requested the APLP to publish pamphlets that would convince the poor that monarchy best served their interests and that a republican government would not improve their situation.[59]

Burke's view of the utility of having government embodied in a person was borne out by loyalist sentiments. One "T. N." of the London Coffee House informed the APLP that this principle was particularly relevant to the lower classes: "I think we cannot at this time speak too highly on the subject of royalty to the common people, in arguing with whom we can only oppose prejudice to prejudice, and leave it to their reason to find a medium. To talk to them of the constitution is vain: They can only respect the constitution in its true representative and visible emblem, the King's person." Yet some loyalists seemed to buy into this sentiment as well. Joseph Moser, author of the rustic "Strap Bodkin" letters, sent the APLP a less condescending, poetical effort entitled "Compassion." His cover letter explained that the work was inspired "from feelings excited by a contemplation of the dangers, that a Life of the utmost importance to the happiness of this Country, was exposed to in the Chace." He asserted that affection for the king and concern for his welfare could never be too strongly impressed upon the public.[60]

Like the anti-Paine pamphleteers, the authors of association tracts sought to convince Britons that they enjoyed true liberty under the monarchy and that they should not be deluded by the illusory liberties claimed by the French revolutionaries. These writers also made use of ideas about the supremacy of the law and the balanced constitution. They described how all ranks in society enjoyed equal security of life, liberty, and property under the law. Under the supremacy of the law, the inviolable power of the king counterbalanced the considerable power of the people and maintained the nation's order and unity.[61] Unlike the responses to Paine, however, association pamphlets did not describe the British constitution as republican in any way. In fact, John Reeves, the APLP's founder, took a stand against this tendency in 1795 with his *Thoughts on the English Government*. In supporting his position, Reeves impugned the Revolution Settlement, a move that allowed the Foxites to initiate a prosecution against him for seditious libel. Although Reeves was acquitted, the fact that the Pitt administration allowed one of its staunchest supporters to be treated in this way illustrates how important it had become to clarify the administration position on the powers of the Crown. Intervening in the prosecution would have constituted tacit approval of Reeves's views.

Reeves accused British radicals in general and the Foxite Whigs in particular of serving as a conduit for pernicious French principles. He pointed out that the Foxite Whigs misrepresented the constitution in order to graft republican principles onto monarchical government. They used the rhetoric of "Republicans, Sectaries and Presbyterians," whose first step in deceiving the people had been the misapplication of the term *revolution* to the events of

1688. In this pamphlet, and in a sequel written in 1797 but not published until 1799, Reeves attacked the notion of the people's sovereign will. He claimed that kings did not derive their power from the people but from law and usage. The people had no inherent power, only rights and liberties given them by law. Moreover, the legislature did not represent the power of the people and, accordingly, did not have ascendancy over the executive. The executive power resided in the king, who presided over the legislative branch of the constitution. Although the king relied on the legislature's advice and consent, it was he who enacted the law. Terrible misunderstandings sprang from the mistaken notion that the events of 1688 had changed the constitution. The precise and useful nomenclature of *king, king's servants, king's subjects,* and *limited monarchy* had been supplanted by vague and misleading terms: *executive power, legislative, chief magistrate, the people,* and *mixed monarchy.* Reeves made the astute observation that Charles I had foolishly subscribed to the false metaphor of the three branches of government and the idea of coordinate authority. No wonder Parliament had rebelled, having been infused with such inappropriate ideas of its own self-importance.[62]

It was Reeves's use of metaphor that landed him in trouble. To illustrate his idea that the Lords and Commons owed their existence to and derived their authority from the Crown, he compared the monarchy to the trunk of a tree, with the Lords and Commons as its branches. Then he drove home his point with a trifle too much energy: "They may be lopped off, and the tree is a tree still, shorn indeed of its honours, but not, like them, cast into the fire." Impolitic language, yes, but not an unprecedented view of monarchical inviolability and immortality. The Foxite Whigs pounced nonetheless. Reeves had claimed that the monarchy could function just as well without the Lords and Commons and thus was liable to prosecution for sedition.[63] Reeves's accusers could hardly have expected a conviction; in order to establish that the work was seditious, they would have had to prove that one of the government's most ardent champions had written it in a deliberate attempt to vilify the government and promote disaffection. But Reeves's trial did offer yet another forum for hammering out the ideological foundations of the British polity.

In presenting the case for the prosecution, the attorney general, John Scott, gave much attention to establishing the official view of what occurred in 1688. He reaffirmed the propriety of describing the events as a revolution, but in the pre-1789 sense. They constituted a return to fundamental principles, not a change in the system. The authors of "the most solemn proceedings in this country" had not intended to set the precedent for violent change; rather, they had intended the British people to be sensible of the rights and liberties that these proceedings restored and preserved. True, the constitution had been clarified, not changed, in 1688, but this process had involved an energetic correction of abuses. The Bill of Rights set down more strongly than ever before the monarch's obligation to convene Parliament frequently for the redress of grievances and the preservation of the law. Where the official position deviated the most from Reeves's stance was in its conception of the basis of political power. Taking for his authority Joseph Jekyll's speech at the Sacheverell trial, Scott declared: "As the law is the only measure of the prince's authority, and the people's subjection, so the law derived its being and efficacy from common consent."[64]

The Reeves trial confirmed the administration's commitment to mixed monarchy. Yet as loyalist propaganda illustrates, although asserting monarchical supremacy would no longer do, other aspects of High Toryism remained current. John Gifford's prefatory address in *The Anti-Jacobin Review and Magazine,* founded in 1798, was at once coy and cheeky: "By some we have been accused of adopting the doctrine of *Divine Right of Kings;* but, to whatever extent we may incline to carry our marked preference to *Monarchy,* over every other form of government ... however disposed, even, we may be to contend ... that it is the only true legitimate form of government, yet most certain it is, that we never advanced such doctrine; but have confined ourselves to the support of the *Divine Right,* or rather *Divine Origin* of GOVERNMENT."[65]

The doctrines of Christianity and the principles of political obligation continued to be intertwined. Although most thinking people rejected the more extreme aspects of Filmerism, patriarchalism remained too deeply ingrained to be easily discarded. Gordon Schochet shows that even the seventeenth-century radicals harbored patriarchal assumptions. Although Locke destroyed patriarchalism as a political theory and scientific discovery, and Enlightenment philosophy shook the authority of religious tenets, patriarchalism survived in eighteenth-century conceptions of society, preserved in the institution of the family.[66] During the 1790s patriarchalism also had a safe haven in the domesticity of George III's monarchy.

The development in loyalist discourse of a historically constructed monarchy gave the institution an ideological flexibility that allowed it to accommodate a wide range of political attitudes. Fear of upheaval allowed certain High-Tory ideas to recover some of the respectability they had lost in 1688. These ideas gained additional strength as they became melded with aspects of the seventeenth-century republican tradition. Most loyalists realized that preaching the ideology of order and obedience was inadequate in the face of the republican challenge and spirit of inquiry issuing from France. By manipulating conceptions of the public and private characters of the monarch, loyalists created a monarchy that could inspire both empathy and deference in subjects. They built an image of George III as fair, law-abiding, and receptive to his people; this gave them a foundation from which they could allow a satisfying yet tamed republican spirit in the British polity. The notion that a historical process had helped produce the present character of the monarchy—George's virtuous attention to the duties of kingship—allowed loyalists to boast of the people's power to resist tyrants while simultaneously rendering this power obsolete. The loyalists' recasting of the monarchy's ideological foundations, particularly in making peace between previously hostile ideas, forced reformers to undertake a similar reconstruction.

FOUR

The Republican Tradition, the Reform Movement, and the Monarchy

*W*HEN Charles I subscribed to the notion of mixed monarchy, he compromised royal power; but during the next century, the trope of balance offered a language for debate and a safe outlet for protest against Crown prerogatives. At the same time, the discussion of constitutional balance provided an avenue by which republicanism could gradually insinuate itself into the British polity after the failure of the republican experiment under Cromwell. The upheavals of the mid-seventeenth century spawned a republican rhetoric that was kept vital after 1688 by the constitutionalist political theorists known as the Real Whigs, or eighteenth-century Commonwealthmen, then by the Dissenters, metropolitan radicals, and extraparliamentary reformers of George III's early reign.[1] Such rhetoric had dangerous implications, however, after Louis XVI went to the guillotine in 1793.

The radicals of the 1790s—in which group I include all proponents of amending British civil and religious institutions—had to deal with the loyalist recasting of the British monarchy on two levels. First, loyalist assertions that mixed monarchy and the balanced constitution already realized republican ideals opposed reformist claims that the present system left a significant proportion of the polity unrepresented in Parliament, the "democratic" branch of the constitution. Second, loyalists' insinuations that anyone who disputed their vision of church and state secretly harbored regicidal designs placed reformers on the defensive. Moreover, accusations of anti-monarchical intent were reinforced by arrests and prosecutions of reformers on charges of high treason and sedition. Members of the reform societies realized that they needed to accommodate their idealistic republican visions to the existence of a long-established and increasingly popular monarchy, which their opponents had encased in a protective rhetoric. As a result, although a minority of committed republicans survived the reform agitation of the 1790s, the reformist mainstream eventually developed a position on monarchy that reinforced loyalist argument. By using the monarchy as an organizing metaphor, loyalists successfully contained republican expression within certain parameters and, by so doing, tamed it.

The nature and intentions of these late eighteenth-century radicals remain contentious. Perceptions of the reform movement have been colored by the political complexion of its chroniclers. In his work of the 1960s, E. P. Thompson, with his vision of burgeoning class consciousness, paints a picture of potential revolutionaries brutally repressed by draconian legislation. When the propertied and manufacturing classes united in common panic, the moderate, educated middle-class reformers fled the movement. Nonetheless, Thompson claims, a democratic tradition had been established, and continued to flourish underground. Historians of the 1970s depict the 1790s in less dramatic hues. Studies of the reform movement emphasize its overall moderation; only a small minority of republican extremists formed a revolutionary underground in the latter part of the decade. Furthermore, these historians contend, internal dissensions, rather than the government's repressive measures, contributed the most to the movement's dissolution. On the heels of these studies, two investigations into the underground societies of United Irishmen, United Englishmen, and United Scotsmen reassert the significance of the extremist element of the movement. Marianne Elliott reveals extensive collaboration between British and Irish revolutionaries working to coordinate a French invasion, Irish rebellion, and insurrection in London. Roger Wells takes Thompson's argument further with his assertion that the United Englishmen were not a mere appendage to the militant Irish movement; they were organized, widespread, and serious about establishing a republic in England.[2]

The two current divergent views of the 1790s are encapsulated in the concluding essays of a collection that seeks to evaluate the impact of the French Revolution on British popular politics. Wells's Britain, racked with dissension stemming from religious and political antagonisms, economic crisis, and war-weariness, narrowly escaped revolution. The Britain of I. R. Christie, on the other hand, was overwhelmingly conservative and united in support of king, constitution, and country. Mark Philp's contribution to the volume bridges these two notions by suggesting that conditions continually shifted.

He describes radicalism as "a developing political practice whose principles and ideological commitments are as much forged in the struggle as they are fetched from the arsenal and brought to it." Like the phenomenon of loyalist association, the reform movement was not a "discrete entity." Along these same lines, in a separate study, John Dinwiddy's investigation into the radicals' revolutionary intent turns up wide variations, ambiguity, and ambivalence. Although the reform societies drew back from overt attempts at overturning the government, individual radicals entertained the fantasy that the system would fold on its own; "the threat of revolution was more of a political stratagem, more of a feint, than a matter of serious intention or conspiracy." As Craig Calhoun points out, by casting these "reactionary radicals" as a nascent working class, Thompson's earlier account ignores the traditional community structure and social relations, with their attendant mentalities, from which the radicals could not easily extract themselves.[3]

A closer examination of the radicals' approach to the issue of monarchy shows republican aspirations contained by the framework of British society and tempered by the pressure of events. Reformers of the 1790s attempted to give their ideas respectability by grounding them in historical precedent. Although they did not succeed in effecting the changes to the political and religious establishments that they sought, their arguments played a key role in recasting the ideology of monarchy. To some degree, the republican challenge contributed to the formation of a royalist tradition. As John Neville Figgis observes, "Dogma never takes definite shape, save as a result of its denial by some thinker or leader. Thus the enthusiastic attachment to the notion of Passive Obedience was due to the Civil War and to the anarchy and tyranny that followed it."[4] Concurrently, republicanism developed into a set of ideals against which monarchies could be evaluated. In spite of the conservative backlash produced by events in France, the radicals' retooling of seventeenth-century republican thought helped preserve the democratic component that contributed to the resilience of the modern British monarchy.

Like the radicalism of the eighteenth century, republican thought of the seventeenth century had encompassed a wide range of views. The classical republicans, or Commonwealthmen, are best represented by the writings of James Harrington, chiefly *The Commonwealth of Oceana* (1656). Harrington believed that landed property conferred political power because landowners determined where the loyalty of the soldiery lay. Once the king no longer stood as sole proprietor of England, monarchy lost its meaning; the obsolete institution only caused tensions within the realm. Harrington argued that extending political power to the small landowners was the only way to achieve balance and harmony. While other republicans wished to be governed by a single legislative assembly, Harrington's disgust with the oligarchy of the Rump Parliament induced him to recommend that the government consist of a senate and a legislative assembly. An aristocratic oligarchy would be prevented by an agrarian law that limited the size of landed estates. The machinations of party politics would be thwarted by rotating the high offices of state and thus allowing equitable access. State control over the religious establishment would keep the clergy from interfering in politics. A state church would thus not preclude freedom of worship. Although Harrington's republic sought freedom, justice, and the rational pursuit of the general good, in it the sovereignty of the people rested in the gentry.[5]

The Levellers took republicanism farther than the Commonwealthmen by seeking institutional reform in order to defend what they saw as natural rights, and thereby achieve popular sovereignty. Yet they were not true democrats either. Although they firmly opposed the privileged orders, few Levellers advocated universal suffrage. Most believed that those with complete autonomy should vote, which excluded women, servants, criminals, the destitute, and in some cases waged laborers and royalists. Levellers called for the annual election of a paid assembly of representatives. They worked from the premises that government had originated by consent and that sovereignty remained in the people, not their representatives. Perez Zagorin characterizes the movement as lower middle class; their reform platform stressed improving the lot of the struggling small shopkeeper, craftsman, and merchant. In contrast to the Levellers, the Parliamentarians who overthrew the monarchy considered themselves inseparable from "the people"; in other words, the sovereignty of the people rested in the people's elected representatives.[6]

Radicals of the 1790s thus drew from an ideological tradition that opposed royal absolutism but fell short of true democracy. In order to support their demands for universal suffrage and annual parliaments, reformers had to reconstruct the republican tradition. They combed the Stuart annals for tales of tyranny and its resistance by republican martyrs—acts of resistance that reformers considered vindicated by the fall of James II in 1688. Republicanism became mythologized with its personification in what Peter Karsten calls patriot-heroes, in particular, John Hampden and Algernon Sidney. Hampden's fame derived from his stand against ship money, a levy that Charles I imposed to pay for strengthening the navy. At Hampden's trial in 1637, the judges were not impressed with the defense's argument that extraparliamentary taxation was unlawful except in cases of dire emergency. They ruled that it was up to the king to determine what constituted an emergency. (They thus helped win the judiciary a prominent place in the Parliamentarians' catalogue of abusive institutions to be purged in the Civil War.) As Karsten demonstrates, supporters of American independence transformed Hampden into the patron saint of property rights. During the 1790s, moderate reformers summoned the memory of Hampden and his cohorts to present their activities as part of the long-term struggle for liberty, while radicals invoked patriot-heroes to conjure up a sense of righteousness in the face of repression.[7]

Sidney became a martyr to the cause of liberty in 1683 for his alleged involvement in the Rye House Plot. His writings, published fifteen years later under the title *Discourses Concerning Government*, helped create his legend. Incomplete and unrevised—his arguments against Filmer differed little from Locke's and were supported with far less skill and historical accuracy—they were bundled up at the time of his arrest and used as evidence against him, which gave the work added poignancy. They also displayed a more personal, bellicose, and straightforward (albeit long-winded) style than Locke's *Treatises*. But the circumstances of Sidney's death, rather than the subtleties of his arguments, were more important to his legacy. Sidney was tried before Judge George Jeffreys, soon to become the personification of judicial despotism. Judge Jeffreys spun new interpretations out of the treason statutes to compensate for the vagaries of the evidence. Jeffreys enjoyed brow-beating and putting on high-handed shows of contempt for defendants in his courtroom. He made no secret of his determination to have Sidney hanged, drawn, and quartered. Charles II had to step in at the time of execution and commute the sentence to a simple decapitation. Jeffreys then presided over what came to be known as the Bloody Assizes of 1685, following an attempt by the duke of Monmouth and his supporters to overthrow the newly crowned James II. The brutality of Jeffreys's sentencing secured his place in the annals of Stuart iniquity.[8] His image would be reincarnated in the figure of the eighteenth-century Scottish judge Robert Braxfield, as reformers of the 1790s invoked the martyrdom of Sidney.

Had reformers not been so intent upon collecting historical precedents, they might have realized that although the Stuarts provided stunning exhibitions of despotism—and ultimately got their comeuppance—the regime also revealed the source of monarchy's resilience: the institution's flexibility and ability to adapt to change. The execution of Charles I demonstrated that monarchy could weather even a challenge to its central tenets of immortality and inviolability. The Revolution of 1688 thus illustrated the institution's capacity for accommodating ideological innovation. The late eighteenth-century radicals made a tactical error by employing an aggressive republican rhetoric in their effort to inspire followers and intimidate foes. The monarchy, they would find, commanded a certain degree of respect, if only for its propagandistic power.

It is often difficult to determine how reformers really perceived George III and monarchy, for government and loyalist repression promoted self-censorship and political posturing. Members of reform societies left themselves vulnerable to charges of conspiracy against the king with their intemperate gloating over the collapse of tyranny in France after the storming of the Bastille; their support of the French revolutionaries in spite of the September Massacres and the execution of Louis XVI; and their championing of the outlaw Paine and his *Rights of Man*. The emergence of Napoleon in 1798 and the threat of a French invasion of Great Britain, perhaps even more than the prosecutions and other repressive measures, brought the activities of constitutional reformers to an end. The constitutional reformers left behind an organization of militant republicans, who destroyed their work of constructing a radical reform plan compatible with monarchy. The reform movement of the 1790s did not bring universal suffrage, annual parliaments, or a more equitable system of representation; instead, reformist speeches and writings contributed to the dialectic that helped endow the monarchy with new relevance.

The bellicose tone of reformist rhetoric was not the only provocation for a conservative backlash; the composition of the societies themselves had disturbingly democratic implications. Before the 1790s, agitation for political reform came from Whig politicians; educated, prosperous Dissenters; and country gentlemen.[9] The establishment in January 1792 of the London Corresponding Society (LCS) by a shoemaker named Thomas Hardy marked the beginning of a plebeian involvement in British politics and thus the growing alarm of the upper echelons of society. Cobblers and tailors earnestly discussing the sovereignty of the people in the back rooms of public houses was very different from the duke of Richmond casually throwing out the idea for consideration in the Upper House. When Major John Cartwright had established the Society for Constitutional Information (SCI) in 1780 as a means of educating the general public on the benefits of parliamentary reform, he had not anticipated the wide-reaching impact of the society's tracts. The centenary of the Revolution of 1688, followed by the fall of the Bastille, revived in-

terest in existing political societies and inspired the creation of corresponding societies by a class of men who had previously been excluded from the
political arena. Moreover, during the decade of the French Revolution, the
plebeian element dominated the movement. The SCI lost its aristocratic associations as it began following the LCS in its principles and activities as well
as in the sort of membership it attracted. Like Cartwright, Hardy had sought
to foster political education and initiate a move toward more equitable parliamentary representation.[10] Both organizations found themselves forced into
precipitous action, however, in response to the government's foreign and domestic policies, as well as to the activities of the loyalist associations.

As early as 1792, reform society leaders realized that they had to discourage impolitic manifestations of anti-monarchicalism as well as find a politic
means of expressing their republican ideals. In the societies, internal tensions
increased as members disagreed on how to respond to repression and what
tactics to pursue for political change. Before this, during the period between
the publication of *Rights of Man* in March 1791 and the royal proclamation of
May 1792, reform activities had adopted a relaxed, free-spirited attitude. Proponents of reform in Britain were exhilarated by the spectacle of the French
people resisting oppression and asserting their sovereignty. Political societies
up and down the country held Bastille Day celebrations on 14 July 1791. Although the speeches, toasts, and songs at these celebrations did not express
overt hostility toward George III, they posed a direct challenge to royal power.
The Norwich Revolution Society listened to the dissenting preacher Mark
Wilks deliver a sermon that referred to Jesus Christ as a revolutionary sent
to liberate the oppressed. Dr. John Taylor, a Unitarian deacon, led the company in a song called "The Trumpet of Liberty," whose refrain ran: "Fall,
Tyrants! fall! fall! / These are the days of Liberty! / Fall Tyrants fall!"[11] The societies' correspondence with Jacobins in France led them to embrace an aggressive revolutionary rhetoric. At the London SCI's celebration, Dr. Joseph
Towers read an address from Nantes: "The decrees which have established
the French liberty have been like the trumpet sounding the resurrection of
the world: at our voice, the nations have raised their degraded fronts; tyrants
have turned pale upon their thrones; and such is the probable effect of this
great revolution, that in a short time nothing will be remaining of them but
the sorrowful and shameful remembrance of their faults, and of their
crimes."[12]

By the following year, some society members were voicing their uneasiness with this revolutionary fervor. The controversy that threatened to split

the Manchester Constitutional Society (MCS) illustrates how those who harbored republican ideals came to practice dissimulation for the sake of maintaining unity. In April 1792 Thomas Cooper and James Watt went to Paris to transact business for a company owned by the society's president, Thomas Walker. Without the society's authorization, they addressed the Paris Jacobin Club in the name of the English reform societies. Walker's letter of introduction, presented to the Jacobin mayor of Paris, Jérôme Pétion, represented the British people as ripe for revolution: Paine, he wrote, "has wounded [aristocracy] mortally, war he has put an end to; Taxes can go no further, and monarchy will not, I think, continue long in fashion." When Cooper returned to London in August, he sent Walker a triumphant account of the mob's invasion of the Tuileries on 20 June that concluded, "Te Deum laudamus."[13]

Unknown to Cooper, Burke had made a speech to the Commons on 20 April condemning Cooper and Watt. Burke's denouncement prompted the MCS to publish their correspondence in order to show that their association with the French was neither secret nor improper. Another member of the MCS, George Lloyd, then published a protest against the society having any communication with the Jacobins. Lloyd argued that consorting with republicans was improper; it deviated from the society's goal of reforming the government by constitutional means. Aspiring republicans took heed of the political temper and moderated their speech. In fact, they became so circumspect that the local loyalists who sought to prosecute them for sedition in 1794 could not collect solid evidence against them. The loyalists resorted to blackmailing a local drunkard into testifying against Walker, with predictable results; the trial embarrassed the government, resulting as it did in the star witness's perjury.[14]

Nothwithstanding the problems of evidence, the reform societies' words and actions gave a sufficiently vivid impression of an international crusade against monarchy to support a series of prosecutions. Because Paine held membership in the SCI, the society helped distribute his writings; on 6 July 1792 the LCS sent thanks to the SCI for sending two hundred copies each of the Letter to Dundas and A Letter Addressed to the Addressers of the Late Proclamation, Paine's response to the King's Proclamation for Preventing Seditious Meetings and Writings of 2 May.[15]

· The SCI also conferred honorary membership on Joel Barlow, another American revolutionary intent upon exposing the fraudulence he saw in monarchy. In his Advice to the Privileged Orders, Barlow called the various arguments used to justify monarchical power—the right of conquest, divine right, compact, and utility—"perpetual shifts of sophistry." He expressed astonishment that the first two even attracted rational debate: "The first is the logic of the musquet, and the second of the chalice; the one was buried at Runnimede on the signature of Magna Charta, the other took its flight to the continent with James the Second." The third, said Barlow, had long been moribund, until it was revived in desperation by Burke. Barlow also disputed Burke's claim that the French had temporarily retained their monarchy because of its utility. The French, said Barlow, were burdened with a king who had managed to gain the love of the people in spite of the mischief he had done them. Since Louis also had powerful family connections in other countries, the revolutionaries had given him a place in their new government to hide the magnitude of the changes taking place. They wished to avoid alienating other nations to allow their society to undergo regeneration in peace.[16]

The societies' uncritical championship of *Rights of Man* gave some reformers pause. In April 1792 Christopher Wyvill communicated his fear that the SCI's patronage of Paine's "ill-timed, and . . . pernicious counsels" would cause moderate members to be overwhelmed by republicans. Jeremiah Batley replied that the society had issued a resolution supporting Paine in order to "re-animate the society." He trusted that the wording of the resolution did not imply full agreement with Paine's principles. Indeed, the provincial societies sent testimonials in favor of the book to the LCS and SCI that conspicuously ignored Paine's injunctions against kings. The provincial reformers preferred to focus on Paine's concern for the poor, his ideas for social and economic reform, and his sentiments against war. Nonetheless, as a result of the resolutions in support of Paine, some SCI members resigned and requested that their names be removed from the society's books.[17]

At the LCS, Maurice Margarot voiced misgivings when the society announced on 15 June 1792 that it was establishing a defense fund for Paine. Margarot counseled against defending Paine before they knew the aspect of his works on which the prosecution would be grounded. He worried that the fund-raising would imply the society's approbation of Paine's works in their entirety, a stand that certainly did not represent the sentiments of a majority of its members. Margarot had just cause for concern: the indictment against *Rights of Man* focused on its anti-monarchical passages, and the government subsequently considered support of Paine as indicative of designs against George III.[18]

During the period between the 1792 Proclamation and the 1794 treason trials, the societies issued declarations that contained ambiguous statements regarding the monarchy, as reformers wrestled with conflicting impulses to represent themselves as the king's friends and to take him to task. The LCS responded to the proclamation by issuing an address that brazenly assumed that the king could not be referring to reformers because they shared his goals: to maintain domestic tranquility, secure religious and civil liberties, and prevent the subversion of government. The LCS further observed that the king, considering his "great goodness of heart and paternal care," must naturally approve of the LCS's activities "of canvassing such subjects as we think proper, of instructing our fellow citizens, of uniting our endeavours to obtain a perfect representation in parliament." Working from the same premise, Cooper published a letter in the Manchester *Herald* that expressed his grief over seeing the king's name attached to the proclamation, which was so obviously the work of corrupt politicians.[19]

Leaders of reform societies used the underlying threat of republican revolution to give their demands more clout. In response to Burke's attack on the MCS, Cooper remarked that he hoped for the sake of the privileged orders that the people's cries for reform would not be ignored. If the people had to demand the restoration of their lost rights, "Kings and Bishops and Nobles, [might] be irrevocably swept away in the dreadful torrent of public resentment." Sharpening the "evil ministers" argument, Cooper and Charles Pigott of the LCS both pointed out that the king had a duty to steer a new course; why should they pay a million pounds a year for a monarch who allowed his ministers to plunder the nation?[20]

Other writings emerging from Manchester at the time implied that the proper relationship between subjects and sovereign set down by the constitution had been undermined by political corruption, but it could be recovered by constitutional means. A handbill addressed "To the Affrighted Nobles of the Land," which circulated in August, explained that subjects would happily submit as a free people to a "patriotic king": an executive authority constituted by law, not one that shackled the people with threatening proclamations.[21] On 17 November 1792 the Manchester *Herald* recommended that the British people indicate their disapproval of the government's preparations for war by replacing loyal addresses with petitions to the king for the dismissal of his ministers.[22]

The societies indulged in a certain degree of license in their manner of address to the king; after all, many of the king's current champions had not always been reverential. Reformers insisted that their principles and activities were no different from those pursued in the previous decade by such worthies as Burke and Pitt, both of whom had offered George III some stern rebukes. As an LCS address observed: "Who can not have forgotten the popularity of Mr. PITT, when he, with so much apparent zeal, contended in the House of Commons ... '*I scorn to approach the Crown with Servility and Adulation;* ... IT IS NOT A CHANGE OF MINISTERS, BUT A TOTAL CHANGE OF SYSTEM AND MEASURES that I look for; and till I can have some pledge, that in this my wishes shall be gratified, *I will oppose Privilege to Prerogative,* and vote, that NOT A SHILLING BE GIVEN BY THE PEOPLE TO THE CROWN.' Such, fellow countrymen, was the language of the present heaven-born minister, out of place."[23] Society addresses quoted liberally from speeches and writings of the 1780s to showcase ministerial apostasy as well as to prove that declamations against Crown influence were neither new nor threatening to public order.

The societies' refusal to abandon their support for the French Revolution led them into anti-monarchical rhetoric that attacked George III more directly than they perhaps intended. The king's position as Elector of Hanover, of little consequence during most of George's reign, reemerged as an explosive political issue. When the societies hurled abuse at the German despots who were trying to thwart French liberty, they found their king in the line of fire. In the summer of 1791, when France went to war against Britain's traditional allies, Austria and Prussia, reformers campaigned for British neutrality. At the end of 1792 the LCS initiated a scheme for the societies as a whole to address the French National Convention. Margarot, who drafted the address, intended it to encourage the struggle for liberty by assuring France that the societies sought to thwart "underhanded ministerial attempts" at drawing the nation into the conflict. The address pointed to "a restless and all-consuming aristocracy" as the "real enemies"; but it also declared that God had not created people "to hate, and to be ever ready to cut each other's throats at the command of weak and ambitious kings and corrupt ministers": "With concern, therefore, we view the elector of Hanover, join his troops with traitors and robbers; but the king of Great Britain will do well to remember that the country is not Hanover—should he forget this distinction we will not." This statement became more menacing in the context of the address's conclusion, which could be interpreted as a plan for a British republic: "If you succeed as we ardently wish, the triple alliance (not of crowns, but) of the people of America, France and Britain, will give freedom to Europe, and peace to the whole world." Judging by the convention's reply, the French appear to have interpreted the LCS's statements in this way. Apparently, they also imbibed the LCS's patriot-hero worship: "The shades of Pym, of Hampden, and of Sydney, are hovering over your heads, and the moment cannot be distant, when the people of France will offer their congratulations to a national convention of England."[24]

The vacillations in LCS rhetoric confused and exasperated the members of provincial corresponding societies who were still fired up by republican ideas. In the autumn of 1792, the Stockport Friends of Universal Peace and Rights of Man tried to pin down the LCS: What had the society meant by the address that stated, "Numerous other reforms would undoubtedly take place"? The Stockport reformers did not entertain much optimism regarding the prospects of Parliament's reforming itself; they inquired: "Would not all the evil be done away at once by the People assembled in convention?" The Norwich SCI, after cataloguing for the LCS all the contradictions to be found in the publications of the various societies, left them with a question of such breathtaking indiscretion that the LCS suspected it was a trap: "It is only desired to know whether the generality of the societies mean to rest satisfied with the duke of Richmond's plan only, or whether it is their private design to rip up monarchy by the roots, and place democracy in its stead." Instead of answering, the LCS issued a public declaration on 29 November stating that they sought liberty and equality, not "no kings, no parliament."[25]

What exactly did this mean? Even the Sheffield reformers—bold satirists and champions of Painite ideas—lapsed into ambiguity when they tried to state their precise intentions: they professed a "determination to obtain a radical reform of the country, as soon as prudence and discretion will permit, and to establish it upon that system which is consistent with the Rights of Man."[26]

Scottish reformers had been much more decisive than the English. While the LCS and its provincial correspondents endlessly debated tactics—whether to petition Parliament or the king, or whether to hold a convention—delegates from the Scottish societies convened in Edinburgh in December 1792. When the meeting led to the arrests of two of their leaders, Thomas Muir and Thomas Fyche Palmer, Scottish reformers decided that strength was in numbers; at their second convention, held the following April, they proposed uniting forces with the English and forming a national convention. The English societies agreed to send delegates to Edinburgh, but their participation turned out to be half-hearted. The summons had come at the last minute, and they had not been able to decide upon a course of action.

In choosing an open forum for electing their delegates—the meeting attracted some thousand spectators to a field in Shoreditch on 24 October—the LCS initiated what would became a staple tactic for attracting more members

and worrying the government: the open-air mass meeting. The English delegates arrived in Edinburgh late but in time to garner the laurels of martyrdom.
Deliberations of the "British convention" ended abruptly on 5 December with
the arrests of the Scottish leaders William Skirving and Charles Sinclair as well
as the LCS's Margarot and Joseph Gerrald. All the society members arrested
on charges of sedition in Scotland were transported to New South Wales after a series of sensational show trials officiated by Robert, Lord Braxfield.

The Scots' impetuousness pushed the English reformers into hasty and
ill-planned action. Seeking to stir public outcry against the treatment of the
six "Scottish martyrs," the LCS held open meetings at the Globe Tavern on
20 January 1794, and at Chalk Farm on 14 April. These meetings produced arrests of the LCS and SCI leaders during the following month; on 17 May, the
government suspended the Habeas Corpus Act. Remaining members of the
LCS's Central Committee continued to meet in a Committee of Emergency
as the Treasury solicitors built a case for high treason against the twelve defendants. Hardy came to trial in November and won an acquittal, as did John
Horne Tooke, leader of the SCI; the government dropped the charges against
the others. The trials precipitated a major schism in an already divided movement. They left the constitutional societies in debt and with falling membership; militant members became convinced that the system could be reformed
only by a French-assisted revolution.

Reformers intent on sticking to a constitutional path faced the perennial
problem of devising a position consistent with both the so-called rights of man
and the power of the Crown. This proved to be a problem even for the decisive and impetuous Edinburgh conventioneers. According to their minutes,
when drawing up resolutions on the need to correct abuses of the constitution in December, Muir "said if he were to object to any part of this resolution, it would be the words 'strike at the root of,' as the enemies of reform
might construe this clause into treason, for the *root* of these abuses was well
known. The House of Commons had voted many years ago that the royal influence 'had increased, was increasing, and ought to be diminished.' (A laugh)
To put it out of the power of our enemies, therefore, to say we mean to strike
at the royal power, he proposed to insert the words 'in order to remove.'" As
the debate wore on, the level of exasperation as well as levity rose: "Muir said
that he was not willing to dispute about words, or to spend the time of the
Convention in mere verbal criticism, although the metaphor of 'removing a
source' did not quite please him. But gentlemen would do well to attend to
the inferences that might be drawn from such a mode of expression. 'What

is the source of these abuses?—the royal influence. What! Are you to remove the king?' Then gentlemen, according to this, we shall find ourselves in the same predicament with those foolish fellows who got drunk with the soldiers in the Castle the other week, and drank, 'George the Third and Last' (A Universal Laugh)."[27]

Reformers found that the old Bolingbrokean rhetoric on Crown influence, revived during the 1780s, now had different connotations in light of events in France. Although countless reform speeches and writings stressed that Pitt had usurped the power of the Crown, the source of corruption remained the monarchical system; hence, reformers found themselves straying from the province of parliamentary reform and threatening the monarchy.

Leaders of reform societies seemed to share Muir's preference for republican government, but they acknowledged the impropriety of discarding monarchy after its long tenure in England. Thomas Holcroft, one of the LCS members indicted for treason in 1794, claimed that parliamentary reform presented the only practicable course; everyone knew that were the king to die, his heir would succeed him, and the monarchy would go on as it always had. Yet underlying this sentiment was a hope that someday circumstances would arise that would allow the establishment of a British republic. Horne Tooke compared kings to wives: nations and individuals were likely to be happier without them, but if one chose either, one must keep each within the bounds of their duty. Divorce was regrettable, he mused in a private jotting, but he had "no religious or political superstition" to prevent him obtaining one by "*canon*, Ecclesiastical or military." Daniel Isaac Eaton, a London publisher, proclaimed, "Whenever it pleases God to deliver a people from a tyrant, and enable them to set up a freer form of government, it is scandalous neglect in them not to avail themselves of the opportunity." Henry Redhead Yorke, the fiery orator of the Sheffield SCI who landed in jail after a speech warning of an impending "grand political explosion," lamented that the principles of liberty had not been sufficiently understood at the time of the Civil War. The fears generated by those convulsions, and the false hopes engendered by the "dazzling lustre of the crown," had impaired the British people's judgment and kept them from effecting real change in 1688.[28]

Other reformers tried to temper their revolutionary ardor and worked on developing a republican ethic that did not threaten the British monarchy. The writings of Cooper, Pigott, and James Parkinson of the LCS reasserted the Real Whig definition of republicanism as government conducted for the public good.[29] In early 1794, after Eaton had been acquitted for publishing John

Thelwall's cheeky fable of a tyrannical gamecock who received a barnyard guillotining, Thelwall bragged to a friend that he was a republican, *sans-culottes,* and admirer of Marat's. Thelwall also displayed a fondness for histrionic gestures: after the Chalk Farm meeting he allegedly blew the head off his pot of porter and declared, "Thus I would serve all kings" (witnesses disagreed over whether he had actually said "tyrants"). In the face of the impending prosecutions in May, however, Thelwall qualified his position on monarchy by denying the inherent harmfulness of the institution. He placed all blame for national misfortunes on the politicians whose corrupt dealings had shackled both king and people.[30]

By 1796 Thelwall had developed the notion of a republican "kingly power." In justification of his anti-monarchical rhetoric, he explained: "By monarchy, the reader is to remember, that I mean something very different from kingly power. The former means a government *by one man,* who holds his power by some supposed or assumed *individual* right: the latter is a delegated trust, conferred by and held for the acknowledged *benefit of the people.* Where monarchy begins, kingship ends; and the people who bargained for a king, are not bound to submit to a monarch." He defined the true checks of a free government as the salutary awe of public opinion, enforced by the vigilance of the people in observing the conduct of their governors and making their opinions known to them. He explained that the different possible forms of government required that these checks have correspondingly different organizations and modes of operation. If the principle of liberty were alive in the people, "monarchy itself may be attempted with a degree of liberty; without it, republics are but despotism in masquerade."[31]

Thelwall's change of attitude mirrored the societies' shift in tactics after the treason trials. Speeches and addresses during 1795 revived the image of Bolingbroke's patriot king. The LCS drew up an address at their St. George's Fields meeting of 29 June that reminded the king that his people were risking their lives to ensure that he enjoyed what should be his chief treasure, their love. Meanwhile, his ministers were betraying him—endangering him, even—by misrepresenting them as disloyal. The address left the king with this warning: "The Nation itself stands tottering upon the Brink of Ruin, and YOUR EXISTENCE IS COUPLED WITH THEIRS!" The Sheffield reformers who met on Crooke's Moor on 10 August to protest the war against France and the high cost of provisions also directed a personal plea to George III: "Let not our prayers for peace be drowned in the thunder of war; when we ask for Bread, let not the Father of his People give us a stone."[32]

When the Father of his People did not respond to these remonstrances by October, the LCS members reiterated them more forcefully at the Copenhagen House meeting. They reminded George that the House of Hanover had come to the throne by the will of the people and expressed the hope that "an eternal gratitude would bind your house to support the freedom and happiness of that nation," particularly considering the high taxes they paid to support his large family. At this meeting, the reformers stressed that a remonstrance to the king was the last constitutional recourse of an aggrieved people. They remained purposefully vague, however, regarding the next step, should George again ignore their plea.[33]

Within the constitutional reform movement, republicanism became a set of standards by which governments could be judged. Reformers argued that a king who pursued republican ideals by acknowledging the proper relationship between himself and his subjects ensured his own security and happiness. William Godwin developed this theme in *Political Justice,* published in 1793. Although the book's price kept it out of popular circulation (as well as out of the way of government prosecution), its ideas were disseminated through Thelwall's lectures and through essays in the popular magazines published by Eaton and Thomas Spence.[34]

Godwin argued that a king could not help but be a despot in his heart, for his upbringing cut him off from everyday society and surrounded him with the corruption of wealth and flatterers. Princes became prisoners of the state. They could not cultivate the independence of mind essential to virtue and the perception of truth; they learned to trust everyone implicitly or to trust no one. Inactivity produced indolence, and ignorance bred arrogance. Treated as if they were higher beings, princes became immune to the sufferings of others. Godwin considered Britain's mixed government a cruel hoax on both king and people. The king was paid an immense sum, all measures were transacted in his name, and everything was done with grand parade while he was actually "a vacant and colourless mirror" of ministerial opinion.[35]

During the Panton Street debates of 27 October to 19 December 1795, LCS members treated the bills introduced against treasonable and seditious practices and against seditious meetings—which became the Two Acts—as typical of the ministerial despotism that had dominated the polity. On 16 November, John Gale Jones, the LCS's new leader, asserted that the bills were part of Pitt's scheme to place himself on the throne. Jones declared that George's refusal to sign the bills would absolve him of all past errors and make him a true king of his people. If he did sign, the king would place himself in danger: governments that did not allow the citizenry a voice suffered the highest rates of political assassination. Jones confidently pointed out that the reformers had power in their numbers. Forty thousand members would not be easily disbanded; the jails could not hold them all. By 25 November a mood of pessimism had descended, and the debaters became more bellicose. They decided that the bills violated Magna Carta and the Bill of Rights and, as such, infringed the compact between king and people. An impetuous young man suggested that by signing the bills, the king would break his coronation oath and be a traitor to his people, thus absolving them from allegiance. Jones tried to address the implications of the bills in a way that was consistent with the society's principles. He declared that the ministers intended to establish an absolute monarchy, with Pitt on the throne. If the king signed the bills they should "shut up their shops and meet the King, dressed in mourning for the loss of their Constitution and of their King," for "he will have signed his Abdication of the Government, and absolved the People from their Allegiance."[36]

The LCS held a mass meeting at St. Mary-le-Bone Fields on 7 December to draw up a remonstrance to the king, which George III, of course, did not acknowledge. On the day the Two Acts passed, Jones morosely observed that he saw no point in picking up a musket, either to assist or to oppose a French invasion, "for if I am to be a slave, it matters not whether I be the slave of an English, or of a French Tyrant."[37] By February 1796, however, Jones was touring Kentish towns in an attempt to assess the degree of support the reform movement still commanded. The LCS devised means by which reformers could continue to meet without contravening the Two Acts and sent emissaries into the provinces to spread the word.[38]

The reformers exhibited their reluctance to throw off allegiance to the king by attempting to hold a mass meeting at St. Pancras on 31 July 1797 to make one last plea. In justification of this apparently futile enterprise, the address declared that evil ministers had kept the king ignorant of their previous remonstrances. Although the reformers tried to satisfy the terms of the Seditious Meetings Act, the meeting resulted in the arrests of six of the speakers.[39] The government's coup de grâce came with their raid of the LCS committee room in Wych Street on 19 April 1798. Ironically, at this meeting reformers were voicing their discontent with revolutionary France and debating whether to join the Volunteers to help fend off a French invasion.[40]

Meanwhile, the United Englishmen and United Scotsmen, underground societies of militant republicans, had begun meeting sometime in 1797.[41] They made contact with the United Irishmen, an organization that had begun as a constitutional reform society in 1791 but that by mid-1796 was armed and insurrectionary. As was the case with their English and Scottish counterparts, the Irish reformers' espousal of a revolutionary republicanism took place gradually, as meetings and petitions failed to effect change. These secret societies tried to arrange a French invasion to coincide with an Irish rebellion and an insurrection in London: an organizational nightmare, to say the least. Fueled by anger against government repression, both the British and Irish movements used anti-monarchicalism as a sign of their commitment to political change.

Scattered evidence suggests that a spirit of militancy began to develop as early as the winter of 1793. Crudely written antiwar handbills posted around Norwich on 3 November expressed violently anti-monarchical sentiments. One proclaimed: "Behold a Despotic Whelp, by some called a King on the Throne of England, making unavailing Excuses by Declarations and such like Nonsense for this unjust and Ruinous WAR which so distress and burden the Sovereign People." The author called upon people to overthrow the "damned Constitution." Another handbill announced a meeting at Chapel Hill that never transpired; at this stage such sentiments were the product of a momentary republican afflatus rather than a revolutionary cell.[42]

By the summer of 1795, loyalists in towns all over England suspected any assembly of artisans spouting inflammatory rhetoric of being the germ of a revolutionary movement, and every suspicious stranger who spoke sedition in front of soldiers of being a Jacobin agent. Antiwar propaganda usually attacked ministerial policy, but the occasional anti-monarchical pieces bespoke a strongly republican spirit. Handbills that appeared in Lewes and Chichester during food riots began: "Soldiers to arms, arise and revenge your Cause / On those bloody numbskulls, Pitt and George." The bills protested sending men to France "to be murdered like Swine, or pierced by the Lance."[43] Judging by the papers confiscated from Wych Street, however, republicans did not break away from the corresponding societies and form an underground network until 1797.[44]

The anti-monarchical rituals that became a feature of these United societies suggest that members viewed the inspiring of hatred and contempt for kings as essential to a republican revolution. The United Englishmen who met at Furnival's Inn Cellar in London drank such toasts as "May the King and Ministers all hang together" and "A Speedy downfall to Spoony the Third and his Ministers."[45] Spies reported that the various groups of United Englishmen took pleasure in talking about political assassination; their writings certainly did not shrink from the implications of their principles, as the LCS publications had done. A handbill that catalogued the supposed insolence, folly, impiety, and tyranny of kings concluded: "Fellow Citizens;—Do not your bosoms swell with indignation; are you not resolved to crush these serpents, and rid yourselves and mankind for ever of the worst of plagues? Let them exhibit the glittery magic of their usurped authority; let them threaten to crush us with their frown; let them plead their divine hereditary right, and issue their pompous proclamations. Alas how vain! how weak and imbecile, when opposed to a nation brave and unanimous, that wills to be free."[46]

The Irish republicans turned out to be the most active revolutionists in the isles, in spite of a late start. Many Irish began to see the king as the higher authority behind the Protestant ascendancy. In *The Press,* a Dublin paper, the United Irishmen issued warnings to the king to stop his servants from murdering and pillaging the Irish people. The *Northern Star,* the organ of the Belfast United Irishmen, also professed loyalty to the king and abhorrence of his ministers. The *Union Star,* an irregularly produced Dublin newssheet, on the other hand, laid the blame on the king:

> Let the indignation of man be raised against the impious wretch who prophanely assumes the title of reigning by the grace of God, and impudently tells the world *he can do no wrong*—Irishmen! is granting a patent and offering premiums to murderers to depopulate your country, and take your properties, no wrong? Is taking part of the spoil no wrong? Is the foreign despot incapable of wrong, who sharpens the sword that deprives you of life, and exposes your children to poverty, and all its consequent calamities? O, man! or rather less, O King! will the smothered groans of my countrymen, who in thy name fill the innumerable dungeons you have made for asserting the rights of man, be considered no wrongs?

This particular piece went on to lambaste the king for involving the nation in foreign wars and for "taking the church into partnership, and encouraging its idle and voluptuous drones to despoil industry of its reward." It warned that the execution of Louis XVI and his followers by "the national axe" heralded a new era of justice.[47]

In spite of the hardline position that members of the United societies espoused, when it came to the the royal family itself, they wavered as much as the constitutional reformers had done. True, in Manchester, republicans joined in extravagant anti-monarchical rituals, particularly the swearing of colorful oaths. One man proclaimed: "I wishe the King was in a necessity House up to the Knees in filthe, and that he might be choaked with the Perfume before he got out." Another, whom the informer pronounced quite sober, fell to his knees and swore, "God for ever! Damn George the 3rd, King of England," adding, "If I was in St James's and had a sword, I would make him George the last instead of George the 3rd." Nonetheless, the conspirators could not come to agreement on the fate of the king: Should he and his heirs be killed privately before the French arrived, should the whole royal family be publicly guillotined, or should the king and his heirs be banished or imprisoned?[48]

The Commons Committee of Secrecy, originally appointed in May 1794 to monitor radical activities, took an interest in the Spensonians as well. Like the United society members, this association of self-professed republicans indulged in inflammatory toasts. Spence, an active propagandist throughout the decade, had been one of the reform-society leaders imprisoned between May and December 1794. He and some of his followers were arrested in April 1801 for distributing a pamphlet propagating his agrarian socialism. In making his case against landed proprietors Spence claimed to have inadvertently threatened the monarchy: "We must scalp them, or else they will soon recover and pull our Temple of liberty about our Ears. We must not leave even their Stump in the Earth, like Nebuchadnezzar though guarded by a band of Iron. For ill destroyed Royalty and Aristocracy, will be sure to recover and overspread the Earth again as before." Spence told the court that he had accidentally stumbled upon the subject of royalty with his reference to the biblical king and claimed that his plan for the redistribution of landed estates should make no difference to kingly power: "We know that Kings existed in Sparta for many Centuries, in company with iron, Money and small divisions of Land. Therefore let Royalty not despair." Spence was being disingenuous here; in a pamphlet published in 1798, he envisioned people reading his tracts and spontaneously beginning a process of confiscation and redistribution of landed estates, "and thus would a beautiful and powerful New Republic instantaneously arise in full vigour."[49] Whether this included confiscation of the king's estates, Spence did not specify. Unlike the moderate reformers, he refused to be pressured into accommodating the monarchy in his scheme. Spence appeared so focused on government from the grassroots that monarchy had little meaning for him.

Those who endeavored to establish a British republic had fortunes similar to that of the Jacobites who had sought to restore the deposed Stuarts. The French attempts at invasion in December 1796 and August 1798 failed, owing to bad timing and adverse weather. Government agents apprehended the United Irishmen's emissaries, James Coigley and Arthur O'Connor, in February 1797 at Maidstone, Kent, where they had been seeking passage to France with the intention of talking the French into another attempt. The authorities rounded up various United Englishmen whom they suspected had been involved in the invasion plan. Like the LCS meetings, the "secret" deliberations of the United English and Scotsmen attracted spies. Throughout the second half of the decade, agents caught a number of association members in England and Scotland administering illegal oaths to soldiers and sailors. In spite of the apparent infiltration of the military, loyal soldiers easily subdued the Irish rebellion of May 1798 and captured its leaders, who were hanged. Finally, the authorities moved in on Edward Marcus Despard and his fellow conspirators at Furnival's before they could put into motion the insurrection allegedly planned for 23 November 1802. It is unlikely that the extent of Despard's network will ever be known. Roger Wells and A. W. Smith are probably correct in their assessment of Despard's death as the start of the "physical force" radicalism that emerged in the next century, rather than as the end of the revolutionary underground.[50]

The strength and flexibility that the British monarchy's ideology and image had achieved by the 1790s allowed political radicals to indulge in republican fantasies and schemes while guaranteeing that these would not pose a threat to the institution. The treason trials did not deter John Baxter of the LCS from asserting the people's right to resist oppression, but he did so in the course of arguing that the purpose of the reform movement was to preclude the need to act upon this right. Baxter recommended that political associations add a democratic element to the government by organizing parish meetings to send petitions to Parliament. After the waning of the idealism inspired by the fall of the Bastille, reformers settled down to work within the system. Richard Dinmore's *Exposition of the Principles of the English Jacobins* (1797) explained that reformers wished no harm to George III, for "the senseless glitter of a coronation, and the noisy enthusiasm which would attach itself to a new king" would distract the public from the evils attending an unreformed parliament. A British republic would have to remain a distant ideal, a goal that could be achieved only in slow steps, as the majority of Britons became sufficiently educated to participate in the political process. Reformers had to accept what loyalists had recognized and capitalized upon: in the words of Samuel Taylor Coleridge, "If Monarchs would behave like republicans, all their subjects would act as royalists."[51]

The execution of Louis XVI in January 1793 produced both a heightened awareness of George III's vulnerability and a new appreciation of his virtues.

Loyalists had drawn upon Britain's republican past and its peculiar ideology of the mixed constitution to create an image of a monarchy that incorporated republican virtues. Their success in commandeering the rhetoric of liberty and grafting it onto the ideology of order forced reformers to be particularly careful about how their politics affected the king. What resulted was a British species of republican thought that was distinct from those of France or America. Loyalists and constitutional reformers wound up with similar models of monarchy: one that possessed the republican quality of providing responsible and accessible government. The main difference was that loyalists claimed that this model already existed, while reformers saw it as an ideal that would be realized only through parliamentary reform.

FIVE

Religious Sanctity

*O*N JUNE 1798 Richard Watson, bishop of Llandaff, a man of reformist leanings, instructed his clergy to urge their congregations to give full support to the war against revolutionary France. He pointed out that the revolution posed a threat more critical than any other Britain had ever faced: "For the Question is not now, as it has usually been, whether this or that man shall be the Minister of the Crown, but whether we shall have a Government to be administered?—Not, whether the Ministers or their opponents are not the wisest and most disinterested Statesmen, but whether both parties are not infinitely wiser, more disinterested, and fitter to serve the Country, than the self-erected Committee of England, associated with a French Directory?—The Question is not now, as it was in the Rebellions of fifteen and forty-five, whether we shall have a Monarch of the House of Brunswick, or of the House of Stuart; but whether we shall have any Monarch at all?—The Question is not now, as it was in the great Rebellion, whether the Church of England shall be governed by Presbyters, or by Bishops, but whether we shall any longer have a Church of any kind?" Like the unfortunate corresponding-society members arrested as they contemplated joining the Volunteers, Watson could no longer support the principles of a revolution that had spawned Napoleon Bonaparte. The bishop's old reform-minded associates saw this change of position as apostasy. Yet Watson did not abandon his reformist stance on domestic issues and continued to make a respectable showing as the last of the latitudinarian prelates. He remained active in his support of religious toleration, freedom of the press, and the abolition of the slave trade until his death in 1816.[1] The Bishop of Llandaff's espousal of the loyalist prowar position in 1798 epitomizes the impact that the French Revolution had upon religion in Britain: Anglicans of all tendencies as well as Dissenters had to clarify their attitude toward George III's monarchy. As was the case with reformers and loyalists, this clarification entailed adaptation and compromise.

This chapter explores the relation of mutual protection and support maintained between the institutions of the monarchy and the church, and the problems presented by the demise of divine-right ideology. Because the threat of revolutionary France allowed Anglicans to intensify their campaign against Dissenters, expositions from the pulpit on the implications for Britain of the French Revolution were as concerned with the role and power of the established church as they were with those of the monarchy. As Dissenters defended themselves against charges of treasonable intent by professing their dedication to King George, they contributed to the reformulation of monarchical sanctity. The dialectic between Anglican and dissenting sects reveals why divine-right doctrines were so enduring and how the monarchy developed its resilient, multifaceted image and fluid ideology of legitimacy. Religious argument helped the monarchy reconstitute its divinity by pursuing an idea of royal sanctity that was practical and relatively secular.

The seventeenth-century assault upon the ideology of divine right had plunged the established church as well as the monarchy into an identity crisis. Religious sects proliferated during the Civil War and Interregnum with the disestablishment of the Church of England. Although Anglicanism did survive on a popular level and Presbyterianism did not take hold, dissent became an established part of the religious landscape. The restoration of the Church with the monarchy made it clear, Norman Ravitch observes, that in England, more so than in the rest of Europe, the "conviction of 'no bishop, no king' was more than a pious platitude or a piece of special pleading." The monarch's religious proclivities now had more of an effect than ever on the fortunes of the Anglican establishment. The Restoration clergy had to cope with two monarchs who held strong ties to French papists and who tended to tolerate nonconformists, a failing shared by a growing number of the populace. James II's alienation of his supposedly inalienable sovereignty put the supporters of the church-and-state alliance in an untenable position. Some clergy found themselves unable to swear an oath of loyalty to William III, given that it would overturn the sacred oath they had already pledged to the Stuart dynasty.[2]

Technically, the new king was a Dissenter. Although the provisions of the dual monarchy allowed William to leave ecclesiastical appointments to the Anglican Mary, his natural gravitation toward Whigs and latitudinarians prompted choruses of "the Church in danger." Churchmen also had to contend with universal gravitation: the rise of scientific inquiry impinged upon the domain of the spirit and paved the way for such abominations as rational arguments for God's existence and the dismissal of Christian mysteries. Anglicans saw the rage for Newtonian mathematics and Lockean theories of human cognition giving rise to anti-clericalism and heterodoxy. The expected restoration of what churchmen viewed as the Stuart golden age of clerical strength and prestige did not materialize with the succession of Queen Anne. Her attempt to steer a moderate course by granting preferments to high churchmen while maintaining Whig parliamentary ascendancy created the frustration and party animosity that erupted in the Sacheverell controversy. Even the resulting Tory takeover did not yield its anticipated rewards. The queen's coyness regarding the identity of her successor caused some unfortunate political jockeying between the Hanoverian and Jacobite camps.[3]

The ascension of George I in 1714 placed on the throne yet another king who had not been brought up in the Anglican tradition and who favored a policy of religious toleration. Robert Walpole eased Anglican anxieties in 1724 by bringing to London Bishop Edmund Gibson, a Whig dedicated to the church establishment. Gibson, however, proved too zealous in his promotion of high-church interests. Although George II, who came to the throne in 1727, did not concern himself much with church affairs, his consort, Queen Caroline, did; and she leaned toward heterodoxy. Walpole, wishing to stay in the queen's good graces as well as to win back radical Whigs and Dissenters angered by the drift away from religious toleration, decided to curb high-church pretensions. In 1736 he supported the Quakers' Tithe Bill, which protected Quakers from prosecution in ecclesiastical courts for not paying tithes. But when the Dissenters and radical Whigs took the opportunity to introduce a motion for repeal of the Test and Corporation Acts, Walpole voted against it, thus showing his commitment to the Church establishment. Gibson's open opposition to the Tithe Bill, in defiance of his patron, then allowed Walpole to rid himself of the bishop's influence and remind the ecclesiastical establishment of certain Erastian realities. This is the kind of maneuvering that H. T. Dickinson presents as an example of the brilliant political management that kept Walpole in power for so long.[4]

In Stephen Taylor's view, the fall of Gibson represents not a Walpolean triumph but a consequence of the minister's "dulled appreciation of the mentality of the Church." Until Gibson's revolt against the Tithe Bill, Walpole, although he recognized the political expediency of silencing the refrains of "Church in danger," did not realize that most clergymen were committed to the institution above any political interests or allegiances. Consequently, in making further recommendations for preferment, the duke of Newcastle, who replaced Gibson as Walpole's main adviser in ecclesiastical affairs, took as much care in ascertaining the orthodoxy of the candidates as in avoiding Tory high churchmen. Taylor's observations sum up the predicament in which orthodox Anglicans found themselves: "In some respects the Church was always in danger under a whig regime. In the absence of a sitting convocation, deprived of any effective political allies, and with a foreign whiggishly inclined sovereign, it was vulnerable to parliamentary and lay encroachments. Not only was whig erastianism perceived as a threat, but so too were dissent, Catholicism, deism, and spreading immorality. These 'enemies on all sides' imbued some clergy with a sense of crisis, even defeatism."[5]

With George III, Anglicans at least had a leader who joined them in their efforts to curb impiety and vice and in their concern for the preservation of the established church. Nonetheless, as I showed in chapter 2, his reign also brought the resurgence of a noisy nonconformity. The specter of atheism and anarchy in France offered the perfect opportunity to reassert the importance of a strong church-and-state alliance and respect for the established faith. Church participation in the anti-Jacobin movement, however, proved to be a double-edged sword. In a study of the impact of the French Revolution upon British Protestantism, Nancy Uhlar Murray concludes that by the end of the decade, Anglican clergy had alienated more people than they had kept loyal with their excessive conservatism and repressive policies. She believes that much of their preaching had been motivated by a wish for preferment, judging by those who, when the rewards did not materialize, found that "disappointment nourished a hitherto latent reforming streak." Murray notes a difference in strategy between the orthodox clergy's defenses of the Test Laws and the anti-Jacobin pamphlets and sermons produced by high churchmen— those of an Arminian bent, in particular: although the orthodox clergy based most of their arguments upon utility, the high churchmen stressed scriptural authority. She postulates that in the atmosphere of heightened scrutiny attending the Burke-Paine debate, to make claims about the Church's contributions to society was risky because it drew attention to its institutional abuses, inflexibility, and intolerance of sectarians. At the same time, the horror of French atheism allowed the clergy to reformulate divine-right doctrines without risking a Sacheverellesque pillorying.[6]

As a number of the anti-Paine pamphlets illustrate, some loyalists combined assertions of the monarchy's spiritual basis with secular justifications of kingly power. The event marking the official reentry of divine-right ideology into political argument was the King Charles Day sermon preached by Samuel Horsley, bishop of St. Asaph, to the House of Lords in 1793. Horsley produced an explication of divine right that was couched in the language of contract theory, in what Helen Randall aptly describes as "a sleight-of-hand performance which was quite satisfactory to his audience."[7] Horsley declared that the king of Great Britain reigned both by God's providence and by a compact between himself and his people. This compact, however, had not taken place in a state of nature: people had never lived without government. God had placed people directly in a state of civil society; the governments they formed were thus divine in being works of human policy directed by providence. Horsley explicitly distinguished his conception of kingship from the exploded notion that sovereigns inherited a divine right to rule. Since kings acted as God's vicegerents, as St. Paul stated, obedience to their rule constituted one of the general duties of Christianity: "a conscientious submission to the will of God." Horsley explained that the British constitution made the king's ministers responsible for misgovernment in order to reinforce good rule as well as to preserve the king from the "degrading necessity" of being accountable to his subjects.[8]

Horsley based his sermon on Romans 13:1—"Let every soul be subject unto the higher powers." His interpretation of this passage diverged significantly from that of William Lucas, chaplain of the Lord Mayor of London, the previous year. The contrast between the two sermons illustrates the shift from utility to spirituality in Anglican conceptions of kingship. According to Lucas's account of the origins of government, holy men had anointed kings to produce rulers who could effectively maintain God's laws, distribute justice, and protect the people from anarchy, the worst plague imaginable. He observed that the same arrangement applied in England but that the king was now aided by the two other estates. The clergy accordingly preached the moral code set down by God. When the "mild Admonitions of the Church" proved ineffectual, the king stepped in; he wielded his secular power to reinforce morality. Lucas described the relationships between subject and sovereign and between church and king as social compacts that brought reciprocal benefits.[9] Although Horsley's sermon used the idea of a compact in order to delineate God's provisions, and although he placed the king in a higher realm, Lucas's compact constituted a pragmatic arrangement that presented the king in a more worldly capacity.

Sermons of the early 1790s in support of the Test Laws sought to undermine the Dissenters' use of scriptural authority in arguments against the privileges of the church establishment. Many took the position stated with refreshing bluntness by George Croft, chaplain to the earl of Elgin: "He *whose kingdom is not of this world,* and who never usurped the authority of a civil magistrate, neither changed nor disputed temporal rights and privileges."[10] Some Anglican anti-Jacobin sermons, in contrast, treated these two kingdoms as inseparable and preached pure Filmerism. John Whitaker argued that monarchy was "the primary, the natural, the divine form of government for Man." The formation of the first parental pair, from whom God constructed the government of man, established the subjugation of one sex to the other and of children to parents. Along the same lines, Charles Daubeny stated categorically that all resistance to authority smacked of the Devil's sin of rebellion against order. Preaching these doctrines must have occasioned some nervous shuffling in the pews, however, judging by Richard Bullock's reassurance to his congregation that the slavish notion of divine right had been exploded, so they need not perplex their minds with what could not happen; the tenet "Fear God, honour the king" did not apply to kings only, but to any constituted authority.[11]

Like Horsley, many orthodox and high churchmen claimed that monarchical authority was based on a dual foundation—divine providence and the British constitution—in order to endow the monarchy with sanctity but spare it the appearance of slavishness. William Hawkins, a Dorset vicar, explained that absolute monarchy as it appeared in the kingdom of heaven represented perfect government. This divine monarchy should provide a standard for judging all human governments. Unfortunately, because human societies did not have the same degree of justice and righteousness as the kingdom of heaven, they resorted to human contrivances to compensate for human failings, as the British people had done with their mixed monarchy.[12]

Robert Nares, chaplain to the duke of York, presented the two bases of monarchical power as interdependent. He argued that the sanctity of the king, as expressed in the religious service during his coronation, was vital to the preservation of the constitution. A king needed to be distinguished from all other members of the state because he ruled as one man over many. Moreover, he required considerable power, majesty, and autonomy in order to protect his people from foreign and domestic enemies. More important, according to the Bible, he was God's vicegerent: he upheld the laws that God had established to maintain harmonious societies. Nares combined the divine and constitutional bases of monarchy in order to acknowledge the right of resistance while effectively denying that it could be used against a king. He defined resistance as a God-given right to self-preservation that was limited to the rejection of arbitrary and life-threatening impositions or repression. Because removal of a king inevitably ushered in the worst possible political dangers, the constitution preserved his inviolability by placing responsibility upon his servants. Nares admitted that according to the constitution the king's power came from his people, but, given his sanctity, it did not follow that their arbitrary will could overstep his wisdom.[13]

Like Burke, some clergymen softened the notion of kingly divinity by conflating religious teachings and natural law: God's laws, they argued, embodied necessity and common sense. After the Fall, a government had to be constructed from the dictates of religion to control our evil nature. Fear of God produced human wisdom by discouraging sin and promoting order. The affiliation between the civil and religious establishments of every state remained sacrosanct for good reason. Clergymen produced countless examples of a decline in religious observance being closely followed by the dissolution of a state. They usually tacked on a disclaimer: they did not intend to suggest that kings reigned by God's direct command but rather that kings received God's wisdom through religious devotion and the workings of providence.[14]

Murray's study suggests that orthodox and high churchmen often appeared more concerned with institutional arrangements than with matters of belief. Orthodox clergymen generally accepted their subsidiary position while high churchmen, although they took pride in their role of supporting the government and maintained a reverence of authority, insisted that political concerns should not dominate the Church.[15] By claiming that the church-and-state establishments both had their origins in a charter by God, churchmen could depict the Church of England as simultaneously autonomous and intertwined with the state. They stressed the spiritual rather than the practical benefits of the alliance to head off any awkward discussion about the balance of power between church and state. Similarly, enumerating the sacred qualities of kingship was more comforting and less confusing than attempting to delineate the monarch's precise constitutional position. Nares and Thomas Rennell both soothed their congregations with sentimental, intellectually undemanding accounts of God's having bequeathed kings with fatherly authority to turn mankind into a brotherhood. This arrangement forged fraternal bonds among subjects based on real obligations, and encouraged a natural feeling of veneration toward their devoted spiritual father.[16]

George III's habits of personal piety provided the established clergy with strong support for these conceptions of benign patriarchy and religion's gentle melioration of government morality. Newspapers left their readers with affecting images of George and his numerous family, heads bowed in prayer, deriving strength and succor from their regular attendance at divine service. Moreover, the king displayed his epicurean taste for sermons in a material way; he evaluated the preaching ability of a clergyman before making decisions on preferment.[17] Yet, George's qualities also gave the evangelical Anglicans a stick to beat the orthodox and high clergy. Evangelicals, disgusted by what they saw as the neglect of the true principles of religion by the higher clergy, government ministers, and aristocracy (whom they blamed for the licentiousness of the lower classes), expected the king to lead a movement for the general reformation of morals: "Let the King and Queen continue to set an example of Piety, Regularity, and Sobriety, and conjugal Fidelity to their Children and Servants, and all their Subjects. Let them drive from their Councils, and their Court, all Adulterers and Adulteresses; all Gamblers; all, in short whose Characters are notoriously *bad,* of either Sex, and of every Rank." George and Charlotte were the only public figures to emerge unscathed from this, the most popular evangelical tract of the decade, which carried through its eight editions the uncompromising title *Reform or Ruin: Take Your Choice!* Its author, John Bowdler, a layman, blamed all the distresses in Europe on the wickedness of the ruling elite. He argued that if the upper classes reformed, everyone would cheerfully obey authority. If people loved the king and one another, they would produce a nation so united that they would never have to fear a threat from abroad.[18]

Evangelicals viewed the Bible as God's means of saving us after the Fall; earthly authorities had a duty to live by and encourage a general observance of its teachings. The country's strength and security could be preserved only by personal reformation. Charles DeCoetlogon, chaplain to the mayoralty, developed a novel interpretation of divine-right monarchy along these lines. The model monarch, the Patriot King, said DeCoetlogon, "acts under the habitual Conviction, that 'the divine Right of Kings is, to govern *well.*' Because *good Government* alone can be in the divine Intention God had made us to desire Happiness; he has made our Happiness, in a great measure, depend on Society; and the Happiness of Society depend on good or bad Government. His Intention therefore must be, that *Government should be good.*[19] DeCoetlogon pronounced theories on the origins of government, hereditary right, and the divine character of kings irrelevant in the face of the fact that political power was a trust, "a kind of Stewardship." Only a sycophant or an atheist would deny this. The Patriot King conducted God's government: his was the rule of morality.[20]

Methodists shared this evangelical notion of self-reformation, but they did not consider the king a vital participant in the process. Their precise position on the role of religion in the political system is hard to pin down; on the eve of the French Revolution they were divided over whether to break away from or cultivate a closer relation with the established church. John Wesley and his followers had a strong conservative streak in their reverence for constituted authority, but the group's spiritual egalitarianism, individualism, and itinerant preaching left them open to accusations of promoting Painite doctrines. When the conservative reaction to the French Revolution brought sectarians of all sorts under fire, Methodists responded by closing ranks and aggressively preaching obedience in the style of the orthodox and high clergy.[21]

Elie Halévy's thesis regarding the impact of Methodism on British society, although overdrawn, makes telling points regarding the nature of political and religious discourse of the 1790s. His introduction to the subject of religion in the first volume of his magisterial *History of the English People in the Nineteenth Century* encapsulates his position:

> During the eighteenth century England had been the scene of a great religious movement, unparalleled on the Continent—the last Protestant movement which has given birth to permanent institutions. This was the "Methodist" or "Evangelical" revival. To this movement, in combination on the one hand with the old Whig political traditions, on the other with the new *ethos* produced by the industrial revolution, British Liberalism of the opening nineteenth century owed its distinctive character. We shall witness Methodism bring under its influence, first the dissenting sects, then the Establishment, finally secular opinion. We shall attempt to find here the key to the problem whose solution has hitherto escaped us; for we shall explain by this movement the extraordinary stability which English Society was destined to enjoy throughout a period of revolutions and crises; what we may truly term the miracle of modern England, anarchist but orderly, practical and businesslike, but religious and even pietist.

In his conclusion to the volume, Halévy notes the great irony in the government's perception of Methodism as a subversive force when they should have realized that it was "the antidote to Jacobinism, and that the free organization of the sects was the foundation of social order in England."[22] The value of Halévy's interpretation lies in its recognition of the dichotomies present in English society at the end of the eighteenth century. Although the established church's rigidity of ideology and image would not allow the compromises necessary for preserving its position in the face of social, political, and economic change, the monarchy proved a more supple institution.

Bernard Semmel points out that historians who try to determine the correctness of Halévy's central contention—that Methodism prevented revolution in England—fail to appreciate the challenge of his argument, of coming to an understanding of the movement's paradoxes and their implications. Indeed, Eric Hobsbawm refutes the Methodism-as-an-antirevolutionary-force thesis by showing that no correlation existed between concentrations of Methodists in particular areas and political moderation. Rather, most of the regions of England that harbored Methodist movements had a simultaneous growth of radicalism. This leaves Hobsbawm with an unanswerable question: Did radical agitators drive others to seek solace in religion, or did Methodist and radical movements attract similarly motivated adherents? In any case, he asserts, the Methodists never had the degree of organization or influence needed to produce either the firmly directed group of revolutionaries or the crisis of the established leadership necessary for revolution. Moreover, there were not enough Methodists to make a significant impact on the nation's political climate. Hobsbawm touches upon but does not pursue the significance of the wide political spectrum Methodists represented. While Wesley and the movement's elite occupied the conservatist camp, the Methodist masses had a more democratic bent. Indeed, Alexander Kilham's New Connexion of 1797 and later breakaway groups seceded because they found mainstream Methodism's ethos and organization too rigid.[23]

Similarly, E. P. Thompson, although he employs the Halévy thesis in explaining the disintegration of the political reform movement, acknowledges "a shaping democratic spirit which struggled against the doctrines and the organisational forms which Wesley imposed. . . . Wesley could not escape the consequences of his own spiritual egalitarianism." For Thompson, "Methodism never overcame this tension between authoritarian and democratic tendencies." In order to support the antirevolutionary force idea, Thompson argues that the New Connexion's secession siphoned off the Jacobinism from the mainstream movement and left the poor members of the sect to sublimate their revolutionary impulse in the "chiliasm of despair." Firmly ensconced in the Marxist paradigm, Thompson describes Methodism's paradoxical mix of emotionalism, inhibition, and discipline as "a ritualised form of psychic masturbation."[24]

Both interpretations fail to place the Methodist movement in the larger context of eighteenth-century political as well as religious discourse; combining democratic and authoritarian ideas was nothing unusual. Methodism seems more the product of revolutionary times than a revolutionary force acting upon the institutions of the state, as Halévy would have it. Semmel's work agrees with Halévy in considering Methodism and utilitarianism as the main forces shaping industrial society. Yet unlike Halévy, who falls just short of calling Methodism a bourgeois plot to entrap the working poor, Semmel does show Methodism's apparent contradictions to be a function of eighteenth-century economical and societal changes and their accompanying muddle. The Methodists embraced Arminianism but not the Laudian Arminianism associated with Charles I and divine right. Their Arminianism had a contractual quality: Christ's sacrifice allowed salvation for all who accepted divine grace and strove to live a godly life through good acts. Being one of the elect, then, depended on accepting these conditions. Along the same lines, Methodists accepted the patriarchal model of kingship, which accorded with the familiar family construct, and duly adapted it as the rigid biblical paradigm gave way to practical notions of paternal guardianship.[25]

Methodist sermons intimate that members of the sect often became annoyed with the defensive stance that the loyalist movement forced them to take. One such preacher, Joseph Benson, blamed the mob violence stirred up against Nonconformists in Oxford on the anti-Methodist sermons of Dr. Edward Tathem. Benson pointed out that the clergy were meant to encourage love of king and country, not hatred of loyal citizens. He denied an intention to dispute the dictum *"Fear God and honour the King,* by which religion and loyalty are coupled together," cited by Tathem. He noted, however, that Methodists were "careful to *render to Caesar the things that are Caesar's, as well as unto God the things which are God's."*[26] Methodists often cited Matthew 22:21 in their sermons after professing their loyalty to a king who followed God's laws; one wonders whether this was an oblique allusion to Jesus' first response to the Pharisees when they asked him, "Is it lawful to give tribute unto Caesar or not?"—"Why tempt ye me, ye hypocrites?" (Matt. 22:17–18).

Nonconformists also expressed irritation over the need to continually defend themselves against allegations of regicidal intent. Supporters of the established church lumped together nonconformists of all denominations under the blanket term Presbyterian, and represented them as the direct descendants of the rebels against Charles I. Joseph Priestley and other Dissenters angrily denounced these aspersions and presented historical accounts in illustration of their particular loyalty to the crown. They pointed out that their initial agreement to the Test Laws showed a willingness to sacrifice their own interests for the sake of supporting limited monarchy. In any case, Dissenters did not form a party with a particular creed, but a temporary union of persons of various beliefs who agreed on one issue, the repeal of the Test Laws. They insisted that their religious concerns had been turned into a political issue by corrupt churchmen. Dissenters maintained that religious worship should properly be kept separate from political institutions. George Walker argued that the Church of England was an innovation, not an inextricable part of the constitution, as its supporters liked to claim. After all, the constitution had existed without the Church for many centuries.[27]

Nevertheless, Dissenters had become political with their involvement in the reform movement and had to devise a viable position on the monarchy that would show they were not the king's enemies. In doing so they took the offensive against established churchmen, whom they represented as the real enemies to the balanced constitution. Priestley asserted that he believed in the utility of monarchy, but he considered its current influence too great. He observed that the clergy's preaching of passive obedience had given the Stuarts their excessive and fatal power; in contrast, the Jacobite sympathies of churchmen during the reigns of the first two Georges prevented the power of the crown from tipping the balance of the constitution. Samuel Heywood argued that the Dissenters' views of monarchy followed the principles of the Glorious Revolution. Dissenters extended their loyalty to monarchs who followed God's laws and held to the solemn contract between themselves and their people, as set down in the coronation oath. The established clergy, on the other hand, still preached High-Tory doctrines. Heywood quoted sermons published over the previous hundred and fifty years to illustrate the church's adherence to passive obedience and nonresistance. The established clergy had made no alterations in their articles or canons; this impaired the ingenuity of constitutional monarchy.[28]

Dissenters cast the established clergy as the evil advisers behind the king. Churchmen, they claimed, tried to increase Crown prerogatives, their means of gaining preferment. Dissenters argued that the clergy's preaching of slavish doctrines clouded kings' minds and corrupted their morals until they could no longer recognize the word of God.[29] This stance enabled Dissenters to join Whig politicians in opposition to the war against France without appearing to be against the monarchy. As Charles James Fox and his party attacked William Pitt's war policies, dissenting clergy and laity represented the established clergy as the source of Pitt's wrongheadedness. George III provided opportunities for making this point when he followed the custom of designating certain days for public fasting and humiliation after military setbacks. "Surely our divines cannot be so much mistaken as to imagine these harangues gratifying to the Head of the Church?" Daniel Stuart inquired as he decried the brutal rhetoric issuing from Anglican pulpits. The religious services held on fast days not only were a vehicle for ministerial propaganda, they were an excellent platform for making the dissenting case.[30]

Although they denounced the church establishment, sermons and pamphlets opposing fast days occasionally impugned the king. In response to a fast called in April 1793, Anna Laetitia Barbauld reasoned that by requesting subjects to confess the sins of the nation, the executive and legislative powers implied that responsibility for government lay in the people—to have the people humble themselves before God for sins they had not committed and had no power to amend would be a mockery of God. Barbauld stopped short of asserting the sovereignty of the people; instead she concluded that the people had a responsibility to raise their voice against the war and the burdens it imposed upon the poor. She did not say what the next step should be if the king ignored this supplication.[31]

In a protest against the same fast, another Dissenter, William Fox, questioned outright the propriety of having the king as the head of the Church of England: "A great mathematician of old, said, that there was no royal way to geometry; so I should imagine that even bishops have not been able to discover a royal way to repentance." Fox argued that given the customary untruthfulness of kings when they set down their reasons for going to war, Christian subjects could never be sure whether they could pray to God in its support. According to the Scriptures, they should obey the government except when doing so contravened their duty to God. Like Barbauld, he would only recommend remonstrances. In response to a fast called the following February, Fox emphasized the relevance of Christian duty to kings and put a new spin on patriarchalism:

> When we see them (as sometimes happens) trampling on these duties, we
> are apt, in proportion as we really believe and reverence our religion, to
> look with horror on their conduct; and, however much we may endeavour
> to reverence the King and all in authority, yet, at the most, it will only be

with that degree and species of reverence with which the child beholds his criminal parent when violating the laws of society, and all the civil relations of life, it will not restrain him from remonstrating on his criminal conduct, nor, in some cases, even from endeavouring to obstruct him in the preparation of his crimes, and in guarding society from their baneful effects.[32]

Many opponents of fast days invoked the principle that obedience to God came before obedience to earthly authorities. Most hastened to add that subjects still owed their governors reverence.

Like the political reformers, Dissenters worked on the assumption that if they protested long and hard enough, the government would eventually yield to extraparliamentary pressure.[33] Preachers came close to calling the king unchristian for commanding fasts in support of an unjust war and recommended defiance of them. Sermons, however, were generally immune from prosecution, with two notable exceptions.[34] Perhaps because Dissenters were the first to be targeted by church-and-king mobs and never built organizational networks comparable to the reformers' corresponding societies, the government did not consider them a threat. Or perhaps the king and his advisers felt vulnerable regarding this religious issue and did not want to risk the discussion that public trials would stimulate.

The exchanges between churchmen and Dissenters mirrored the general debate between loyalists and reformers in the way it brought a synthesis on the issue of monarchy. As political argument produced a model of republican kingship, religious argument resulted in what can best be described as an idea of the king's secular sanctity. Heywood presented only a partial picture of the high-church clergy's position on monarchy. True, some churchmen preached unadulterated Filmerism, but others combined the divine with the constitutional. Monarchy, as depicted in the Scriptures, was the perfect form of government, but earthly imperfections had to be compensated for by such human innovations as the constitution and the church establishment. Dissenters, although they maintained that the king should not interfere with the religious life of his subjects, acknowledged that monarchy had a religious component when they insisted that obedience to the king depended on his observance of God's laws. Churchmen and Dissenters, then, both implied that monarchy was divine in respect to its being subject to the workings of providence. Evangelicals most clearly articulated this middle ground when they suggested that the king's sanctity came out of his moral duties: his exalted position required him to be a perfect Christian.

The conceptualization of monarchical divinity in terms of practical morality reflects the shift in clerical preoccupations from political to social issues. Susan Pedersen shows that Hannah More's *Cheap Repository Tracts* were not so much anti-Jacobin propaganda as part of the evangelical campaign against the licentiousness of popular culture. Similarly, William Ward's general study of the impact of the French Revolution on religious life in England suggests that by mid-decade, social rather than political tensions posed the greatest threat to church and state. After church-and-king mobs had destroyed the chimera of Unitarian Jacobinism, churchmen faced the real threat that itinerant Methodist preachers might appeal to the large section of laboring poor who had drifted away from an established religion that had become irrelevant to their lives. This is not to say, however, that Anglican divines abandoned their political aspirations and resigned themselves to pastoral ministrations. In the 1790s, as in the 1690s, voluntary efforts to extend charity and education to the poor did not assuage the aspirations of an institution long accustomed to considering itself one of the pillars of the constitution.[35]

The animosity accompanying the political and religious divisions during the 1790s has encouraged critics to overemphasize polarization, which has tended to perpetuate contemporary propagandistic stereotypes of the decade's partisans. In this regard, F. C. Mather's reconsideration of Bishop Horsley is instructive: "His image as a reactionary royalist and as 'the most powerful and articulate excoriator of French republicanism in particular and change in general,' to use Dr Soloway's phrase, is undeserved." Horsley's life, as Mather presents it, reflects the dilemma of high churchmanship in the latter part of the eighteenth century as well as the subtleties that were often lost in the course of acrimonious political argument. Horsley hailed from a nonconformist background and involved himself in the Royal Society's scientific controversies of the 1770s. During the following decade, however, he became troubled by the encroachment of science upon matters of the soul as well as by what he perceived as extremism among Calvinist Evangelicals and Rational Dissenters. Mather emphasizes that Horsley actively opposed repeal of the Test and Corporation Acts more in the interests of religious truth than out of conviction regarding the Church's constitutional position. Moreover, the bishop's support for a strong monarchy was motivated by a fear of mob rule in the name of democracy rather than by devotion to divine-right principles. Famous for his injunctions against the common people who agitated against the laws, Horsley also participated in the campaigns against the slave trade and missionary encroachments in India, a fact that tends to be forgotten. Ultimately, Mather describes him as "a conservative constitutionalist of mixed Whig and Tory pedigree"; although he dedicated himself to "the principle of establishment and the union of Church and State in a single society under the King's Majesty," he also believed in the episcopacy's spiritual independence.[36]

As churchmen directed their attention to the lower classes their preaching became more ethereal. Latitudinarianism faded and revealed religion made a resurgence. George's dedication to the church establishment, coupled with his example of personal piety, furthered this trend. His regnal style made patriarchalism and ceremonial grandeur and ritual admissible again. At the same time, Dissenters continued to push the state toward an acceptance of rational Christianity and religious toleration. J. C. D. Clark captures this long process of compromise with his description of the 1660 Restoration Settlement as having "decisively fused the warring factions into that composite sovereign the King in Parliament, the Anglican Trinity of monarchy, lords, and commons." Clark notes that divine-right ideology evolved from support of the authority of kings to upholdance of the entire social hierarchy.[37] The monarchy maintained its power and centrality by adjusting to shifting tensions in society and continuing to provide a point of unity for conflicting political, religious, and social groups.

Legal Sanctity

ECASTING the ideological foundations of the monarchy and endowing it with a secular sanctity involved a bit of arm twisting. The monarchy remained the center of attention because the decade's sedition and treason trials continually reminded the public that religious and political dissenters threatened the king's life, a life that had to be cherished to preserve the welfare of the nation. Legal argument became a key element in the discourse on the monarchy. The judiciary, after all, had long served as a vehicle of propaganda, albeit in support of more general aims. Douglas Hay observes that charges to grand juries usually set out the government's philosophy, the state of the law, and the duties of gentlemen. They also conveyed a paternalist message to the general public: "a secular sermon on the goodness of whichever Hanoverian chanced to be on the throne, the virtues of authority and obedience, the fitness of the social order." During the early eighteenth century, these charges touched on such matters as the devilish confederation of Jacobitism and the incendiary speculation about who was responsible for the South Sea Bubble.[1] Judges and prosecution counsel of the 1790s turned this message into an injunction to aid the authorities in protecting the king's life. The courts of law became another arena for debate on the position of the Crown, an arena in which loyalists possessed a distinct territorial advantage.

This is not to say that the legal system acted as an unimpeded instrument of government repression. The relation between the monarch and the law involved numerous vagaries that not only aroused contention between Crown and Parliament but also complicated prosecutions of seditious libels. Regarding the first problem, Howard Nenner cautions historians against seeing the disagreements between James I and Edward Coke as a conflict between Crown prerogative and the common law. Nenner finds it more productive to view the struggles of the seventeenth century as a contest between the Crown and Parliament over who would control the law and its accompanying rhetoric of historical legitimacy. When considering the status of the law, he points out, one must distinguish between the common law, an object of great reverence, and the common lawyer, a necessary evil who had to be overseen. Ironically, however, although Coke idolized the common law as the bastion of English liberties—a sentiment shared by subsequent jurists, most notably William Blackstone—it was the common law that bequeathed discretionary powers to the Crown: prerogatives stretched to the breaking point by Charles I and James II.[2]

Contestation over the legal positions of the Crown and Parliament as well as the tension between common and civil law caused difficulties when the common law of libel was applied to attacks on the government.[3] Elizabeth's ministers found it easier to employ statute law in the form of licensing acts to squelch censure from the press. The difficulties inherent in prosecuting flagrant press challenges to Elizabeth's authority as treason inspired Parliament to pass an act in 1581 that designated as a felony any written calumny against the queen that could not be prosecuted as treason. But Parliament balked when Elizabeth tried widening the statute to encompass all antigovernment propaganda in 1585, and, faced with uncooperative juries, the Crown increasingly turned to the Star Chamber to handle such matters. During the first two years of the Restoration, with no prerogative courts or licensing act in force, Charles II resorted to prosecuting libels against him as sedition, much to the surprise of jurors, who by this time had no recollection of such an offense under the common law. In 1662 the king availed himself of a new licensing act and also dusted off the old Roman law of *scandalum magnatum*—against slandering high personages—which William Scroggs, chief justice of the King's Bench, duly conflated with the common law of libel. Other judges proved less cooperative regarding the Crown's efforts at censorship, so Charles had to rely on his right to prosecute unlicensed news deemed likely to breach the peace. Consequently, most seventeenth-century trials for seditious libel actually proceeded as violations of the Licencing Act.

William III had allowed the Licencing Act to lapse by 1695, however, having successfully employed the treason statute to silence a Jacobite propagandist permanently in 1693. Yet this practice provoked outcry, and the Treason

Trials Act of 1698 gave defendants the same rights in treason cases—such as the right to counsel—as in other criminal proceedings. Finding the treason law unwieldy for prosecuting scandalous literature against him, William turned to scandalum magnatum. Meanwhile, operations of the common law against attacks on the government in general further clarified the procedures in seditious libel cases. Whereas the licensing acts had made any unlicensed publication liable to prosecution by virtue of its existence, the court now had to prove both the fact of intentional publication and whether by law the writing constituted a seditious libel: that it had been published with a malicious intent to alienate allegiance to the government. Once the province of the Star Chamber, the determination of fact and law now fell to the court. During the eighteenth century, the source of dispute in sedition trials concerned the relative powers of the bench and the jury. Charles James Fox's Libel Act of 1792 placed responsibility for determining seditious intent upon the jury, which made for controversy in sedition and treason trials alike.

The means by which juries assessed intent became sticking points in the English treason trials of 1794 in particular. John Barrell declares that these trials "put the nature and function of the law itself in question." So much judicial opinion had attached itself to the treason statute by 1794 that prosecutors were treating high treason as if it fell within the auspices of the common law. Judges cited much of this interpretive literature in an effort to establish the meaning of the statute's definition of treason as "compassing or imagining the king's death." Barrell contends that the prosecution's use of analogies, as in common-law proceedings, allowed the defense to exploit the wide-reaching definition of *imagining* as an opportunity to present opposing analogies: "The prosecution was doing the imagining, and . . . its imagination was hopelessly disordered. . . . The Common Law, it seemed, had usurped the functions of reason and judgement." The trials fueled Jeremy Bentham's crusade against Blackstone's apotheosis of the common law in his *Commentaries* and inspired William Godwin's fulminations in the *Morning Chronicle* against "constructive treason." In the same way as Nenner, who sees the conflict at the heart of the Civil War as the contest to gain control of the law and its legitimating rhetoric, Barrell notes that maintaining command over the law involved excluding rival discourses. Failing to accomplish this, the proceedings of 1794 brought the very location of sovereignty into question. Common-law constructions—associated with the royal prerogative—prevailed over laws passed by the legislature.[4]

The treason trials of 1794 resulted in acquittals, but they did not lead to the demise of the judiciary. Emotionally charged monarchy-in-danger rhetoric overcame esoteric discussions of the intricacies of the law. The government won some important convictions, and even when judgments favored the accused, prosecutions still involved imprisonment and financial hardship for defendants awaiting trial.[5] In the years following, the real threats of French invasion and rebellion in Ireland reinforced the fiction that a treasonable conspiracy had existed in the early 1790s. More important, the trials succeeded in building an atmosphere hostile to reformers by repeatedly representing them as potential regicides who had to be suppressed in any manner possible.

This was not a premeditated strategy on the part of the government. Prosecuting antigovernment rhetoric as sedition had never been easy, so punishment had to be terrifying enough to discourage those who might be tempted to risk the odds of being convicted. During the 1790s, additionally, the wording of the sedition and treason laws dictated the prosecution policy. In the statutes and commentaries, definitions of these crimes stressed activities that posed a deliberate threat to the king's life. Since little evidence existed that the reform societies were plotting an armed insurrection against the king, prosecutors had to present interpretations of reform activities and ideas as indicative of an intent to bring down the monarchy. As I have shown in chapter 4, reformers had been fairly inattentive to the issue of the monarchy until they began to be accused of harboring treasonable intentions. References to the monarchy—serious and satirical—proliferated in reformers' speeches and writings in response to government and loyalist allegations. This served only to provide more evidence for the prosecution and to whip up public concern for the king's welfare.

The first state trial of a reform-society member for seditious words, in May 1793, favored the government. Nevertheless, the proceedings drew attention to the difficulty of applying the sedition laws to reformist ideas and activities. The prosecutors employed dexterity of argument, not to mention a special jury.[6] The defendant, John Frost, a London attorney, had belonged to the whiggish Thatched House Tavern Society and even corresponded with William Pitt during the 1780s. Unlike Pitt, however, he remained committed to reform and joined both the Society for Constitutional Information and the London Corresponding Society (LCS). On 6 November, recently returned from Paris and fortified with coffeehouse punch, he began holding forth on French equality. Asked what he meant by equality, Frost replied, "No kings." In explaining why Frost's words fell within the dictates of the sedition statutes Attorney General John Scott cited Edward Hyde East's *Pleas of the Crown* as his authority: "In general, it is sufficient to observe, that all contemptuous, in-decent, or malicious observations upon his [Majesty's] person or government, whether by writing or speaking or by tokens calculated to lessen him in the esteem of his subjects, or weaken his government, or to raise jealousies of him amongst the people, will fall under the notions of seditious acts, as well as all direct or indirect acts or threats calculated to overawe his measures, or dis-turb his government, not amounting to overt acts of high treason, or other-wise punishable by particular statutes." Although Scott gave the impression that the sedition law was wide-ranging and discretionary, the law made it plain that the seditious effect had to be "calculated." Scott maneuvered around this by referring to Robert Foster's *Crown Law*, which, in discussing the inter-pretation of seditious words, stressed that the surrounding circumstances had to be taken into account. Scott pointed out that the doctrines of "equality" and "no kings" had occasioned such horrifying consequences in France that any-one propagating them in Britain had to be regarded with suspicion.[7]

In Frost's defense, his barrister Thomas Erskine argued that the attorney general was setting a precedent that would ultimately endanger the monar-chy: "I might say, that I do not know an individual, who seriously wishes to touch the crown, or any branch of our excellent constitution; and when we hear peevish and disrespectful expressions concerning any of its functions, depend upon it, it proceeds from some obvious variance between its theory and its practice. These variances are the fatal springs of disorder and disgust." Erskine also invited the jury to examine the circumstances across the Chan-nel: the least expression of support of royalty brought the guillotine blade down upon the speaker's neck. Is this what England wanted? Erskine ob-served that Frost could have traversed every coffeehouse in London ex-pounding the dangers of republican government and nobody would have paid him any mind, although the Commons was just as important a part of the gov-ernment as the Crown. The special jury would have none of it. Frost was dis-barred and spent six months in Newgate, which included a daily hour in the pillory. Reformers tried to counteract the impact of the trial by gathering to cheer Frost upon his release; the crowd took the horses from his carriage and pulled it through the streets past St. James's Palace and Carlton House.[8]

The wording of the sedition statutes required the prosecutors to present every antigovernment utterance as indicative of a design against the king. This practice is particularly striking in the trials of William Winterbotham for seditious words. He committed his first infraction in a sermon that he de-livered in 1792 on the anniversary of William III's arrival in England. Realizing that he had caused offense, he preached a follow-up sermon on 18 November to clarify his position, only to have that sermon serve as the basis of a legal prosecution as well. In his first sermon, the Baptist preacher had assessed the legacy of 1688 and found unjust taxes and abuses of the law. He expressed astonishment that the people did not stand up for their rights, observing that England needed a revolution similar to the one in France. Although the fourteen-count indictment included these passages, the prosecutors focused on Winterbotham's statement, "His Majesty was placed upon the throne upon condition of keeping certain laws and rules; and if he does not observe them he has no more right to the throne than the Stuarts had." Winterbotham's defense counsel pointed out that the words were true, and challenged: "Does any man pretend to say his majesty sits on the throne by *divine right*—no one will dare to do this—no one can do it without making himself an offender against the constitution of the country." The counsel for the Crown replied that it was improper to investigate the terms of the king's rule; soon everyone would consider themselves fit to judge royal behavior and absolve themselves from duty with the flimsiest of excuses. Plainly, the government's concern centered on pulpit politics. The judge instructed the jury that determination of Winterbotham's conscious intent was academic; he had delivered it to "some of the lowest class of people" immediately after His Majesty's Proclamation against Seditious Meetings and Writings, which specifically warned against holding such discussion. The jury, almost certainly packed, accommodated the prosecution in spite of contradictions in the witnesses' testimonies.[9]

Prosecutors successfully used circumstances to assign intent during the Scottish sedition trials of late 1793 and early 1794. Speaking in his own defense, Maurice Margarot put up the biggest fight against this application of the law. He declared: "The indictment only pretends to know, what I am sure the Almighty never commissioned the lord advocate to inquire into, namely, our secret intentions. I did not know before that there was an inquisition in Scotland, and that he was grand inquisitor; and for certainly, otherwise, the minds of the people are only to be gathered from their behaviour."[10] Nonetheless, the lord advocate convinced the jury that the reformers had betrayed their intentions by calling their assembly a convention, in imitation of the French regicides. In the next trial, Joseph Gerrald's attorney argued that one could not place constructions upon speeches and actions that were open to different interpretations by different persons at different times. He disputed the sedition charge: if their speeches had excited disaffection, participants in the

Edinburgh Convention should be charged with seditious words; if they had plotted to overthrow the constitution, they should be tried for treason. The solicitor general replied that holding a convention that purported to represent the people, coupled with the tendency of the speeches, showed a seditious intent.[11]

The government's decision to prosecute the English reform-society leaders for high treason is hard to fathom. The prosecutors could hardly have expected to win convictions: when Spencer Perceval, M.P., assessed the societies' papers at the request of the attorney general, he reported that no matter how alarming the societies' activities were, they did not add up to high treason. "But if the reason for not prosecuting them for a misdemeanor is the expectation that they will soon proceed to some clearly treasonable offence, I much doubt if they will ever be prosecuted at all." In a reassessment of the treason trials from a present-day barrister's point of view, Alan Wharam defends Scott's decision to pursue the treason charge. Wharam cites Scott's memoirs to show that the attorney general was aware that it was possible to escape conviction for sedition by proving that the charge should have been treason. Moreover, Scott did not want to proceed on partial evidence: "Unless the whole Evidence was laid before the Jury, it would have been impossible that the Country could ever have been made fully acquainted with the dangers, to which it was exposed . . . and it appeared to me to be more essential to securing the public safety that the whole of their Transactions should be published than that any of these Individuals should be convicted."[12]

This at least suggests that the Pitt administration was more interested in propaganda than in convictions. Had the reform-society leaders been convicted and executed, their martyrdom might well have stirred public outcry and provided a rallying point for the reform movement. The acquittals stood as monuments to trial by jury and English freedom and undermined the reformers' complaints of government oppression. Moreover, the proceedings probably left many people wondering whether the reform movement was a front for a treasonable conspiracy. Indeed, the designation "acquitted felons," coined by William Windham while discussing Thomas Hardy's trial in the Commons, entered the language.[13] It also does not seem likely that Scott feared the defense tactic of proving that the accused should have been indicted for high treason rather than sedition, for it fell flat in Gerrald's case. Scott might have felt confident about the charge after the conviction of Robert Watt for high treason in Edinburgh on 3 September 1794.

Watt's trial was the first time prosecutors applied the treason statutes to reform-society activities. The lord president's address to the grand jury noted that the crime of high treason had a certain unfamiliarity because the present reign had produced general contentment. He discussed the sections of 25 Edward III that were most relevant to the case: "When a man doth compass or imagine the death of our lord the king, or of our lady his queen, or of his eldest son and heir. Or if a man levy war against our lord the king in his realm, or be adhered to the king's enemies in his realm, or elsewhere, and thereof to be proveably attainted of open deed by the people of their condition." As noted above, the definitions of "compass and imagine" and "open deed" proved to be the controversial points in the law. The lord president cited Matthew Hale and Foster, who each specified that "compassing" was a state of mind that had to be evinced by overt acts. Yet because the king was so important, overt acts could not be limited to direct attempts on his person. They included any act that presented a probable risk to his life, for instance, "the entering into measures for deposing or imprisoning him, or to get his person into the power of the conspirators." Experience had shown that "between the prison and the graves of princes the distance is very small." Likewise, overt acts included insurrections designed to force the king into changing his measures or removing ministers: this fell under the rubric of levying war. In short, any attempt to restrain the king in any way constituted a conspiracy against his life.[14]

Watt's counsel argued that the prosecution had placed a labored construction on the evidence to make it fit the statute. An overt act required a conscious design and evidence of its pursuit. Watt had allegedly conspired to. seize Edinburgh Castle, subdue the soldiery, take possession of the banks and excise office, and hold captive the justice clerk, lords of council, lords of session, lord provost, and members of the judiciary. Watt responded that he never intended to cause the king harm. He had planned not to spark an insurrection in London but rather to protest against government corruption. He envisioned reformers presenting the king with a petition that called for a dissolution of Parliament and appointment of ministers who had the people's confidence. The only evidence that the scheme went beyond Watt's imagination consisted of a small collection of arms found on his premises. As his barrister observed: "It is impossible to conceive that the practicability of so absurd and ridiculous a plan could have entered into the head of man."[15]

Watt's case is particularly intriguing because he had in fact been a government spy between 1792 and 1793. He had filled his reports to Henry Dundas, then home secretary, with tales of anti-monarchism, such as declarations by society members that a king should be sacrificed every hundred years. In the confession he wrote on the eve of his execution, Watt admitted that he had started working for Dundas in the hope of gaining favor and attaining the social status he thought he deserved. He had at first believed that the societies posed a threat to the nation's tranquility; however, once he began attending their meetings he had become aware of the government's abuses of the constitution. Convinced of the need for reform, Watt had conceived his plan to bring it about. Watt's hanging took place while Hardy's trial proceeded in London. In the middle of his defense of the LCS's founder, Erskine pointed to Watt as an example of the extremes to which the government had gone to frame reform-society members. He presented Watt as an agent-provocateur run amok who had had to be destroyed by his employers to hide his embarrassing mistakes.[16]

Erskine's assessment is more convincing than the claim that Watt's confessions represented the ravings of an unbalanced individual who had become a fanatical reformer. It is also conceivable that the government used Watt as a scapegoat to cast further obloquy upon the Scottish reform societies and to legitimate the harsh sentences meted out to participants in the Edinburgh Convention. At the least, the Watt affair illustrates how alarm for the king's life generated tales of fantastic conspiracies.

Erskine's view also seems plausible in light of the case that became known as the Pop-Gun Plot, a straightforward tale of greed and revenge that hit the press shortly before the start of the English treason trials of 1794. Members of the LCS had allegedly constructed an airgun capable of killing a man thirty feet away with a poison dart. This ingenious weapon was, of course, to be used for "Royal Game." As far-fetched as the story sounded, it gained sufficient credibility to have three of the four suspects imprisoned, without any significant public outcry, from September 1794 until the following May. When their trial finally took place a year later, cross-examination of Crown witnesses revealed that the plot existed only in the mind of a vengeful former society member who had been expelled when members found out that he had set fire to his house in order to collect insurance money. The disgruntled arsonist then went to the authorities with tales of an assassination plot and left reams of sworn statements in evidence, only to stage a drowning death and disappear before the case came to trial.

In spite of these irregularities, the government did not abandon the prosecution. Legal authorities focused on the guilty behavior of the main suspect, Robert Thomas Crossfield, who took a position as a surgeon on a South Seas whaling vessel under an assumed name at the time of the arrests. After Cross-field antagonized the crew by objecting to practices that defrauded the ship's underwriters, they testified that Crossfield had bragged about the assassination plot, sung republican songs, and appeared to be in league with the French who captured their vessel. Gross inconsistencies in their stories and the suspicious absence of the star witness brought Crossfield an acquittal, and he and the other suspects finally gained their freedom.[17]

In the case of the reform leaders indicted for high treason, the evidence was abundant but largely circumstantial. During Hardy's trial, the prosecutors argued that as soon as a "wicked imagining of the heart is acted upon" the crime of sedition turned into treason. Moreover, the judge's summation instructed the jury that a distinct imagining was not even necessary; any act which in its natural consequence might endanger the life of the king was considered an act in pursuance of an intent to compass and imagine his death. Erskine demonstrated that the prosecutors had resorted to magnifying any hostile reference to kings in order to make all reformist activities appear to be specifically targeted at George III, and launched a successful attack on constructive treason. He pointed out to the court that the dreaded British Convention consisted of little more than "ten gentlemen, appointed by two peaceable societies, conversing upon the subject of a constitutional reform in Parliament, publishing the result of their deliberations, without any other arms but one supper knife."[18]

Erskine's argument disputed "against all appeals to speculations concerning *consequences* when the law commands us to look only to INTENTIONS." He observed that intentions had been ascribed to behavior by using false analogies drawn from events in France. Dismantling the convoluted reasoning prosecutors had employed to assign speculative consequences to reformist activities, he stressed the absurdity of the charge: "The conspiracy imputed was not to effect a reform by violence, but, as in the case before us, by pamphlets and speeches, which might produce universal suffrage, which universal suffrage might eat out and destroy aristocracy, which destruction might lead to the fall of monarchy, and, in the end, to the death of the king—Gentlemen, if the cause were not too serious, I should liken it to the play with which we amuse our children. 'This is the cow with the crumpled horn which gored the dog, that worried the cat, that ate the rat,' &c. ending in 'the house which Jack built.'" Articles in the *Morning Chronicle* critically assessed the way the government interpreted and applied the treason statutes. One writer inquired whether prosecutors cited Foster's statement on the proximity of the prison and the grave of a king as a witticism or as a positive truth upon which a new species of treason was to be constructed. If the statement were true, why had the last deposed king [James II] "lived to a good old age in France and at last died quietly in his bed?" And were his deposers guilty of treason? If they were, then on what was the present king's title to the throne based? In any case, when Edward III's parliament stipulated that treason consisted in levying war against the king, compassing his death, or adhering to his enemies, did they intend that other acts be treasonable as well?[19]

An attack on George III's coach in October 1795 provided the opportunity for the administration to reinforce its interpretation of the treason and sedition statutes. "An Act for the Safety and Preservation of His Majesty's Person and Government against Treasonable and Seditious Practices and Attempts," introduced on 16 November, declared that "by writing, Printing, Preaching or other Speaking, [to] express, publish, utter, or declare, any words or Sentences to incite or stir up the People to hatred or Contempt of the person of His Majesty, His Heirs or Successors, or the Government and Constitution of the Realm, as by Law established" was a misdemeanor punishable by banishment or transportation of up to seven years.[20]

Clive Emsley argues that this and the accompanying Seditious Meetings Act, forbidding meetings of fifty or more without previous permission or advertisement in a newspaper, did not mark any significant departure in the law. Moreover, the government never applied the former and only used the latter against reform meetings on a few occasions.[21] The significance of the Treasonable Practices Act, however, lay in its confirmation of the government's success in labeling the reform movement a cover for a republican conspiracy against the king. The act stood as a reminder to proponents of change that for all the judicial system's vagaries, it could still be used to turn public sympathy against reformers. The act was not applied because it was not needed. After the treason trials, as we have seen, there was in fact a conspiracy to coordinate a French invasion, an Irish rebellion, and an insurrection in London. The activities of the plotters fell under the Traitorous Correspondence Bill, introduced shortly after the commencement of the war, which rendered virtually any contact with the French a treasonable offense.[22]

Defense counsel for John and Henry Sheares, the first conspirators to be tried for their part in the Irish fiasco of May 1798, attempted to argue that a rebellion in Ireland could not be treason because it did not threaten the king's person. The absence of significant French assistance on that occasion gave the lawyers leave to argue that the rebels had not adhered to the king's enemies; the prosecution thus had turned the evidence of one crime into another, "a constructive treason, calculated as a trap for the loyalty of a jury." This line of defense was doomed, given that David Maclane had been hanged the previous year for fomenting rebellion in Quebec, a place even farther removed from the king's person. As the prime sergeant of Ireland remarked during the Sheares case: "Treason does not depend on the local residence of the king; the order and well being of society require that his person, wherever he may be, should be sacred."[23]

Meanwhile, as prosecutors and defense counsel thrashed out the meaning of treason, the government pursued its campaign against sedition with varying success. As Emsley's study of sedition prosecutions demonstrates, use of the judicial system to check antigovernment agitation continued to be haphazard. Trials for seditious libels were often overturned for faulty indictments, and inconsistent testimony dogged cases of seditious words. The authorities were reluctant to proceed unless they had a watertight case, so prosecutions predicated on revenge or other ulterior motives usually did not receive support.[24]

On the other hand, because convicting reform leaders proved to be so difficult, arrests and punishments took an erratic course. The government relied heavily upon the exemplary function of the law; every state trial pounded home the message that reformers intended to overturn the monarchy. Even when seditious words or acts did not involve the king directly, prosecutors presented them in terms of how they affected him. The indictment against Henry Redhead Yorke and other Sheffield reformers, for example, indicated "a conspiracy to villify, and traduce, and defame the Commons House of parliament." Crown counsel, however, presented the crime as "a conspiracy to excite disaffection against his majesty's government." Similarly, Archibald Hamilton Rowan published an address by the United Irishmen against the Protestant Ascendancy, "that faction, or gang which misrepresents the king to the people and the people to the king." Nonetheless, the indictment charged him with inciting disloyalty against George III.[25]

The haphazardness of the prosecutions made the government's policy appear arbitrary, at the least. The need to set an example to deter others seems to have been the motivation behind the excessive punishment of Kyd Wake after the assault on George III's coach. In spite of the rewards offered, no one identified either the culprits who threw stones or the so-called miscreant in the green coat who tried to force open the coach door. Because the most thoroughly documented and consistent evidence was collected against Wake, he served as scapegoat. Wake claimed that he did not belong to a reform society and that he had merely been expressing his disapprobation of the war with the rest of the crowd by hissing and shouting as the king passed. Nonetheless, he caught the eye of constables and other "respectable persons," who testified against him. Wake received a sentence of five years' hard labor, an hour in the pillory, and £1000 in sureties as a condition of his release, which he did not live to see. Prosecutors argued that Wake's crime approached high treason; he had insulted the king as he discharged one of his most solemn and important duties. A Treasury-sponsored newspaper asserted that the fate of Wake should "operate as a seasonable admonition to the Sons of Sedition, the active pupils of the Corresponding Society."[26]

The government exploited the popularity of Thomas Paine's *Rights of Man* in its effort to pin anti-monarchical intent on reformers' ideas and activities. Paine and his writings had been outlawed in 1792. Although other of Paine's ideas appeared more likely to foment rebellion, particularly his schemes to reduce taxes and improve the situation of the poor, seven of the eight passages cited in the indictment touched upon the monarchy.[27] During the trials of reform-society leaders, prosecutors sought to establish that interest in Paine indicated a design against monarchy. Prosecutors worked so hard to connect Thomas Muir to *Rights of Man* that the proceedings turned into a trial of Paine. Witnesses claimed that Muir lent *Rights of Man* surreptitiously during meetings. According to others, however, Muir stated that the book had a tendency to mislead weak minds and was foreign to the societies' purpose. Muir himself testified that he had lent the books before they were declared libelous; in any case, he did not recommend Paine's works to the reform societies because of the republican spirit that pervaded them. He added that he nonetheless did not see the harm in such writings; if Paine's critique made people aware of defects in the constitution, it would contribute to the repair of those defects. Muir further argued that the passages cited in the indictment were taken out of context and presented a distorted view of *Rights of Man.* Judge Robert Braxfield brushed these arguments aside with the pronouncement that Paine's works were pure sedition; it was immaterial what passages the indictment cited.[28]

The authorities harassed reformist printers, publishers, and booksellers by sending agents to purchase Paine's works. Daniel Holt, publisher of the *Newark Herald,* described a clergyman appearing at his shop to buy Paine's *Letter Addressed to the Addressers,* then offering a large sum for *Rights of Man,* which Holt had refused. Holt received a sentence of four years' imprisonment and a £100 fine for selling Paine's *Letter* as well as reprinting a 1782 reform tract by Major John Cartwright that others had printed with impunity. To Holt, the government's selective application of the law had a galling shamelessness: "Had *every* Bookseller been prosecuted who had sold the popular but obnoxious writings of THOMAS PAINE ... I imagine not fifty would have escaped."[29] Indeed, judging by the trials as a whole, the government found it much easier to punish propagandists by establishing their association with writings that had already been declared libels than by proving the seditious character of other printed works. When William Holland displayed caricature prints disrespectful to the royal family in his London shop, magistrates sent an agent there to purchase Paine's *Letter;* as a result, Holland spent a year in prison and paid a £100 fine.[30]

Trials for propagating Paine's works were by no means foolproof or easy to arrange. Years before the Manchester magistrates turned to blackmailing a witness to testify against local reformers, a subordinate officer informed the Home Office: "I have used every endeavour to discover whether Mr. [Thomas] Walker had ever given Paine's works to any of our Men, but have not been able to obtain any information that cou'd be depended on." An agent apparently sought to entrap John Bone of the LCS as late as 1797. A Coventry bookseller wrote twice to request that Bone send him Paine's pamphlets as quickly as possible, and to accompany them with a bill or note of the books in the parcel. Bone did not take the bait.[31]

Prosecutors also tried to extract as much propaganda value as possible out of each prosecution. They argued that printers and booksellers should be considered as dangerous as writers: "Mr. Paine shall have my consent to sit down and write till his eyes drop out and his heart aches, provided he cannot find any one to publish it; but it is by means of persons like the defendant ... that injury has been done to society." The defendant in this case was Daniel Isaac Eaton, one of the most active distributors of reformist literature. English juries demonstrated their uneasiness with the manner in which prosecutors applied the sedition laws by reaching the verdict "Guilty of publishing, but not with criminal intent" in two prosecutions of Eaton for selling the works of Paine. His attorney translated the verdicts as *"convicted of innocence."*[32]

The courts of law became another platform for declaiming on the monarchy's role, power, and sanctity. Judges underscored the heinousness of high treason and sedition by stressing the king's importance. In the course of charging the jury in the trial of Crossfield, Scott pointed out: "The king is considered as the head of the body politic, and members of that body are considered as united and kept together by a political union with him, and with each other: his life cannot in the ordinary course of things be taken away by treasonable practices without involving a whole nation in blood and confusion: consequently, every stroke levelled at his person is, in the ordinary course of things, levelled at the public tranquillity." The lord justice declared that allowing libels against the government to circulate "would be a way to shake all law, all morality, all order, and all religion in society."[33]

The example of France always stood in readiness to illustrate such arguments. One of the justices presiding over Muir's trial asserted that Muir's attack on "kingly government, a pillar on which the constitution hinges," posed particular danger, given recent events in France, where similar crimes "had like an earthquake swallowed up her best citizens, and endangered the lives and property of all." In response to the claim that Yorke's ideas were no different from those of the aristocratic reformers of the 1780s, a prosecutor replied that those men had not harangued large assemblies in such a manner as to inflame the minds of the multitude. Another Crown counsel reminded the court of the licensed abuse of public figures that had preceded the French Revolution. He exclaimed: "In God's name, how is the parliament of the country—how is the king, who presides at the head of that parliament, to be obeyed, if the people are to be taught to treat them with habitual contempt!"[34]

The king stood not only as a lofty, abstract figure who upheld the nation's institutions; as a person he deserved respect and protection. Promoting disaffection should be considered "a vice of the most odious and dangerous tendency" because all good government had its basis in the mutual affection and regard between subject and sovereign. Without it, neither could live in comfort and prosperity.[35] One of the presiding justices contemplated the wickedness of the sentiments expressed by three Edinburgh printers charged with attempting to seduce soldiers from their allegiance to the king. In a fit of loyalist ire, he digressed: "Openly to avow a desire to overturn the constitution; an impious wish that our beneficent sovereign, distinguished by private and public virtues; his sacred majesty, the father of his people, would be damned!— What can be more criminal? But this is not the crime meant to be here charged." During Watt's trial, the lord advocate, Robert Dundas, presented George III as an innocent victim of disaffected persons motivated by "restless ambition, or the mad desire of innovation." Dundas observed that it was inexcusable to have "the life of the monarch not only endangered but forfeited, merely because he has the misfortune to be the chief magistrate."[36]

As much as the reformers' advocates might protest, and in some cases successfully, against the government's application of the laws, it would have been impolitic to disparage the prosecutors' praise of the monarchy. Defense counsel tried to diffuse the alarm for the king's life by drawing attention to how the inherent prejudice regarding alleged crimes against the king had been exploited by the prosecution. As he began his defense of John Horne Tooke, Erskine pointed out the ease with which one could whip up emotions by invoking "that deep and solid interest which every good subject takes, and ought to take in the life of the chief magistrate appointed to execute the laws, and whose safety is so inseparably connected with the general happiness, and the stability of the government." Moreover, he "had farther to contend with an interest, founded upon affection for the king's person, which has so long been, and I trust, ever will remain the characteristic of Englishmen." Erskine concluded with the hope that this natural awe should not interfere with impartial consideration of the evidence. In the case of one of the Catholic Defenders accused of consorting with the French in 1795 and administering unlawful oaths to soldiers, an Irish barrister enumerated the implications of having the king as the prosecutor. The king was a figure to whom "the law attributed immortality and perfection ... ascribes to him so great and so transcendent a nature that ... the people are led to pay him the most awful respect, and to look to him as superior to other beings."[37]

Defense counsel also indulged in loyalist grandstanding of their own, when they argued that their clients could not have had any design upon their most gracious king. During Hardy's trial, one of the defense counsel disputed the prosecution's contention that the reform societies were following the French Jacobins: it was, he said, impossible to compare two monarchies of such different characters. Unlike Louis XVI, George III had never attempted to subvert the constitution; more fundamentally, his public and private virtues gave him a place in the hearts of his subjects. Watt's counsel stressed the improbability that anyone would wish to commit high treason. Such an act would cut an individual off from the benefits of a government "where the road to prosperity and happiness is laid open to all; where the lives of the subjects are not wantonly sported with, but where security and stability exist, and I trust, ever will remain, as the desirable and ultimate object of all our wishes and desires!" Barristers stressed that reformers did not believe themselves a risk to an institution so firmly established and venerated; the British monarchy could not easily be eroded by criticism.[38]

Collectively, sermons and legal prosecutions endowed the king with a practical sanctity enforced by, but not completely dependent upon, a particular species of Christianity. Prosecutors did not seem troubled by Erskine's assertion that prosecuting Paine supported Edmund Burke's revival of Filmerism. In a Crown lawyer's condemnation of Winterbotham, the legal establishment and Burke's beloved church-and-state establishment merged: "It has been laid down by divine authority, that there is no power but what is derived from the supreme Being—therefore to cry out against the government where there is no occasion, is a crime. And for a man living under mild and equal laws, to preach sedition and discontent, is blasphemy against the majesty of Heaven. Till of late, there has been no attempt to deny these principles, but in a neighbouring country, never remarkable for religion, there has been a new light sprung up."[39] Yet such a defense required a monarch who exhibited moral probity and dutifulness of the same caliber as George III. The sons who succeeded him did not have the presence to withstand the reformist challenge. As J. C. D. Clark stresses, the Reform Act of 1832 came on the heels of the repeal of the Test and Corporation Acts and Catholic Emancipation. He asserts that "the roots of reform lay in theology."[40] The dissolute regency and reign of George IV and the impotent exertions of William IV might have had something to do with the passage of the Reform Bill too.

The support network formed by the triad of monarchy, church, and law tied in with the entire social hierarchy. Support of the social status quo was a subtext in a great many of the sermons and trials. The outspoken Judge Braxfield brought the issue into the open with his fulmination: "Mr Muir might have known that no attention could be paid to such a rabble. What right had they to representation? He could have told them that the parliament would never listen to their petition. How could they think of it? A government in every country should be just like a corporation; and, in this country, it is made up of the landed interest, which alone has a right to be represented; as for the rabble, who have nothing but personal property, what has the nation of them?"[41] The message broadcast from the bench and the pulpit—that reformers were potential regicides who had to be suppressed in any manner possible—justified a new species of loyalist activity, the church-and-king riot.

SEVEN

Court Culture, Royalist Ritual, and Popular Loyalism

ELEMENTS of past regimes pervaded George III's court. In conjunction with the personal qualities the king projected, these remnants of past majesty reinforced the images of fortitude, legitimacy, and paternal care that loyalists invoked. Linda Colley notes an increase in public enthusiasm for royal ceremonies after 1786: George's attention to ritual and patronage, combined with his steadfast belief in the glory of Britain, helped his subjects to shake off the humiliation of losing the American colonies. The British began to develop a national consciousness by focusing on the king as the representation of everything of value in the state. After hostilities with revolutionary France began, supporters of the government looked to the royal family for displays of grandeur in defiance of the enemy. As Colley observes, press coverage of the royal family's activities expanded significantly during this decade. Yet these accounts were not always adulatory.[1] Newspaper reports of the royal family's public appearances became another forum for debate. Royal celebrations sometimes turned into literal battlegrounds between loyalists and reformers. Notwithstanding the conflict that royalist rituals provoked, the loyalist values they propagated proved difficult to undermine.

Like the monarchy, the institution of the court never dies, whatever the behavior of its inhabitants, and every royal household also carries with it the memories of past regimes. As is the case with most memories, these connections with the past tend to be shaped by the imperatives of the present. Various circumstances act as catalysts upon the legacies of previous reigns; the particulars of royal style determine which elements of the past resonate in court culture and how these memories will be interpreted. Hence, for an institution steeped in form and tradition, the royal court varies significantly in its political role, atmosphere, and efficacy with each succession. The personality of the monarch and the character of the preceding reign help determine the court's capacity for influence. In order for the court to enhance the strength and status of the regime, the monarch's personal qualities must accord with the values held in esteem by the leading ranks of society.

James VI of Scotland began his reign as the first Stuart king of England at a distinct disadvantage. In spite of the escalating discontent that characterized her last years, Elizabeth I would have been a tough act for anyone to follow, particularly a Scot. The queen revived the spirit of chivalric dazzle in her crusade against the Spanish. James I, in contrast, was not only a pacifist, but he also wished to reestablish diplomatic relations with the papists. He even tried to negotiate a marriage between his son Charles and the Spanish Infanta. Nor did James maintain the Elizabethan tradition of image-building. He disliked the elaborate Elizabethan progresses and refused to indulge his subjects' desire to see their monarch on parade. He much preferred the homey comforts of his court, which, in the absence of carefully cultivated royal splendor, became branded with the image of elitism, debauchery, and conspiracy, both Scottish and Jesuit.[2]

The emphasis on family relations—real and imagined—at James I's court, however, laid the foundation for a divine-right monarchy that ultimately did not have to depend on rigid theories of royal lineage and right. By drawing upon the patriarchal aspect of royal divinity and stressing the "father" part of their association with God the Father, the early Stuarts paved the way for later monarchs to enjoy the reflected majesty of their relation to God without making any threatening claims about the specific powers that this relation engendered.

Although patriarchy had a troubled history in English constitutional theory, its practice became a key element in English royal style. Gordon Schochet's study of patriarchalism shows that political philosophers did not use family authority as a justification for political obedience until Robert Filmer's work appeared in the late seventeenth century. Since the time of the ancients, philosophers, politicians, and theologians had grappled with the nature of the relation between the institution of the family and the political state. In sixteenth-century England and Scotland, theologians began suggesting that the commandment "Honor thy father" applied to thy magistrates as well. Although an awkward argument to support during the reigns of female mon-

archs, the idea did have appeal in the post-Reformation era, with its emphasis on the family's importance. The sanctity of the father's role became a matter of interest and debate. The shaking of the Catholic Church's grip on historical interpretation also opened up new inquiries into the state of nature
and the origins of political authority. How did people move from the family
to the political state? Were familial and political relations contractual? Did
kingly authority devolve from Adam?

Noting the familial analogies in James I's *Trew Law of Free Monarchies,*
Schochet credits the king with having launched the development of, but not
established, a patriarchal doctrine of rulership. In his theories of royal absolutism, James failed to maintain any consistency in his assertions regarding
the origin of kingly authority. Nor did he ever clearly define paternal and
monarchical power. Nevertheless, in spite of the demise of divine right, the
trope of king as the father of his people not only survived, it evolved into a
standard by which monarchs could be judged. Locke demolished the patriarchal theory of political obligation based on a particular view of monarchy's
historical foundations, Schochet points out, but other forms of patriarchalism persisted into the eighteenth century. A patriarchal undercurrent ran
through early modern English society. The habit of obedience to God, fathers,
and political authorities continued to be inculcated by family life and church
preachings.[3]

James's construction of kingly self as father went beyond metaphor. Although unconventional in form, his court had a familial atmosphere, with
James and his beloved "Steenie," George Villiers, duke of Buckingham, addressing each other as father and son.[4] When Charles I became head of his
own household, he attempted to promote a different sort of familial model at
court. After a rocky start, he and Henrietta Maria of France built a strong,
faithful union and produced seven children on whom they doted in a manner
uncharacteristic of royalty. Both also had a love of ritual that, combined with
their devotion to domestic virtue, developed into a cult of idealized Platonic
love. Court masques, paintings, and poetry revived aspects of the Elizabethan
chivalric ideal, but this time exalting peace, order, and morality instead of war
and conquest. The early Stuarts began shaping the royal family as an institution, an idea that George III later exploited so effectively with his public displays of domesticity.[5]

Charles's court also demonstrated the limitations under which even absolute monarchs operated. An effective royalist culture required cooperation

and reciprocity. Notwithstanding Charles I's inheritance of a sense of divine mission from his father, the new king's diametrically opposed taste and personality meant that when James died, in 1625, the court underwent an abrupt transformation. The old king was barely laid in his tomb before Charles let it be known that his father's informality and lack of decorum would no longer do. Charles had what can best be described as a mania for order and propriety and was determined that his court should follow suit. He sought to reform the court financially and morally by replacing its licentious roistering and intrigue with decorous entertainments that advertised high standards of domestic probity. In spite of the royal couple's efforts to elevate the tone of the court, however, scandal and immorality continued to disrupt it. Court masques, which glorified the harmony of the reign, coexisted with a long tradition of satire in poems, plays, and other artistic expression that exposed the regime's problems and weaknesses.[6] Peace and accord simply could not be imposed by force of will.

The virtue and familial devotion Charles and Henrietta Maria projected within their court was not clear to the rest of the kingdom. Instead, their court seems imbued by the sort of baroque piety that the English associated with Continental despotism. In justification of his rebellion, Oliver Cromwell linked parliamentary right with Puritan virtue and simplicity. Ironically, once installed as Lord Protector, the leader of the "godly reformation" moved with his family into Whitehall Palace, and laid claim to the other former royal residences for himself and his heirs. Royal paintings and tapestries again graced the palaces of London and Hampton Court. Heirlooms of the royal family even found their way into the Lord Protector's bedchamber. The man who refused to be called king had no objection to courtiers and ambassadors addressing him as "Your Highness." When receiving visitors, Cromwell used palatial space to enhance his status as adroitly as any monarch; foreign emissaries sometimes trekked through as many as four apartments, with doors opened and closed ceremonially at each point, before reaching the inner sanctum. Barry Coward insists that "such developments should not be interpreted as conservative milestones on the road to the restoration of the monarchy in 1660." Rather, they should be viewed as part of Cromwell's program of "healing and settling," for they were intended to help win over his former opponents. Yet the style of the Protectorate also suggests that court culture could not be effaced even by the destruction of the monarchy. As Roy Sherwood observes, the court stood as "a symbol of the failure to establish a wholly acceptable and lasting alternative to a monarchical form of government."[7] In the reigns that followed, the court showed itself capable of surviving dissipation and neglect as well.

The libertine style of the Restoration court acted as a smokescreen for Charles II's sneaky but ultimately astute political maneuvering. Scholarship shows Charles to have been a more skillful leader than his "Merrie Monarch" image allows. With regard to the development of the monarchy, however, appearances had more of an impact on events than did reality. Shortfalls in the Treasury, despite an apparently generous financial settlement, were the result of crown revenues failing to achieve their expected yields. Appearances, on the other hand, suggested that a dissipated, extravagant court, headed by a frivolous monarch and his mistresses, were squandering the high taxes of an overburdened people. What in retrospect appear to be sagacious political decisions in a precarious political climate, conveyed the impression of royal double-dealing, deceit, and duplicity.[8] The baroque piety that James II added to the scene at his accession in 1685 rankled rather than reassured the nation. With the integrity of divine-right monarchy finally demolished in 1688, the character, interest, and personal style of individual rulers, which had always helped shape the institution of monarchy, became more significant than ever in determining the court's power.

William III was no charmer. Initially hailed as the man who saved England from Catholic despotism, he quickly alienated the political ranks of society with his foreign customs, Dutch favorites, unfashionable tastes, and brusque manner. William had a hard time imagining an aristocracy that was uninvolved in the military and had contempt for the English nobility's dabbling in commercial concerns. Culturally, his interests centered on art, architecture, and gardening, while his new nobility favored literature and music. William did not speak English with confidence; added to his regard for birth, status, and proper decorum, this limitation gave him a haughty, distant air in conversation. The coal smoke and stuffy rooms of London made him cough blood. The roast dinners and wine of the English aristocracy destroyed a digestion brought up on boiled or braised meats and beer. So William sought the quiet and fresh air of Kensington Palace and, when not away on military campaigns, hunted or buried himself in his work, leaving social and ceremonial duties to Mary. Aware of the importance of this aspect of monarchy, he endured ceremony when he had to. At the end of 1692, for instance, when his chief ministers were sighted consorting with known Jacobites,

William resorted to calculated displays of affability. He even suffered through a birthday ball on 4 November.[9]

Anne temporarily restored some of the Stuart charisma to the monarchy. She sanctioned the idea of the divinity of the sovereign by reviving the custom of touching for the King's Evil. In this ceremony, dating back to Norman England and Capatian France, monarchs underwent a day's fast and prayer, then laid their healing hands upon scrofula sufferers, who would line up in the hundreds. William III, as a Calvinist, considered the rite a ridiculous superstition. Likewise, the Hanoverians wanted no part of it. In contrast, James II, as well as the Old Pretender, continued to minister to the sick while in exile, enhancing their mystique. Anne's revival or adaptations of other royal rituals and customs eased the transition to another kind of monarchy. For her first speech to Parliament she wore an outfit copied from a portrait of Queen Elizabeth. She appropriated Elizabethan imagery and mottoes to place herself in the tradition of Protestant avenger, and reestablished Elizabethan progresses and Thanksgiving ceremonies after military victories. Anne's style conveyed an impression of Stuart individualist sovereignty. She scheduled commemorative ceremonies and celebrations for personal days, particularly her birthday, and steered clear of partisan political anniversaries.[10]

Anne ultimately proved to be a tragic heroine, trapped within the vicissitudes of the seventeenth and eighteenth centuries. Her reign featured paradox as well as misleading appearances. Dedicated to the hereditary principle and keenly aware that her status during the reigns of James II and of William and Mary depended on her producing an heir, she ruined her health with eighteen pregnancies that resulted in miscarriages, stillbirths, and children who did not survive infancy. Only William Henry, duke of Gloucester, seemed a possible heir between 1689 and 1700. Anne's invalidism belied the active role she took in politics and prevented her from reestablishing the court's cultural centrality. By the last years of her reign, it was plain that she was as unsuccessful in promoting national unity through ceremony as she was in circumventing party machinations with the use of her managers. Although she won over the common people with royal pageantry, aristocrats had moved away from the court; Tories and Whigs had their own social calendars and meeting places. Robert Bucholz points out that Anne's revival of Tudor-Stuart spectacle proved hopelessly anachronistic, but her efforts to present herself as a mother figure and the monarchy as a nonpartisan symbol of the nation and upholder of virtue showed remarkable foresight.[11] It would be more than a hundred years before circumstances allowed the British to accept a monarch of this kind.

Early Hanoverian court culture starkly reflected the monarchy's post-1688 identity crisis. Although the court continued to be the center of government in terms of political power and patronage, the first two Georges were not dominant figures, as the Stuarts had been. They did not engage in Elizabethan progresses or revive Stuart pageantry. Instead, they attended entertainments in London as if they were private citizens and allowed the aristocracy to gain control over artistic patronage. Like William III, George I did not bother with the ceremonial side of monarchy unless he had to. An intensely private person who disliked spectacle, George restricted access to the royal bedchamber and dispensed with the formal dressing ritual. George came into contact with a limited number of English people and was more comfortable conversing in German or French than in English. For the most part, he left drawing rooms and other ceremonial occasions to the Prince and Princess of Wales. So subjects saw a king who could not be bothered to learn their language or uphold the country's customs, and who could not even bear to leave behind his German servants. Consequently, many Britons found it easy to believe that George I must be sacrificing their country's interests to those of his fatherland.[12]

National xenophobia, coupled with the absence of a well-managed image issuing from the palace, left room for malicious supposition. Contemporary gossip had long-term effects upon assessments of George I as a ruler. Ragnhild Hatton spends most of her groundbreaking biography of the king tracing the source of misrepresentations that have survived as historical record. George's unconventional domestic situation, his German manners and customs, and his court's foreign members, including his exotic Turkish menservants, Mustapha and Mehemet, gave much material for speculation to those who wished to think the worst of him. His wife remained comfortably but firmly confined back in Hanover, after having been caught in a romantic tryst. Her lover, moreover, had come to a mysterious end. The silence surrounding these events guaranteed that they would inspire gossip. George's long-term mistress, Melusine von der Schulenburg, who was a former lady-in-waiting to his mother, and their three daughters accompanied him to England, as did George's illegitimate half-sister, Sophia Charlotte von Kielmansegg. Sophia Charlotte was widowed three years after arriving in England, and many assumed that she became a second mistress to George. The ménage acquired additional visual interest by the juxtaposition of the tall, thin Melusine and the plump, short Sophia Charlotte; they were a gift to caricaturists. Members of London society who knew of the family relationship conjectured that incest would be no barrier to this cuckolded, tyrannical husband who, rumor had it, used Mustapha and Mehemet as panders to help feed his prodigious appetites. As Hatton illustrates, George I actually shared a relatively tame household routine with Melusine and their daughters.[13] Because his domestic stability was unsanctioned by matrimony, however, and hidden from view, the public did not recognize it.

The court of George II suffered from the opposite problem: his devotion to his consort appeared excessive. In spite of his aggressive, extrovert personality, George II gave the impression of being a king in toils. It was commonly believed that Walpole used his influence with Queen Caroline to control the uxorious ruler. Although George, who came to the throne in 1727, was more comfortable in the British political arena than his father had been, he had not learned the importance of cultivating a regal image. As Prince of Wales he received a political education in the drawing rooms at St. James's and set up a rival court at Leicester House between 1718 and 1720 after falling out with the king. Unlike George I, he systematically worked the crowd in the drawing room to demonstrate who was in and out of favor. He also opened up access to the royal bedchamber by reviving the formal dressing ceremony. Fond of showing off his proficiency in English, he would have been mortified to learn that his courtiers found his accent amusing. He could not escape the effects of having spent his early life in Hanover or the negative impressions produced every time he went back to visit his Electorate. Additionally, the post-1688 political settlement and its accompanying change of attitude toward the monarchy ruined his plan of taking command of every aspect of government. Hammering out policy with his ministers and making compromises further detracted from his kingly mien.[14]

Elaborate regal splendor could not save a floundering regime, but a poorly managed court detracted from royal power. Ideally, a royal court was the center of the social and cultural life, which helped keep the upper classes in line; it also provided a seductive yet intimidating venue for communication between the monarch and politicians, created an imposing backdrop for state visits and foreign negotiations, and projected a public image of grandeur without money-wasting indulgence. None of the Stuart or early Hanoverian courts comprised all of these attributes. George III came close to creating such a court only after much hard work, accompanied by a peculiar set of circumstances that turned the quirks of his personality into assets. This first

English-born Hanoverian king managed to revive Stuart grandeur, dispel fears of absolutism, and add an egalitarian twist to Stuart patriarchalism by emphasizing the king's—as well as the royal family's—accessibility and reciprocal relationship with his subjects. The domestic irregularities of George's Hanoverian predecessors had not made them popular with the British people, and they had allowed many people to romanticize the exiled Stuarts, whose personal lives, ironically, would not have borne close scrutiny either. George III's stolid paternalism, in contrast, served him well when British reformers threatened to overturn the traditional social hierarchy and French revolutionaries repudiated the principles of obedience to constituted authority and social subordination. The king's exemplification of bourgeois family values created a potent image for propaganda, as the French Revolution endangered all human relations.

George III's domestic probity and sense of propriety had great appeal for the middle classes, a group growing in size and influence by the end of the eighteenth century. In 1787 the king issued a proclamation for the encouragement of piety and virtue and for the prevention and punishment of vice, profaneness, and immorality. Even more novel, he practiced what he preached. Throughout his life the king attended divine service regularly, eschewed the customary overindulgence in rich foods and fine wines, curbed luxury at court, and took various steps to discourage the aristocracy's penchant for gambling. George's coronation in 1761 had been combined with a marriage ceremony that united him with the seventeen-year-old Charlotte of Mecklenburg, who bore fifteen children by 1783. The queen shared her consort's homely values, sense of duty, and thrift. She could not control her roistering sons, but she kept the six princesses locked in a strict domestic routine. Most evening entertainments consisted of sewing their own clothes, doing needlepoint, and reading edifying literature aloud. When they became old enough to display their own personalities, George and Charlotte's children helped endow the king with the image of paternal solicitude.[15]

As soon as his children were old enough to place on display, George turned family routines into public rituals. His middle-class tastes helped the monarchy develop as an institution that was based on family and provided a foundation for a new sort of patriarchalism. The simple family stroll became the "terracing" ceremony at Windsor. On summer evenings, rain or shine, all available family and guests would be mustered to promenade two by two on the south terrace of the castle, accompanied by a band playing "God Save the King." The nobility took the opportunity to pay their respects, and the king, the benevolent patriarch, would sometimes even receive petitions. In 1795 the *Sun* presented an account of a Quaker woman who made an appeal for peace: "Never was there a finer sight than the attention given to this Religious Petitioner by our benevolent and pious Monarch." When members of the royal family were at Weymouth, they performed this ritual on the esplanade. Spectators also gathered to watch the royal brood working in their gardens or bathing at the seaside. George recognized the importance of subjects being able to see their ruling family. When the queen and princesses felt hampered by crowds during a tour of Cheltenham, the king told them that for the first few days they had to walk about to please the people; afterward they could walk to please themselves. On a similar occasion, the king surprised and delighted the people of Worcester by strolling like a private gentleman, accompanied by only two attendants.[16]

Newspapers assessed the degree of support for government policy by measuring participation in royal rituals. As loyalists and reformers duked it out on the streets, ministerial and opposition newspapers had their fisticuffs in print. In response to the deluge of loyalist proclamations in support of the King's Proclamation of May 1792, the *Times* declared, "A CONQUERED REBEL-LION strengthens the hands of Government, and from the downfall of the Associations in this country, and the overthrow of Democratic tyrants in France, England may soon look to a long system of peace." Emboldened by the loyalist initiative, the paper proclaimed: "The real estimation of the country towards the present Administration, is best proved by the number of Addresses that have at different periods of this duration, been presented to the King thanking his Majesty for his paternal regard to the interest of the nation,— thereby approving of the conduct of those who advised the King to these Measures." After Britain entered the war against France in 1793, the addresses printed in the *London Gazette* evolved into prowar declarations. The *Morning Chronicle* expressed outrage when Pitt derived enough confidence from these addresses by March 1794 to present a scheme for voluntary subscriptions in support of the war. The paper compared the idea to "the old *Star Chamber* scheme of Prerogative Supply, by aids called Benevolences." The *Morning Chronicle* continually censured the administration for creating the impression that loyalty to the king required agreement with ministerial policy; now, opposition to the war connoted disloyalty.[17]

Loyalist papers had the upper hand in the beginning of the decade because court functions tended to be well attended and grand. Reporters drew large deductions from small details. On the occasion of the queen's birthday ball in January 1791, the *Times* praised the palm tree and cornucopia design embroidered on the king's coat as a fitting tribute to the country's condition of peace and prosperity. When the royal family arrived at their summer residence at Weymouth that year, the general illumination included transparencies of what the *Morning Post* described as "emblems strikingly significant of the power and consequence of the English Nation and its most Gracious Sovereign." The loyalist press also stressed the importance of royal ceremonies as demonstrations of national unity in the face of the threat across the Channel. Regarding the king's birthday celebration, the *Times* commented:

> At a time like the present, when Revolutions have overturned the hereditary honours of some Sovereigns, and Royalty and Nobility have in one vast kingdom been levelled to the humble rank of Citizens; the British Court seems proud of the opportunity of testifying its reverence for a wise and perfect form of Government, by giving to surrounding empires, in the persons of their Ambassadors and Envoys, who were witness to the sight, a conspicuous proof, that however the people of England may differ in trifling political matters, there is one grand point, in which they all agree—they love their KING, and revere their Constitution.[18]

Until 1795 the king's birthday celebrations in particular allowed the progovernment press to boast; appearances indicated that "licentiousness had been nipped in the bud by a well-conducted government": "the voice of the people every where loudly cried 'GOD SAVE THE KING'" and had "driven factious Republicanism into its cave of despair." In 1794 the *Sun* implied that the good attendance at court and the celebrations of the populace indicated general support for the war: "Let this day of joyous Celebration impress more strongly the virtuous resolve, which we trust is imprinted on the heart of every TRUE BRITON, to live or DIE with our glorious and unparalleled CONSTITUTION." Before 1793 the *Morning Chronicle* could only rail against the rigidity and impracticality of court fashion and custom. Unlike other papers, it refused to carry detailed descriptions of the participants' dress or court decorations. Once war commenced, the paper made a point of noting the impropriety of giving attention to court splendor when most Britons suffered privations.[19]

From 1795 to 1798, the number of guests at royal birthday galas dropped off, and the opposition papers had their day. In its account of the queen's birthday celebrations in 1795, the radicalized *Morning Post* remarked:

> Never was there seen so gloomy a Birth-Day in this Country as that of yes-

terday. Care and despondency seemed to sit on every brow; the affected smiles of Ministers, shewed that disappointment and despondency resided in their hearts; and instead of being a day of joyous gratulations, a settled melancholy and dread apprehension for the safety of the Nation, pervaded the Assembly, and made them inwardly condemn the measures of those wretched men in whom they had reposed their confidence, and who, if they are suffered to remain in power, must bring certain and eternal destruction on the kingdom.

The *Morning Chronicle*, with its usual terseness, observed: "The Court was not crowded, indeed, for the calamities of war are felt even at St. James's." By 1797 the pro-government press was offering excuses for the thinness of the company, such as the increased demands of court attendance brought by two royal weddings in a short time, that of the Prince of Wales to Caroline of Brunswick in 1795 and that of Elizabeth, the Princess Royal, to Frederick William Charles of Würtemburg in 1797.[20]

The weddings and their attendant preparations generated much discussion about the function and cost of royal splendor. The press coverage further highlights how important royal ceremonies had become as a medium of propaganda. The Prince of Wales's wedding tested the principle that the country's welfare depended on an appearance of wealth being upheld at court under any circumstances. Parliament gave free rein to the prince's extravagant tastes amid increasing wartime distress and public resentment over having to pay his debts, which by that time totaled £630,000, on top of his annual income of £73,000. The *Times* contended that the national celebration of this momentous event in the lives of the royal family guaranteed tranquility at home as well as prestige abroad: "The COURT held yesterday at St. James's in honour of the nuptials of the Prince and Princess of WALES, was the most numerous and splendid ever seen in this country; and it will certainly be a very unwelcome intelligence both to our external as well as internal enemies, to hear of the unanimity which prevailed among all parties of rank in the kingdom, to shew their attachment and obedience to the ILLUSTRIOUS FAMILY now on the throne." The paper also reminded its readers of the material benefits of royal expenditure: "Never were the riches of the country seen to such advantage; and it was no trifling consideration to know, that the looms of our manufactures and the delicate hand of the illustrious female, had been so successfully employed in the decorations."[21]

As the Foxite Whigs sought to preserve their alliance with the Prince of Wales, the *Morning Chronicle* meekly followed suit. The *Morning Post*, however, now out of the pocket of the prince and under the influence of the rad-ical Daniel Stuart, did not extend the same graciousness. During the prepa-rations, the paper reported that the dress and ornaments under contract for Princess Caroline to wear on the day were rumored to be worth £15,000: "Two-thirds of this enormous sum, given for a Head Dress, might have afforded a very great relief to the numerous starving Poor during the late inclement weather—But CHARITY dwelleth not in Palaces." The national interest in royal munificence was argued in court the following February. The jeweler from whom the prince had commissioned jewelry for his new consort filed suit when he was not paid in full. The defendants' counsel argued that to pay £54,684 for jewels worth £45,700 would defraud the English people. Thomas Erskine took time off from championing the rights of reformers to defend royal finery. "He thought the difference in question not worth the time it had occupied—that the splendour of an English Court was the last money which an English public would grudge. It encouraged the arts; it promoted manu-facture; it advanced that condition of social life, which was the sinews of a commercial country, and only brought round in the brisk circulation of com-merce the specie of the kingdom from one English subject to another." Er-skine further pointed out that the arrival of the princess had raised demand and thus the market price of jewels. The case concluded in compromise; the jeweler received £50,997.[22]

During the negotiations for the betrothal of the Princess Royal and the prince of Würtemburg, the opposition press had the opportunity to challenge loyalist claims of the court's power to enchant. The marriage negotiations were protracted, owing to the king's reluctance to let his oldest daughter go, so the prince of Würtemburg had to be kept out of sight and occupied while the palace hastily completed the wedding preparations. The *Times* made much of the fact that his supposedly incognito tour of the country offered an op-portunity to display national achievement. The paper explained that the tour would offer amusement for the prince, but, more important, it was "highly proper that he should have ocular demonstrations of the riches and prosper-ity of the Country and its Manufactures." The *Morning Chronicle* countered that, unfortunately, he had arrived two years too late for such a demonstra-tion. The *Morning Post* suggested that the prince must have received a curi-ous impression of the fleets after the recent mutinies brought on by the min-istry's neglect of sailors' claims. The paper described his visit to the Bank of England as a view of "the Grand National Mausoleum erected in consequence of the death of *Public Credit*."[23]

It is impossible to estimate the impact of the opposition press's efforts to expose the duplicity of court splendor, or the power of royal ceremonial to win popular confidence in the war. George's coach may have been attacked in 1795 by a mob yelling for bread and peace, but the incident also elicited a flood of loyalist addresses congratulating the king on his escape from injury and calling for better legal protection of the monarch. The Chichester address, for example, called the assault a "daring attack on the Constitution itself, in the Person of the first Guardian of our liberties." The loyalist response provided an adequate foundation of support for Pitt's Two Acts; the image of Majesty in peril had great potency.[24]

Yet by 1797 this image wore thin. The National Thanksgiving Day at the end of 1797 was marred by an attack on Pitt's coach and the trampling of a woman by a city volunteer's horse. Although the ministerial papers made light of the disturbances that took place during the course of the procession, the opposition treated the event as a travesty. The *Morning Post* made the immortal observation: "The result of the procession to St. Paul's was that one man returned thanks to Almighty God and one woman was kicked to death." In his study of the liberal press and the antiwar-petition movement, J. E. Cookson suggests that the combination of the two scuttled Pitt's attempt to build a national consensus. Cookson observes that a quarter of the addresses congratulating the king on his escape from harm in 1795 contained condemnations of the war or the Two Acts. He believes that the only period in which government repression had sufficient strength to silence the opposition was during the state of emergency that existed between 1798 and 1799, when financial crisis, naval mutinies, rebellion in Ireland, and French invasion threatened.[25]

Court ceremony emerged triumphant. The opposition press did not exaggerate when it complained that support for the war had become requisite to any claim of loyalty to the king. Indeed, a grand military review dominated the king's birthday celebrations in 1799. The *Sun* noted that George's satisfaction with the display gratified as well as inspired the volunteers present. The *Times* could report that the court was better attended and more brilliant than it had been in years. The paper had the audacity to add: "Hitherto the war has certainly neither diminished the spirits nor the wealth of the country, which were no more than fairly represented by the gaiety and magnificence of the first Drawing-room in Europe." The king had always been fond of elaborate military exercises. He and one or two of the princes would inspect troops on horseback while the queen and the princesses observed the scene from carriages. Before the war began, maneuvers and mock battles at the Bagshot encampment provided entertaining spectacles for the royal family and fashionable society. After 1793 the royal princes and increasing numbers of gentlemen appeared at the Drawing Room in full dress uniform. By 1796 ministerial papers estimated that nearly half the men there sported military attire.[26] Martial display featured prominently during the royal family's visits to Weymouth. Soldiers escorted them into town and welcoming volleys issued from ships and artillery assembled onshore. Vacation pastimes included cruises aboard battleships, inspections of installations along the coast, and military exhibitions.[27]

The Prince of Wales's desire to "addict myself to military pursuits" was not satisfied by his appointment as colonel of a regiment of dragoons encamped near Brighton. Nevertheless, the ministerial press held him up as an example of the volunteering spirit. He and his men presented a romanticized view of military life. They conducted dazzling reviews and enlivened the countryside with their marches from Egham or Staines to Windsor for garrison duty. Loyalist newspapers relished the chance to present the prince in a favorable light. When the king and Frederick, duke of York, reviewed the prince's dragoons in 1796, the *Sun* reported that "the PRINCE gave the word of command in the most General-like manner, and the Troops went through their various evolutions with a precision and ability that did honour to those who have had the disciplining of them, and astonished every military man present. The grand charge was one of the finest manoeuvres we have seen. The KING and the DUKE of YORK, who are both excellent judges of military matters, decided that nothing could be better." The prince's participation reached out to all ranks of society. While he and his friends enjoyed his grand birthday dinner at Brighton Pavilion and a high society ball at the castle, the lower classes had ox roasts, jackass races, illuminations, and other entertainments. The prince customarily participated in the distribution of beef and beer to the populace.[28]

The royal family revived the spirit of Elizabethan progresses. Its involvement in the war effort brought court glamour to provincial towns usually untouched by royalty. The princes cut colorful figures as they traversed the country on military business. By 1797 the twenty-one-year-old Prince William Frederick of Gloucester had distinguished himself in Flanders and commanded a regiment of Fencible Highlanders near Newcastle. He held temporary commands and conducted inspections of troops across the country. On his three visits to Norwich, he not only reviewed troops but also visited public buildings, workshops, and theaters; participated in fund-raising events for charity and the war; and dined with persons of all political persuasions. He also flirted with the daughters of a prominent dissenting family who invited him back for a second visit.[29] After the duke of York returned from the Continent and became commander-in-chief of the armed forces in 1795, he too reviewed regiments and participated in public ceremonies up and down the country.[30]

Victory celebrations also brought the excitement of royal visits to the provinces and, indeed, to newspaper readers at second hand. After Lord Howe's victory off Ushant in 1794, dubbed "the glorious first of June," the mayor of Portsmouth arranged elaborate festivities around the king's presentation of a diamond sword to Howe aboard the ship *Queen Charlotte*. Cannon on the dock fired royal salutes, a band played "God Save the King" and "Rule Britannia," and crowds from all over the country gathered onshore.[31] In the wake of the naval mutinies and growing discontent with the war, the local elite planned an especially grand display for a royal visit to Admiral Duncan's fleet at the Nore. Although the event had to be canceled because of bad weather, the *True Briton* had established its effects two weeks beforehand: "It will present to Europe the proud spectacle of a BRITISH MONARCH *twice*, in the same war, visiting in person a victorious Fleet; and we apprehend it will have the most beneficial consequences with respect to our domestic feelings, and the perfect reunion of the British seamen to the warm wishes of their Country.—To these indeed, and to our gratitude they are fully entitled, by their carriage and conduct in the late brilliant victory; but we are convinced that the presence of our gracious Sovereign in the midst of his victorious Seamen, will be a spectacle which will animate and gratify every British bosom."[32] The ability of the press to take a non-event and turn it into a news item developed well before the media age. Coverage of the canceled Nore visit illustrates the impact of the print revolution on the social influence of the monarchy. Those who did not experience a royal visit directly could be told what they would have seen and how they would have felt had they been present.

Opposition newspapers had their work cut out for them undermining the impact of royal ritual. Provincial celebrations of royal anniversaries meant a day off from work, a break from routine, extravagant festivities, and gestures of generosity. Such treats could not but make an impression on all ranks of society, and they encouraged subjects to associate royalty with sentiments of benevolence and fellowship. Mayors and their corporations customarily participated in a procession, after which different groups had dinners at the principal inns and public houses—royal anniversaries also stimulated business. Tradesmen illuminated their shops, clergy ordered church bells rung, and soldiers fired salutes. The prominent families of each area sponsored dances, fireworks displays, and other events. The lower classes, sometimes even those in jail, enjoyed free beef and beer.[33] After the unpleasantness of the church-and-king riots, commentators liked to stress the harmony promoted by loyalist celebrations. On the king's birthday in 1793, the *Birmingham Gazette* proclaimed that "the day passed with that loyalty and conviviality which had ever distinguished similar public meetings in this town."[34]

Provincial leaders used military victories and royal anniversaries to promote loyalty and support for the war. After the Battle of Valenciennes in August 1793, Norwich loyalists tried to counter the popularity of the local reform societies by investing in a fifty-stone bullock, two thousand loaves of bread, and four barrels of beer. To drive home their point, the loyalist society hired a band to play "God Save the King" and "The Roast Beef of Old England" to accompany the feast. When the mail coach brought favorable news of the war to a small town, residents would illuminate their windows at night and hold meetings to draw up loyal addresses. As was the case with festivities in London, the military component became increasingly integral to provincial celebrations. Regiments of volunteers paraded through their towns, fired volleys, attended divine service, and dined with local worthies. Royal birthday celebrations provided opportunities for military recruitment and promoting good relations between soldiers and civilians. In 1794 two colonels raising regiments in Birmingham added several barrels of beer to the celebration of George III's birthday. The *Sun* reported the following year that the citizens of Yarmouth had raised a special subscription for the purpose of allowing soldiers to drink His Majesty's health.[35]

A caricature print that portrayed the public response to the birth of Princess Charlotte to the Prince of Wales and Princess Caroline in 1796 neatly sums up the allure of royal celebrations: a parson and a preacher receive inspiration for a special sermon, a debtor drinks to an early jail delivery, a wet-nurse and a milliner hope for employment, a self-important member of a corporation revels in the prospect of making the announcement, an artisan gloats over the blow to popery (a reference to the end of the Prince of Wales's liaison with Maria Fitzherbert), an old woman relishes the gossip, and a country bumpkin and a child delight in the excitement.[36] The congeniality between the social orders and the shows of munificence that accompanied royal rituals promoted the idea that members of the royal family acted as guardians to all ranks of society. Court grandeur supported industry and showcased British ingenuity. Royal tastes set the fashion for the nobility, the patrons of the arts and consumers of luxury goods.

John Money attributes the fierce loyalty found in Birmingham to the fact that royal patronage aided the renewal of the town's buckle trade after French imports horned in on the market. The petition that the buckle makers sent to the Prince of Wales in 1791 illustrates the popular conception of the royal family's role as guardians of trade:

> We beg leave to observe, that when Fashion, instead of foreign or unprofitable ornaments, wears and consumes the Manufactures of this Country, she puts on a more engaging form and becomes Patriotism. When Taste, at the same time and by the same means that she decorates the persons of the Rich, Cloathes and feeds the naked and hungry Poor, she deserves a worthier appellation, and may be styled Humanity. We make no doubt but your ROYAL HIGHNESS will prefer the blessings of the starving Manufacturer to the encomiums of the Drawing Room.
>
> We know it is to no purpose to address Fashion herself; she is void of feeling and deaf to argument; but fortunately she is subject to your control: She has been accustomed to listen to your voice and obey your commands.[37]

The prince responded with a gracious reply and an order to his household to discontinue the use of shoestrings. The duke of York and members of the City of London Corporation endeavored to extend the prince's influence by following his example. Reports of the queen's birthday gala in 1794 complimented the prince for his attention to the manufacturers and noted the predominance of fancy metal buttons, shoe buckles, and the "Soho new invented shoe-latchets." The papers expressed hopes that patronage as well as the ingenuity of the new design would "do much toward rescuing a valuable manufactory from ruin." The royal princesses completed this scene of patriotic fashion in their Spitalfields silks. Along the same lines, for the queen's birthday in 1798, George III altered the rules governing mourning when he realized that the custom had become detrimental to trade.[38]

Britons displayed their loyalty as spectators and revelers during celebrations of royal anniversaries and military victories. Alarm over events in France generated a new series of participatory loyalist activities. Attacking supporters of reform became an acceptable way of demonstrating attachment to the king. The first of these confrontations took place in Birmingham, after some ninety Dissenters held a dinner to celebrate Bastille Day in 1791. A well-organized, albeit drunken, mob spent three days pillaging and burning the homes and chapels of prominent Dissenters, most notably Dr. Joseph Priestley, who, anticipating trouble, had left town and had not attended the dinner. The crowd was motivated by religious bigotry, a long-standing resentment against the Dissenters' agitation for full political rights, and envy of the group's success in the commercial sphere. The local Anglican ruling elite neglected to act against the rioters, and even egged them on. The Treasury solicitors then obstructed the victims' efforts to press misconduct charges against the magistrates.[39]

Like the Priestley Riots, all demonstrations against reformers carried an underlying threat of physical violence because church-and-king rioters usually escaped punishment, and the government treated reformers as the instigators. Lt. Col. Oliver DeLancy, who commanded the troops that were eventually sent to restore order in Birmingham, commented: "The sufferings of a few individuals is very far counterbalanced by the advantages that will be gain'd to the publick." He believed that the incident would demonstrate that property was not safe without the protection of the magistracy and army; this would enhance the reputation of these institutions and earn them popular support. George III himself disapproved of the church-and-king rioters' employing "such atrocious means of shewing their discontent" but admitted: "I cannot but feel better pleased that Priestley is the sufferer for the doctrines he and his party have instilled, and the people see them in their true light." The *Times* echoed DeLancy's sentiments on the beneficial results of the Birmingham riots. It portrayed the 14 July celebration as an attempt by mad republicans, excited by the victory of democracy in France, to incite the people of England to rebellion. The Dissenters were so sure that the mob would be with them, the paper claimed, that they did not retreat when confronted with hissing and hooting en route to their celebration of revolutionary principles. They soon, however, discovered differently: "As the great body of the people (some few Dissenting individuals excepted) really loved their King, and in a manner worshipped the laws by which they were governed, it was natural to suppose that some decisive indignation would manifest itself against those factious traitors. . . . The real sovereignty of the Constitution trampled over the mock Majesty of the people."[40] The Priestley Riots set the stage for church-and-king mob actions in Manchester, Liverpool, Nottingham, and a number of small towns throughout the country.

Popular participation in the suppression of reformist ideas and activities was encouraged by the royal proclamation against sedition of 1792.[41] Cities, counties, corporations, and various religious, trade, and political organizations held meetings to draw up addresses in its support, which filled the *Lon-*

don Gazette for a year. By the autumn, opposition newspapers complained that collecting signatures for the loyalist addresses had become a means of intimidating sympathizers of the reform movement. Indeed, a Dissenter from Failsworth recalled that some loyalists approached the task with such zeal that they signed the names of their sons, some as yet unborn. The chronicler's father and some twenty other heads of dissenting families had refused to sign; in response, whenever they appeared in public their neighbors assailed them with cries of "Down with the Rump" and "You are Jacobins, Painites and Presbyterians; you are enemies to your king and country, and deserve to be killed!" Church-and-king supporters went to great lengths to ensure that they reached all members of their community. An enthusiastic associator of Wakefield, for instance, informed the London Association for Preserving Liberty and Property against Republicans and Levellers (APLP) that he had collected 1,700 signatures for their loyal resolutions by going door to door for six days.[42]

In Liverpool, a meeting called to consider the propriety of addressing the king precipitated a confrontation between loyalists and reformers when the two presented rival addresses. The reformers' address, which combined a declaration of loyalty to the Crown with a plea for parliamentary reform, was ripped up by a mob. Fearing further sectarian violence, the mayor discouraged anti-Jacobins from forming an association. A loyalist printer who reported this to the London APLP explained:

> I readily fall into his opinion, from a conviction that the disaffected party are so weak and contemptible that no danger is to be apprehended from them, and the chief object of our care at present is to manage cautiously the temper of his Majesty's good Subjects, who conceive themselves and their beloved Sovereign insulted by the recent attempts of certain Republicans, who have artfully laboured to seduce them from their duty.—Yet I think it necessary for the Friends of the King to keep an eye upon his Enemies. They are subtle and designing, and altho' they have lately been overawed; their malevolence still rancles in their bosoms.—They know themselves weak in number, and therefore act by stratagem on all occasions.— They are the first in all mixed companies to drink the "King and Constitution," but it is easy to discover by their *looks* and *motions* to each other, that they do it in derision only.

Frequently, these initial meetings spawned provincial branches of the APLP. Although a great many dissenting families of the middle classes were intimidated into silence, the artisans who made up the bulk of the corresponding-society membership proceeded with strengthened resolve.[43]

The government stepped up its efforts to repress the reform movement at the end of the year by trying Thomas Paine. The trial inspired the traditional ritual of burning public enemies in effigy. For two months thereafter, loyalists up and down the country held Paine-burnings. A likeness dressed in republican regalia—ragged trousers, Phrygian cap, and tricolor—would be transported from the jail to the marketplace in a long procession of rush carts bedecked with ribbons, bells, and items denoting loyalty to the Crown. Crowds would pelt the figure with stones and shout anti-Jacobin slogans. Sometimes loyalists mounted the effigy on a pole with a halter around its neck or dragged it through the streets to be whipped. A band customarily accompanied the proceedings with choruses of "God Save the King." Church bells tolled, sometimes for days afterward. Organizers usually conducted the event in such a way as to draw in all members of the community. At the marketplace participants shot, hanged, burned, or buried the effigy; particularly zealous crowds employed several methods of execution. Subscribers to public libraries contributed Paine's books, as well as any others considered to be of a similar tendency, to the pyre. In some places, loyalists organized Paine-burnings in retaliation against reform society meetings or else staged them in such a way as to draw attention to sympathizers of reform. These occasions provided opportunities for reinforcing paternalist bonds between ruling elites and the lower classes. When well-to-do members of the loyalist associations enjoyed dinners and toasts in celebration of their loyalty, they often gave money and ale to the poor so they could drink the king's health and burn Tom Paine.[44]

The mock executions of Paine did not usually involve direct attacks on the persons or property of reformers, for they often proceeded unchallenged. According to Alan Booth, of thirty such demonstrations in the northwest of England, only one, in Salford, resulted in violence, when a reformer cut down the effigy that had been placed near his house. A crowd gathered, a punch-up ensued, and the reformer ended the day with his windows broken.[45] After the Priestley Riots, however, the threat of physical violence increased the menacing nature of these public spectacles. Because they represented themselves as the party of law and order, loyalist associators gave particular emphasis in their accounts to the unity and orderly behavior that prevailed. The *Sun* reported that during a loyalist dinner and Paine-burning in Jersey, "One soul seemed to animate the whole on this occasion, and not the least riot or disorder (notwithstanding there was plenty of liquor) happened from beginning to end." A loyalist boasted that at a similar gathering in Frome, Somerset, "not a Single Word or Action was indecorous"; Paine was set aflame "amidst the acclamation of a United Multitude." A Wakefield associate revealed the temper of these events when he wrote that the burning of *Rights of Man* was "executed with great formality: whilst the Populace impelled by a blind zeal hanged and burnt him."[46]

Loyalists who enjoyed harassing their political and religious opponents presented these activities as legitimate expressions of loyalty to the king. After Paine's trial, the Treasury solicitors sent a circular letter to provincial magistrates requesting them to secure reliable persons as agents to collect evidence against the government's enemies. The letter contained instructions on how to procure seditious works, take sworn statements from informants, and send in information for indictments.[47] Protection of the king became a national obsession. Letters poured into the Home Office and the London APLP detailing the activities of loyal subjects who took it upon themselves to confront persons whom they saw showing disrespect to His Majesty. Defining loyalism in chivalric terms promoted heroic poses. A surgeon of Evesham, for instance, described himself as "a Loyal Subject[,] one whom is attached to his King and Country And allways will to my Dieing Day—I have respect for him, and I will Die for him." He wished to be authorized to send reports of the disaffected in order to frustrate "their Diabolical schemes . . . their Evil and unlawful Designs." Others sought more material support. An anonymous correspondent suggested that the public would respond generously should a subscription be opened that would allow the APLP to offer liberal rewards for every one of the "rebellious Villains" apprehended and convicted. In this way all the "Vermine and Wolves" would be exterminated quickly.[48] The prosecution campaign brought those who were disaffected with the king down to the level of beasts.

The arrests and treason trials of 1794 generated tales of bloody regicide plots. In May, for example, an anonymous informer identified a hatmaker's house across from Thomas Hardy's shop as a rendezvous for democrats: "In it there lately might be seen—if not yet been seen, daggers fitting to Destroy Kings—and Tyrants of all descriptions." In August "a Royalist" named several "*damned Jacobinal rascals*" who met in coffeehouses to plot a rebellion. When Hardy's trial began, a Nottingham woman stepped forward claiming to recognize the defendant as the gentleman with whom she had shared a coach from Sheffield the previous November who had damned the king and bragged he could cut George's throat as easily as he could shave himself. She went so far as to identify Hardy at the Tower but backed down when she saw Thomas

Erskine in action cross-examining witnesses. In this atmosphere of suspicion, rumors that freemasons harbored a vast conspiracy against monarchy were sufficiently worrisome to induce at least one lodge to issue a proclamation in support of king and constitution.[49] People who wished to become government agents for whatever reason—self-importance, favor, revenge, monetary gain, or simply as an outlet for loyalist fervor or anxiety—realized that their stories would receive more attention if they included a plot against the king.

Traditional celebrations of the king's birthday in the provinces became opportunities for rooting out and punishing those suspected of reformist tendencies, which loyalists presented as an affront to monarchy. The first church-and-king riot in Manchester took place on the king's birthday in 1792. A portion of the crowd that had gathered to watch the illuminations suddenly turned on the other spectators. Shouting "Church and King" and "Down with the Rump," the mob tore up trees to use as battering rams against the town's dissenting chapels. In Liverpool, a constable reported that on the king's birthday in 1794, loyalists took over a coffeehouse once frequented by reformers and renamed it King and Constitution Tavern. During the fireworks display, he had to rescue from the crowd's fury one known Jacobin and a man mistakenly accused of damning the king.[50]

The custom of singing the national anthem at theatrical performances became a weapon against the disaffected. In October 1792 the *Times* praised the "lusty and vociferous manner in which *John Bull* insisted upon the song of 'God save the King'" and the "ordering of any black sheep who *baa* against it to be disgracefully turned out of the house." The practice soon posed a serious threat to public order; a month later the *Times* gave the loyalists a slap on the wrist: "The constant cry for 'God save the King' at the theatre does not appear to us either prudent or proper. It often times gives rise to much disturbance, and affords the opportunity to the few who are discontented to form parties to show their disloyalty. On particular occasions nothing can be more proper than this call expressive of the good wishes and affections of the people—but to make a nightly demand for this song seems inconsiderate."[51]

Tate Wilkinson, a Yorkshire theater manager, left behind a record of the drunken thuggery that accompanied this loyalist activity in Edinburgh, Sheffield, Hull, and Portsmouth. He concluded that forcing participation in the national anthem was not a demonstration of loyalty but rather an exercise of power. Unable to take a stand against the incessant call for "God Save the King" because he feared accusations of disloyalty, Wilkinson recorded his frustration with the church-and-king vigilantes who were frightening people away from performances.[52]

Government policing agencies sometimes took part in the action as well. According to a 1795 spy report, members of the London Corresponding Society complained of rough treatment at theaters and told stories of people being indiscriminately pummeled or trampled by Bow Street runners.[53] The worst violence involved soldiers. The Edinburgh riots of April 1794 began at a performance of a play about Charles I's martyrdom. When some members of the audience refused to remove their hats for the national anthem, a number of gentlemen and officers of the Argyllshire Regiment of Fencibles insisted on it, brandishing their swords in emphasis. At the next performance, the protesters had bludgeons. Newspapers decried the use of a place of rational amusement for settling political differences. Although the opposition press criticized the magistrates for allowing a politically sensitive play to be performed during tumultuous times and reprimanded the soldiers for dragooning the audience, the ministerial press remained silent regarding the possible causes of the riot.[54]

The tradition of illuminating windows to commemorate military victories provided other occasions for loyalists to menace reformers who refused to participate. Mobs twice attacked the house of Thomas Hardy. His wife died in childbirth as a result of injuries received in her flight after the first attack, in 1794. In light of the tragedy, the mild disapproval with which the *Times* regarded the second attack in 1797 seems to imply that reformers deserved any fate dealt to them: "We are sorry even when we hear of a LOYAL MOB committing any irregularities. It is true, that the JACOBINS must feel themselves extremely mortified at not only witnessing the illuminated joy of the public at large, but still more that they should be forced to become themselves partakers of it, or at least externally, by illuminating their own houses. But on these occasions, Jacobins, as well as Constitutionalists, must comply with what general custom has prescribed, and make a virtue of necessity."[55]

As the confrontations that took place at theaters suggest, reformers were not completely cowed by the vigilantism that had become incorporated into royalist ritual. John Binns left an account of the assault on Hardy's house in 1797 that told a very different story from the loyalist triumph chronicled in the *Times.* Binns claimed that Londoners customarily showed their disapprobation of Pitt and the war by placing few if any lights in their windows. Although street-walkers and glaziers' boys often broke unilluminated windows, in this case, a church-and-king mob had intended to sack the house. Binns bragged that a hundred Corresponding Society members, "many of them Irish, armed with good shillelagh," turned out to defend Hardy in the longest and best-conducted fight of Binns's recollection. A troop of cavalry finally arrived and quelled the disturbance before either side could claim victory.[56]

Gestures of loyalism became a shield against prosecution. Sailors from Great Yarmouth attacked the audience and broke up the hall where John Thelwall lectured in August 1796. Loyalist accounts emphasized that when the constables arrived, the sailors were peaceably singing "God Save the King" with some gentlemen. The *True Briton,* as well as a handbill issued by the mayor in response to the opposition press's outcry against the incident, placed all blame upon Thelwall for holding such a meeting, and compared loyalist actions to a religious crusade. Other interest groups, however, began to use loyalist demonstrations in defiance of the government. In Bath, women angry with the high price of bread boarded a vessel carrying wheat and flour in order to prevent it from sailing. When a magistrate read the Riot Act, the women responded with choruses of the national anthem. The soldiers summoned to disperse them wound up helping the women carry the grain ashore to a warehouse. John Bohstedt's study of eighteenth-century mob actions suggests that ritualistic gestures of allegiance to the king became a regular aspect of food riots. Similarly, protesters against the Militia Act in Lincolnshire combined shouts of "God save the king" with damnings of Pitt and the justices.[57]

Commemorative celebrations could also be altered to demonstrate discontent. After Admiral Duncan's victory over the Dutch fleet at the end of 1797, residents of Nottingham drew attention to the city's depressed economy by replacing the usual celebrations with a meeting to draw up a petition to the king demanding a dismissal of his ministers. On this occasion, citizens of Newark-upon-Trent voted the usual loyal address but opened a subscription for soldiers' widows and orphans instead of appropriating funds for a celebration. Loyalist rituals could be inverted as well. The recruiting party that marched to Joseph Gales's unilluminated house after Lord Hood's capture of Toulon in September 1793 was foiled by an assembly of reformers standing guard and singing "God Save Great Thomas Paine."[58]

Notwithstanding the occasional subversion of royalist ritual to support opposition causes, court culture overwhelmingly supported popular loyalism and, by implication, the administration of government. As the historians discussed in chapters 3 and 4 intimate, the number of people who signed addresses and joined societies organized by loyalists far surpassed those willing to publicly proclaim their support for reform. The impact of repression as well as the material benefits of loyalism remain contentious. The surges of radical agitation, particularly during mid-decade, when antiwar sentiments ran high, however, indicate that a significant degree of low-grade discontent, or even disaffection, lay beneath the surface, waiting for a catalytic issue to spark expression. Gayle Trusdel Pendleton's statistical analysis of reformist publications shows that their authors cannot be relegated to the margins of society: "Reform expressed the grievances of the traditional professions, alienated intellectuals, the middling classes, and artisans and tradesmen who aspired to respectability and opulence." She finds a surprisingly high proportion of pamphlets at both the Whig and republican ends of the reformist spectrum. Yet republican writings enjoyed the highest circulation, judging by the percentage that went into multiple editions.[59] Moreover, republicanism cannot be dismissed as insignificant, given the impact it had on the cult of loyalism that dominated the 1790s.

The royalist fervor that gave shape to the loyalist movement relied upon fear of republicanism as well as of the monarchy's embracing certain republican attributes. George III's ruling style fostered a loyalist culture that was accessible to all ranks of society. The image he cultivated of devoted father to his immediate and his larger families endowed the monarchy with an approachability that encouraged an attitude of protectiveness.

EIGHT

The Public Image of George III

EORGE III is generally remembered as the mad king or the king who lost America. But Linda Colley's studies of British nationalism bring to light something that is usually overlooked: the king's emergence in the last quarter of the eighteenth century as the focus for a growing patriotic movement. Colley points out that the Pitt administration encouraged this cult of the monarchy as a safe outlet for loyalist fervor and describes George III as undergoing an apotheosis in the latter part of his reign. James Sack's investigation into the principles and practices of conservatism challenges Colley's interpretation. He finds "very little evidence of any cult of royalty or cult of George III in the eighteenth-century right-wing British press." Sack stresses the negative images that George III generated during the bulk of his reign and sees little change in the decade of the French Revolution. Even the ultraloyalist newspapers contained criticism of the royal family. Sack claims that William Pitt the Younger, not George III, became the idol of the conservative press, particularly after the statesman's death in 1806. Although the Right appreciated George's piety and domestic virtues, these qualities "invariably ran up against the most assailable activity of the later Hanoverian monarchy, [the princes] whose very existence was in some ways a reproach to George's own obvious role as *pater familias* [of] perhaps the most scandalous royal family in British history."[1]

Although Sack rightly questions Colley's use of the term *apotheosis* to describe George's status in the latter part of his reign, he nonetheless underestimates the monarchy as a paradigm in the late eighteenth century by focusing too narrowly on the right-wing press, particularly in regard to the royal princes. The discussion of the monarchy in pamphlets, legal argument, and radical discourse in the decade of the French Revolution shows that Sack over-simplifies when he deifies Pitt, the minister so often accused after 1788 of usurping the crown. But George III did not undergo an apotheosis either. The secular sanctity attached to the monarchy in the decade of the French Revolution did not so much glorify as humanize the institution. George's com-bination of court splendor and a down-to-earth manner exalted the everyday and commonplace. Accolades and censure converged to project a strikingly human and sympathetic royal image. Allowing the king to be fallible gave him a vulnerability that made loyalist claims of his accessibility believable, en-couraged his protection in the form of active loyalism, and defused criticism by circumventing any surprise and excitement that might reward the oppo-sition should they expose some hidden royal weakness.

Vincent Carretta's study of the satires published during George III's reign, on the other hand, supports Colley's interpretation of the king's apo-theosis in the era of the French Revolution. Carretta, however, sees a contin-uous vein of support for monarchy running through satirical treatments of George, even during those periods in which his popularity reached low points. Carretta's analysis of the change in the king's image stresses the reconcilia-tion between the king's two bodies in this post–divine right age: the body politic became capable of accommodating a corporeal king who was familiar and human. The Farmer George image became conflated with that of John Bull, producing the image of a king who could maintain his majesty while seated upon a toilet as well as he could on a throne.[2]

One of the reasons for the change in the royal image was a growing sense that Pitt had usurped the powers of kingship. This became a common theme in caricature prints by mid-decade; Richard Newton, for example, labeled Pitt and Dundas "Sacred Characters" and portrayed them seated side by side on an ersatz throne.[3] With this change in image came a shifting of blame. For example, James Gillray responded to the attack on freedom of conscience and expression that he saw embodied in the King's Proclamation of 21 May 1792 by using the royal family to represent the hypocrisy of the government. He set out the vices associated with each member of the royal family in four pan-els (fig. 1). George and Charlotte, with their reputations for hoarding and penny-pinching, epitomize avarice. The Prince of Wales is depicted drunk and in bad company. The duke of York is pursuing his passion for gambling as William, duke of Clarence, pursues the actress Dorothea Jordan. In con-

Fig. 1. James Gillray, *Vices Overlook'd in the New Proclamation*, 24 May 1792
(Yale Center for British Art, Paul Mellon Collection, B1981.25.949)

trast, Isaac Cruikshank's portrayal of the public response to the Two Acts of 1795 (fig. 2), supposedly enacted to protect the king, shows Pitt astride the white horse of Hanover. He spurs his royal mount toward the safe haven of the Treasury as the mob assails him with rocks, rubbish, and dead cats.

Likewise, responsibility for the war devolved from George to Pitt. The hardship and frustrations of the Flanders campaign in the spring of 1793 occasioned a lot of grumbling among the officers against the leadership of the duke of York. Stories abounded of the drinking and whoring going on in the duke's camp, all exploited by the caricaturists in London.[4] Gillray's satire of the duke's return in early 1794 made a two-pronged attack against royal nepotism and the senselessness of the war (fig. 3). A goggle-eyed king in hunting dress strains forward from his throne to receive the keys of Paris from his swaggering favorite son. The duke, with a bottle secreted not too well in his tailcoat pocket, boasts of his achievement and offers his father the spoils of war: a sack labeled "Breeches of the Sans-Culottes," as well as a pile of their heads, pots of frogs, boxes of assignats (presumably worthless), a hamper labeled "Wooden shoes of the Poissards," and some broken weapons of liberty. Behind the throne, the Devil scoops coins from a sack representing the Civil List into the apron of a horribly grinning queen. Pitt sits at the king's feet, drawing up "new Taxes not to be felt by the Swinish Multitude"; they include "Bricks—Rum—Brandy—Water—Air."

Two years later, perceptions had changed. Cruikshank's *The British Menagerie* (fig. 4) shows Pitt scooping guineas into the mouth of the Austrian leopard, while the king and queen, rendered as Mr. and Mrs. Bull, look on, gaping in dismay. Dundas, in full Highland dress, points to the latest tamed beast, a scowling pope, identified in the legend as "The *Whore of Babylon* who once was Master of All Europe, but now glad to find a place in this Menagerie." Pitt, aided by his henchman, Dundas, has become the keeper of Europe. George's pockets are turned inside out; he has been robbed not only of money but of power. Now he is thoroughly identified with the people.

The domestication of majesty was at the heart of Farmer George's transmigration into John Bull. The monarchy became a family drama, with the everpresent hope of regeneration for members who had strayed from the path of virtue. In spite of the deprecations of the opposition press, royal rituals served not only as distractions from national woes but also as hopeful parables suggesting that better times would come. In 1795 the hope that the marriage of the Prince of Wales would save him from debt and debauchery became analogous to the belief in the salvation of the nation from economic hardship and

Fig. 2. Isaac Cruikshank, *A Specimen of Light Horsemanship*, 26 December 1795
(Yale Center for British Art, Paul Mellon Collection, B1981.25.1301)

Fig. 3. James Gillray, *Pantagruel's Victorious Return to the Court of Gargantua After Extirpating the Soup-Meagre's of Bouille Land*, 10 February 1794 (Yale Center for British Art, Paul Mellon Collection, B1981.25.944)

Fig. 4. Isaac Cruikshank, *The British Menagerie*, 5 July 1796
(Yale Center for British Art, Paul Mellon Collection, B1981.25.1107)

military defeat. As the poet laureate, Henry James Pye, proclaimed in his ode for that year:

> O that amid the nuptial flow'rs we twine,
> Our hands the Olive's sober leaves might join
> Thy presence teach the storm of War to cease,
> Disarm the battle's rage, and charm the world to peace.

Newspapers anticipated the arrival of Princess Caroline and circulated reports of her beauty, elegance, and virtue, all of which they confirmed upon her arrival.[5] Gillray captured the marriage's implications in *The Lover's Dream* (fig. 5). As the prince clutches his pillow in blissful slumber, a goddesslike princess, with angels attending her, is borne to him on a pillow of clouds. His royal parents hover over him: the queen proffers a book entitled *The Art of Getting Pretty Children,* and the king, in the attitude of a tabby about to pounce on its prey, clutches a huge moneybag representing the prince's new income. The vision has routed the prince's roistering companions: Bacchus rolls off the bed on a port barrel. Beneath the king's seat of clouds, the Whigs have the desperate look of the vanquished; Charles James Fox drops his dice and his political crony Richard Brinsley Sheridan holds up his hand in an expression of no contest. Three scowling prostitutes move out of the scene, and racehorses dash away in the background.

The marriage portended disaster from the beginning, but the press went out of its way to keep up appearances. The papers described the wedding service in tones of awe and respect, choosing to ignore the prince's state of inebriated befuddlement. Although some reporters recorded the prince's stumbling over his vows, and other royal faux pas that hampered the ceremony, they explained that his sensibilities had been overwhelmed by a rite that was "awful, affecting and sublime" for all who witnessed it.[6] After the birth of Princess Charlotte some nine months later, however, it became difficult to ignore the state of the marriage or the prince's affair with Lady Jersey. Cruikshank's *Sketches from Nature!!!* (fig. 6) is just one of the many graphic images of illicit sex, cuckoldry, and innocence betrayed that filled the print shops in 1796. The newspapers turned Princess Caroline into a tragic heroine, abandoned by a faithless husband who had taken up with a scheming old crone. The king became the venerable patriarch patiently waiting for the return of the prodigal and providing a haven of familial affection for the wronged bride and her infant.[7]

George III's paternal mien captured the imaginations of ministerial and

The LOVER'S DREAM.

A Thousand Virtues seem to lackey her. Driving far off each thing of Sin & Guilt. *Milton*

Fig. 5. James Gillray, *The Lover's Dream*, 24 January 1795
(Yale Center for British Art, Paul Mellon Collection, B1981.25.912)

Fig. 6. Isaac Cruikshank, *Sketches from Nature!!!–The Sultan Retiring–Fashionable Pastime–The Discovery–Confidence Betrayed,* 23? May 1796 (Yale Center for British Art, Paul Mellon Collection, B1981.25.1293)

opposition newspapers alike. For years they commented upon his devotion to the newest member of the royal family. Although the christening was private, detailed reports appeared in the papers: "The whole was a scene of domestic felicity calculated to warm the heart of every good Subject, who must feelingly participate in every circumstance so intimately connected with the happiness of a Monarch, who shines with equal lustre in the bosom of his amiable Family, as on the throne."[8] Cruikshank drew George as *Grandpappa in His Glory!!!* (fig. 7), lovingly and messily spooning pap into the mouth of the baby. His dress, a mixture of formal and informal, reflects his environs: palace turned nursery. The king's expression of utter devotion to the infant combined with the cozy domestic details—they share the fire with laundry hung to dry and a basking cat—create a comforting sense of familial warmth. Similarly, accounts of the Princess Royal's wedding and departure to Würtemburg in 1797 allowed subjects an intimate view of the king during an emotional family event. Even the customarily churlish *Morning Post* noted that the departure of the princess drew tears from many of the spectators. The papers reported that the queen and princesses wept openly during the service, while the king and duke of Clarence wiped their eyes frequently. The *True Briton* pronounced all present appropriately affected.[9]

George III cultivated the image of being a father to all. He showed the same sort of care and affection toward children of his subjects as he did for his own. In a report of one royal visit, the *True Briton* noted: "The charming condescension of the royal family, in sitting down at a Table with the Soldiers of a Regiment to witness the happiness which their bounty diffused, must excite the warmest affection of every good heart. The KING, during the repast, carried several of the soldiers' children in his arms to the QUEEN, by whom they were tenderly caressed."[10] Cruikshank captures this sentiment of parental regard, albeit sardonically, in a satire on the growing discontent over taxes during 1795. *Favorite Guinea Pigs Going to Market* (fig. 8) shows Pitt, sporting a "'45" armband and a club, driving an angry herd of anthropomorphized swine through an archway inscribed "Licence office: Pigs Meat sold Here." He admonishes the queen for standing idly by and taking snuff. She snaps back that he shouldn't "hurry any Man's Cattle but your own" and expresses sympathy for his charges as well as appreciation of them: "I have had fourteen of my own & certainly must know the value of Pigs." The king, handling a particularly angry black boar, notes that the herd have been driven long and hard, and have taken to grunting. He cautions Pitt, "If they once turn the Devil can't stop them." Although the king's and queen's words suggest that the royal pair

London Pub. Feb.ry 13 1796 by S.W. Fores No 50 Piccadilly. Folio of Caricatures Lent out for the Evening

GRANDPAPPA *in his Glory !!!*

"There was a laugh & a craw   Goody-good girl shall be fed
There was a giggling honey.   But naughty girl she shall have money.

Fig. 7. Isaac Cruikshank, *Grandpappa in His Glory!!!* 13 February 1796
(Yale Center for British Art, Paul Mellon Collection, B1981.25.1290)

Fig. 8. Isaac Cruikshank, *Favorite Guinea Pigs Going to Market*, 27 July 1795
(Yale Center for British Art, Paul Mellon Collection, B1981.25.1221)

might have their own interests at heart (in addition to reminding the viewer of the royal progeny feeding at the public trough), the conflation of children and subjects, combined with their majesties' criticism of Pitt, convey a well-meaning but flawed paternalism.

Reports of royal ceremonies and public appearances stressed the reciprocal relationship between sovereign and subject. When residents of Plymouth greeted the Prince of Wales with effusions of loyalty during an impromptu visit, the *Sun* observed: "In the present critical state of affairs, nothing could be more gratifying than this display of attachment to a Branch of the royal family, and His Royal Highness seemed thoroughly sensible of it, bowing in the most familiar manner, and taking every opportunity of gratifying the curiosity of the people." The words *sensibility, affability, familiarity,* and *condescension* appear repeatedly in reports of encounters between the royal family and commoners. These accounts leave the impression that the king was accessible to all his people and that demonstrating loyalty was the duty of every good subject. The loyalist press emphasized that the royal family's superior virtue earned them such veneration. For example, audiences reportedly acknowledged the royal attendance at the theater "with that degree of approbation which illustrious birth and elevated station must ever command from a free and grateful People, when accompanied by superiour merit and pre-eminent virtue."[11]

The focus on the paternal qualities of the king in reports of encounters between royalty and commoners supported the idea that submission to authority was natural and, moreover, a duty that elevated, rather than debased, the subject. Journalists popularized Burke's argument that reverence of royalty was an essential quality of a civilized people. In a report on the queen's birthday celebration in 1794, the *Times* waxed Burkean:

> On such an occasion, it was natural to contrast the happy Constitution of Great Britain and the happiness of its inhabitants with the wretched republican mobocracy of France; and, turning the mind's eye to that distracted country, compare the bloody celebrations of Paris with the delightful sensations of an English festival. There, a set of Cannibals, wallowing in the blood of their King and Queen, and thousands of their fellow-creatures, blaspheme all moral virtue and deny their God.—Here, the People rejoicing in the spirit of Loyalty return thanks to the Sovereign of the universe for the blessings they enjoy, and by every mark of respect to the Throne, testify their satisfaction of that mode of Government, which secures their property, protects their persons, and guards their religious and civil rights.[12]

Yet Burke had not understood that a certain degree of irreverence toward the royal family actually protected them. The ethereality of the image of Marie Antoinette that he conjured up in the *Reflections* was the quality that brought her down: the French saw their queen as an abstraction, a symbol of court corruption. Killing her seemed more like abolishing feudalism by decree than like executing a living, breathing human being. In contrast, for the British, to kill the king would not only be patricide but a symbolic act of suicide as well.

Hostile references to kings in general and George III in particular abounded in the 1790s, but they did not necessarily indicate a desire to do away with either or both. In looking at anti-monarchical rhetoric as a whole, one can see two distinct patterns. First, the demystification of monarchy started by Paine continued, but with a different intent. Although Paine endeavored to prove monarchy obsolete, most British reformers simply desired a monarch who was accessible and responsible to his subjects. The ideal king depicted in reformist writings empathized with the common people, recognized that his interests intersected with theirs, and prevented greedy politicians from plundering the nation.

Second, the strongest expressions of hostility toward George III occurred either during peaks of loyalist or government repression or during periods of economic hardship. Anti-monarchicalism often took on the character of blasphemy: like damning God, damning the king was a rhetorical device rather than literal wish. Such oaths appeared to be spoken for effect: to stir a particular emotion or provoke a certain reaction in the listener. Seditious words often seemed expressions of frustration and powerlessness—when pursuing reform by constitutional means proved ineffectual, when the government or loyalists misrepresented reformist ideas, or when the government seemed insensible to the sufferings of the poor. Reformers also responded to repression by parodying the worst possible fears harbored by the ruling classes. Ironically, reformist satires tended to reinforce the very misrepresentations they sought to debunk; the use of irony in tracts, songs, and broadsheets included irreverent portrayals of George III that prosecutors seized upon as evidence of treasonable conspiracies.

Paine pursued the demystification of monarchy as an essential step in the participation by all citizens in British political life. In June 1792, when he found out that the government intended to prosecute him for *Rights of Man,* he reconfirmed his commitment to this cause in *A Letter to Mr. Secretary Dundas,* first published in the *Argus:* "When I look into History and see the multitudes of men, otherwise virtuous, who have died, and their families been ruined, in defence of knaves and fools, and which they would not have done had they reasoned at all upon the system; I do not know a greater good that an individual can render to mankind, than to endeavour to break the chains of political superstition." Urging the British to remodel their government, Paine made a contemptuous allusion to George III. If the people still desired a grand personage at their head, he mused, they could deduct a percentage of the other government officers' salaries to create a more highly paid post, "and stile the person who should fill it, King, or Majesty, or Madjesty, or give him any other title."[13] Paine considered disenfranchised Britons enslaved by an unquestioned reverence of royalty; this predilection had to be overcome before they could understand and pursue their political rights.

British writers tended to use satire rather than exposé to chip away at the mystique of monarchy. In part, this had to do with a desire to avoid prosecution, but it also reflected the sort of anti-monarchicalism found in Britain at the time. Theorists like Paine and Barlow, who were not based in Britain, had no ties to its monarchy; this enabled them to reject royal government without qualms. British radicals, on the other hand, no matter how republican they were in spirit or how much contempt they felt toward George III, had difficulty making the leap into political atheism. Even Charles Pigott, a steadfast republican and audacious satirist, displayed some ambivalence in his writing. His most famous work, *The Jockey Club* (1792), is a witty verbal caricature of royal foibles. Yet it does not reach into the foundations of monarchical legitimacy. One can hear Pigott's despair as he declares, "No nation ever seemed more stupidly rooted in admiration of the glare and parade of royalty than the English" and observes: "The fulsome adulation that fills the majority of our daily prints, is a disgrace to the national character." He positively sputters with indignation when he describes the trappings of royal ritual "erected for the reception of the most insignificant puppets that act in this farce . . . to delude and overawe the minds of the multitude." In keeping with his organizing metaphor he describes the French as a "galled jade" that had finally resisted and thrown a bad rider. George III, however, displays skillful jockeyship. John Bull, a patient steed, would be willing to endure a heavy load until he perished rather than use his natural strength to unseat his rider.[14]

Pamphlets produced in response to the proclamation against sedition employed anti-monarchical statements as a measure of defiance. Many of the satires on royalty displayed an attitude of impudence, rather than malevolence, and seemed more directed at loyalists than at the institution of monarchy. A much-reprinted pamphlet that originated in Sheffield in 1792 ridiculed the arrogance of the loyalist response to Paine. The anonymous author noted with mock horror that Paine and others like him, "who grudge the poor king his salary that he labours so hard for," wished to cut the king's salary from a million a year to two hundred thousand: "What ignorant puppies such fellows must be, to suppose the dignity of the king can be supported with such a trifling sum! Why, it would be scarcely 600l. per day, and what would this be for a king! a mere trifle, a nothing; such a salary would starve him by inches. . . . Horrid miscreants! they would starve their king! I am sorry to find this too much the spirit of the times: and this is the work such ragamuffin, bare breached fellows as you are, would set about, if you were disciples of this TOM PAINE, and fancied you had rights." The passage enumerated the placemen and pensioners who had to be supported by this sum, without whom "a king would be no more than a cypher" and would have no defense against public servants "prating about the good of the nation and the comfort and happiness of the poor." The writer then explored the bowels of the court as well as those of the king: "There is the groom of the stool; that always attends his majesty when he wants to go to stool, and surely this is an office so offensive, no man would like to undertake it for less than 1000l. a year: and what could the king do without such a man? There have been men who have died in the action of disemboguing, and surely a king's life is too precious for him to be trusted in such a situation alone."[15] One wonders whether this was an oblique reference to George II's rather undignified death in the privy, or simply lavatory humor, a common element of the satiric tradition.

Scatological treatment of the British royal family became a common feature of caricatures from the time of the Civil War. Coming to terms with monarchy's compromised divinity allowed exploration of the relation between the king's two bodies. Satirists now had license to expose the frailties of the king's corporeal body as well as to criticize the policies his political body pursued.[16] During the 1790s, most of the caricature prints that depicted royal excretory functions suggested the vulnerability of majesty. The most striking example is Gillray's *Taking Physick:–Or–the News of Shooting the King of Sweden!* of 11 April 1792. A grotesquely emaciated Pitt holds up a paper bearing "News from Sweden" and exclaims, "Another Monarch done over!" as he bursts in on George and Charlotte at their places upon a two-seated latrine. The lion in the royal seal over the privy evacuates his bowels in panic. The queen shrinks as she looks on, horrified. The king half rises to take a better look at the paper, while clutching his distended stomach with both hands. He is wearing a nightcap—which implied infirmity—tied with a ribbon of the Royal

Order of the Garter; the memory of his madness of 1788 could never have been too far from the public mind. George's response—"What? Shot? What? what? what? . . . Shot! shot! shot!"—a stock rendition of his idiosyncratic speech pattern, in this context suggests mental confusion.[17]

Prints depicting privy scenes also implied that the royal family was at the mercy of politicians. The Prince of Wales had received similar treatment at the pen of William Dent the previous year when he was incapacitated by debt. *C–rlt–n House in Want of Necessary Furniture* shows the prince upon a closestool in a recessed alcove, gripping toilet paper made from a treatise on the principles of economy, and looking on in anticipation as various politicians dressed as nurses and doctors argue over remedies. Old Nurse Fox sits in an armchair blubbering over the prince's distress, a bottle of "French Spirits" at his feet. Doctor Sheridan prescribes "Royal Mint Drops" and "Golden Pills," while Doctor Pitt protects the "Public Dispensary."[18] The prince's attitude is one of a child who resorts to a rebellion of the bowels to gain leverage over controlling adults.

Displays of cloacal wit were a stock feature of satire, but using this sort of humor to mock the king is arresting: the highest person in the state is shown engaged in one of the least dignified of human acts. Caricaturists even depicted improper female influence scatologically. Noteworthy is *The Festival of the Golden Rump* (1737), which satirized Walpole's exploitation of the queen's influence with a depiction of Caroline wielding an enema bag for the regulation of George II's wind.[19]

Was this degree of bathos simply irresistible for the satirist, or does such treatment of royalty say something about the character of the British monarchy? By the final decades of the century, representations of the British royal family differed from caricatures of its French counterpart, which tended to use sexual deviance or dysfunction to represent inversion of the natural order of rule within the palace and the consequent weakness of the state.[20] Excretorial imagery was to some degree opportunistic. Although caricature prints were full of the royal princes' sexual misadventures, George and Charlotte did not offer much material along those lines, aside from their vigorous pursuit of procreation. George, on the other hand, was extremely visceral; during his illness of 1788, his mental and physical functions became the subject of great public interest.[21] The ability of artists to muck about in the bathroom habits of the king and the heir apparent signified a new degree of intimacy with royalty after George's illness.

Satires that made use of George III's bodily functions were generally not as censorious as the graphic depictions of Louis XV and Louis XVI had been.[22] In fact, in the latter part of 1793, Gillray reversed the tendency to represent the royal guts as a source of weakness with *The French Invasion;–or– John Bull, Bombarding the Bum-Boats.* Gillray drew George III as a map of England. One leg, consisting of Norfolk, Suffolk, Essex, and Kent, is drawn up; the other, made up of Devon and Cornwall, extends back, giving the impression that the king is engaged in a purposeful, high-stepping march. From the royal posteriors, the border of Hampshire and Sussex, issues a barrage of excreta that scatter the lines of French ships making their way across the Channel and that hit the coast of France, rendered as the profile of an angry, open-mouthed face. This print can be interpreted in a number of ways. In a study of Gillray's political ambivalence, Ronald Paulson emphasizes the travesty of "the body politic metaphor." Paulson notes Gillray's technique of using metaphors of food and digestion to capture his subjects' characters. This print implies that the French Revolution has brought mankind down to a bestial level: "Figures on both sides of the Channel share the lowest common denominator of regression to orality and anality." Linda Colley argues that beneath the ostensible "scatological disrespect" in the "Bum-Boat" print lies an extraordinary merging of king and country. The counties "give him shape, but he gives them identity." Moreover, Colley notes, this sort of image, at once irreverent and ennobling, disarmed hostility and promoted "an amused tolerance for royalty."[23] Indeed, acknowledging that the king goes to the privy like everyone else, and being able to imagine him doing so, gave the monarchy a sympathetic, human quality that was not possible in an absolutist, divine-right regime.

A primitive drawing tentatively dated 1794 stands out as one of the few prints that employs scatology in a cruel rather than humorous way. *Farmer Looby Manuring the Land* shows a clearly demented George III with his breeches lowered, squatting in the middle of a field. The accompanying verse reads:

> Is Looby only fit
> To dung the verdant plain?
> Yes, Looby has got wit
> to sack the golden grain,

followed by a toast

> May every tyrant fall from power and state,
> To be made Ploughman quickly be their fate;

> But that same care of these fine Lads be taken
> May Kate be made to boil their broth and bacon.[24]

The print never turned up in state's evidence or was mentioned in the papers of the reform societies. It is representative of a narrow but serious strain of anti-monarchicalism in Britain that finally found an outlet in the militant republican network that formed in the second part of the decade.

When material associated with the reform societies showed disrespect toward the king, however ironic, it was usually interpreted by prosecutors as revealing secret intentions to overthrow the monarchy. The infamous "La Guillotine" handbill that circulated at the LCS's Chalk Farm meeting of April 1794 was trotted out in evidence during Hardy's trial for treason, although it is hard to read it as anything other than an April Fool's Day joke:

For

The Benefit of JOHN BULL

At the

FEDERATION THEATRE in EQUALITY-SQ,

On Thurs. the 1st of April 4971

will be performed,

A new and entertaining Farce, called

LA GUILLOTINE;

or

GEORGE'S HEAD IN THE BASKET!

Dramatis Personae

Numpy the Third, by Mr GUELP

(Being the last time of his appearing in that
character)

Also among the cast were "Grand Inquisitor" played by "Mr Pensioner Reeves," "Don Quixote, Knight of the Dagger, By Mr Edmund Calumny," and "Billy Taxlight." It featured "Tight Rope Dancing, from the Lamp-post" and the singing of "Ça Ira" and "BOB SHAVE GREAT GEORGE OUR ——!"

The whole to conclude with

A GRANDECAPITATION

OF

PLACEMEN, PENSIONERS & GERMAN LEECHES[25]

The piece's playfulness suggests more a thumbing of the nose than a shaking of the fist. Given the time of the handbill's appearance, it seems to have been motivated by outrage over the Scottish sedition trials and is a typical example of reformist parody of loyalist misconceptions. David Bindman notes that such broadsides "caused panic out of proportion to their numbers and indeed their content, which is invariably mischievous rather than sinister."[26]

Reformers produced the most pointed satires of George III when they perceived the government's repressive measures to be the most unfair, in a sort of tit-for-tat. In September 1794, for example, reformers' resentments ran high as their leaders sat in jail and their colleagues stood accused of a fanciful scheme to assassinate the king at the theater with an airgun and a poisoned dart. A poem commemorating the "Pop-Gun Plot" exploited the stereotype of George as gormless:

> But sure your hair will stand on end when once I do begin sir,
> The dreadful story to relate of our most gracious King, sir;
> How that a *poison'd arrow*, by some base *plebeian hand*, sir,
> In his most *sacred guts* was intended to be cramm'd sir.
>
> But, ah, the dark design!—what a blessing for the nation!
> Was happily discover'd while 'twas in contemplation:
> For had it pierced his Royal paunch, he surely had been dead, sir,
> Tho' possibly he'd not been hurt if it had struck his head, sir.

The poem described the invention of the fantastic tale and how eager ministers were to believe it. Ultimately, it targeted the king's servants, not the king:

> But, Britons, be not dup'd by such base insinuations;
> For *those that cry* "Stop thief!" are the *rogues that rob the nation*
> Of their *treasure* and their *liberty*—but soon the times will alter,
> And they'll be all rewarded with *Gu–t–ne* or *h–lt–r*.[27]

The old "evil ministers behind the king" theory appeared often in these writings because many reformers genuinely seem to have subscribed to it. John Binns, who joined the LCS in the aftermath of the treason trials and later became involved in the underground republican movement, stated in his memoirs that during the 1790s, most reformers believed that Pitt was the one who was determined to wage war against republican France. Upon reading the memoirs of various cabinet ministers, Binns decided that the public had been duped: "George the Third was an obstinate, self-willed king, who much more frequently compelled his ministers to adopt *his* opinions and carry out *his* measures, than they succeeded in inducing him to adopt theirs."[28]

Although the people at large might conceive Pitt to be the brains behind the operation, they did not believe that this should absolve the king from responsibility. The records of seditious words spoken by people who were un-involved in the reform movement show revolutionary and Painite rhetoric moving beyond the corresponding societies and being used to articulate long-standing economic discontents. The poor's expectations of paternal care on the part of the local gentry—what E. P. Thompson called "the moral econ-omy"—extended to the king, who, after all, was the father of his people. After enclosure riots in Sheffield in 1791, a magistrate requested that troops remain because of "the Number of treasonable Inscriptions on Walls and Doors and frequent nocturnal Exclamations in the Street such as 'No King.' 'No Corn Bill.' 'No Taxes.' etc. and the incendiary letters which have been sent to dif-ferent persons." A cleric of Durham voiced alarm at the sentiments of liberty and equality spreading through the collieries. He reported that the poor blamed high taxes on the Prince of Wales's debts and the failure of the king—the richest monarch in Europe—to pay them.[29]

Disaffected persons learned that using anti-monarchical rhetoric brought them attention. Judging by the letters that poured into the Home Office and the London headquarters of the loyalist associations, the well-to-do feared a Jacobin insurrection and their local ne'er-do-wells enjoyed the new sense of menace they were able to wield. For instance, patrons of a Birmingham pub-lic house became concerned when a group of men, including a suspected Ja-cobin spy, formed a Rights-of-Man club. The loyalists policed the scene as best they could; they threatened to eject one man after he declared that all kings were useless beings set up for fools to worship and that the people had cer-tain burdens—such as taxes and allegiance—to throw off. When confronted, the man allegedly boasted that he had said the same in front of a larger com-pany elsewhere and nobody had objected.[30] Most indictments for seditious words in late 1792 showed simple Painite oaths, declarations that French re-publicanism was superior to monarchy, or exuberant damnings of the king.[31] Judging by the number of incidents that occurred in public houses, a good proportion were the product of loyalist provocation or drunken belligerence.

While early anti-monarchical statements seemed the product of bravado inspired by events in France and impatience for change in Britain, by 1793 dis-affected people had begun to associate the king with the hardships brought on by the war. Seditious oaths became more elaborate, an indication either that the reform movement had politicized the lower classes or that loyalist propaganda had inspired witnesses to embroider their statements. While vis-iting his former place of employment, a London baker became angry when his old workmates praised the king's latest speech and allegedly retorted that "he wished he could see the King forced to take a coal sack, and to walk up and down Wapping and to Look after a Job without either Shoes or Stockings or Money in his Pocket, and then to sit down upon the step of a door and be damned." Such sentiments were not confined to the laboring poor. A Cambridgeshire farmer had a similar reaction when his workers informed him that they should not work on a fast day. The workers claimed that he asked them whether the king would send them the eighteenpence in earnings they stood to lose. They testified that he then declared: "If the People of this Nation were sensible of the Distress they labour under, they would not have burnt Tom Paine, but instead of Him they would have burnt their King. Take off the Heads of the Nobles and set their Land at Liberty."[32] With the debates on war and reform raging around them, individuals who were not political-minded began to see their own grievances in terms of the national situation. Distress and the heat of argument provoked them to use violent words against the king to emphasize the seriousness of their plight and to show solidarity with their fellow citizens who were agitating for change.[33]

The duke of York's conspicuous role in the campaign against the French republic made him a target for the disaffected as well. A London publican, hearing a commotion outside his door, testified to a harangue against the duke delivered by a tailor to a swearing and hissing crowd.[34] The recurring theme in these angry or drunken declarations was that the royal family had no conception of the real state of the nation because they were insulated by wealth and flatterers. Paine's *Rights of Man* and the national reform movement had caused the people at large to focus on the king as the key to achieving redress against all perceived oppressors.

The idea that the king had a paternal responsibility to feed his people received physical expression in the attack on George III's coach on 29 October 1795. Contemporary analyses of the meaning of the incident demonstrate that anti-monarchicalism defies straightforward interpretation. Loyalists' reactions were predictable; their accounts presented the confrontation as part of a radical plot to assassinate the king and compared the mob that surrounded his coach to the French rabble that had confronted Louis XVI on his way to St. Cloud. William Pitt and George Grenville took the opportunity to introduce the Two Bills, which, after considerable public and parliamentary debate, became law on 18 December 1795.[35]

The reformist response was more complicated. The bills put reformers on the defensive; consequently, they showed little sympathy for the king. Constitutional reformers and militant republicans agreed that the attack was a

spontaneous act of desperate persons, but they were divided about its implications. Francis Place, who tended to play down the republican component
of the reform movement, argued that the loyalist press had exaggerated the
seriousness of the assault. He claimed to have met the so-called miscreant in
the green coat. Place heard the man explain to assembled society members
that he had stepped into the street to see what the commotion was, had found
himself in danger of falling under some coach wheels, and had grabbed onto
the handle of what turned out to be the king's carriage door. Place presented
the escapade as just another instance of the people taking the opportunity to
protest parliamentary policy by hissing and groaning as the king passed. He
added that on these occasions the ministerial press usually reported that the
crowd had greeted the king with displays of affection.[36]

Binns, a committed republican, also claimed to have met the "miscreant
in the green coat"; but he placed the man at one of the LCS division meetings
that evening and told quite a different story as a result. The man admitted to
having gone into the coach and seized the collar of the king, who had slumped
to the carriage floor in fear. Binns insisted that no preconcerted plan was in
operation that day but speculated that if the king had been dragged out of his
coach and killed by the angry mob, the Cabinet would then have been assas-
sinated. He believed that impatience with war and privation might have induced the people to overthrow the government, establish a republic, and make
peace with France.[37]

Allegations that the events of 29 October were part of a treasonable conspiracy inspired a parody of loyalist attitudes that treated the sanctity of
monarchy with heavy sarcasm. The pamphlet speculated that the worst shock
George III had suffered was coming into contact with "the swinish multitude":
"Unfortunately, the *Lord's Anointed* was discovered on his return to the
Queen's House, and stopped by his outrageous subjects; who, too horrible to
relate! were proceeding to lay their Harpy hands upon *The Representative of
the King of Heaven.*" It asserted that George's great distance from his subjects
made him blind to their wretched condition. How strange that all but placemen and pensioners should demonstrate against a king, "who, while he en-
joys a MILLION *per year* (fixed Wages) ... would never permit a single Debt
to remain unpaid, or the existence of one *Object in Distress,* in the whole NA-
TION, *if he knew it.*"[38]

Cases of seditious words indicate that hostility toward the king reached a
peak during 1795, as people felt the pinch of an increasingly unpopular war.
When told of the attack on the king's coach, a Richmond man who witnesses

said generally showed loyalty to the government, reportedly responded: "Damn him. I wish they had stoned him to Death for he is a Monopolizer and Forestaller and Damn him I sho'd like to see his Head upon Temple Bar."[39] This was also the year in which the infamous republican printer Richard "Citizen" Lee circulated such tracts as *King Killing* and *The Happy Reign of George the Last* at LCS meetings. Lee had been expelled from the society twice but remained undeterred in his mission to disabuse the British people of what he saw as a superstitious reverence for the idiot on the throne. His tracts included insolent poems that ridiculed George's mental capacity and exulted in images of royal trappings being trampled to dust.[40]

After the Two Acts passed, reform agitation waned, but the quiet was deceptive. On 1 February 1796, a hissing and hooting group of twelve or so assailed the king's coach in Covent Garden after their Majesties attended the theater. The culprits hit a coachman with a brick-bat and threw "a very sharp-edged and dangerous flint stone" which broke the window, grazed the queen's cheek, and landed in the lap of a lady-in-waiting. This time the government treated the incident as the work of cowardly individuals who were unlikely to have associates. According to Binns, the royal family received a frosty reception at the theater that evening; yet, as reviled as they were at that point, they were still more popular than the ministers.[41]

Street ballads in circulation during 1796 alternated between the "evil ministers behind the king" position and aggressive anti-monarchicalism. In the latter category, an antiwar song entitled "The King's Service" began:

> You *boys* who doat on a *King*,
>   Attend and I'll sing you a song,
> You must very well know 'tis a maxim,
>   Our monarch *can never do wrong*,
> But as it is know he did *never*
>   For *his* people a praise-worthy thing,
> Wo'nt it open your eyes to discover,
>   That a LOG *is as good as a King?*

The ballad lamented the lives lost for the vanity of kings, pointed out the contradiction of George being both king of England and elector of Hanover, and voiced outrage over court opulence in such lean times.[42] Public sentiment soon shifted, however, as the invasion scare and dread of Bonaparte drew people together in defense of the nation. Anti-monarchicalism went underground with the republican movement.

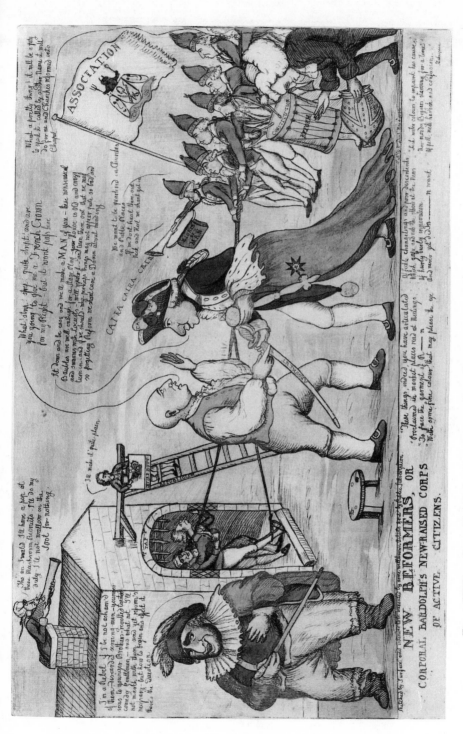

Fig. 9. William Dent, *New Reformers, or Corporal Bardolph's New-Raised Corps of Active Citizens*, 4 May 1794 (Yale Center for British Art, Paul Mellon Collection, B1981.25.1772)

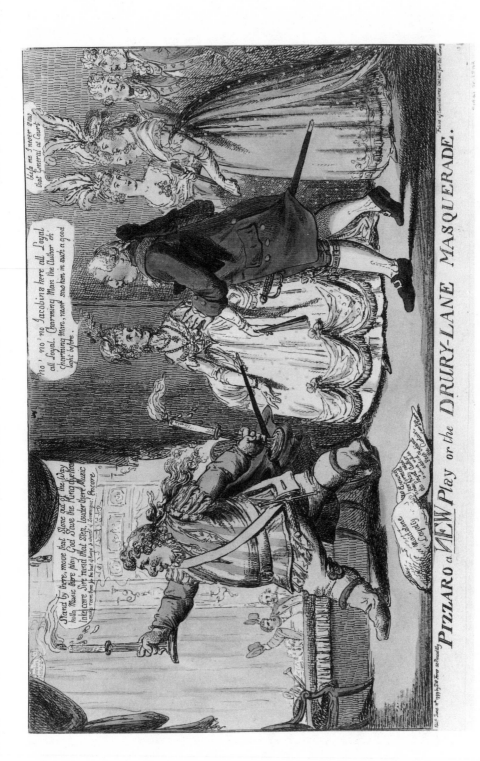

Fig. 10. Charles Ansell, *Pizarro, a New Play, or The Drury-Lane Masquerade*, 11 June 1799
(Yale Center for British Art, Paul Mellon Collection, B1981.25.1203)

The monarchy that emerged in the 1790s synthesized reformist and loyal-ist positions: it was a mix of formal patrician grandeur and informal republi-can accessibility. Yet the quirks of the king's personality shaped the monar-chy more than theories on his role and legitimacy. The force of the king's character, as well as the power of court culture, are captured in two prints that feature the king and Sheridan. A satire published by William Dent on the alliance between the Foxite Whigs and the reform societies shows Sheri-dan relieving George III of his crown, scepter, and royal robes (fig. 9). He ex-plains to the wigless, plainly dressed king that these are outdated baubles, use-ful only to theatrical performances. As Sheridan tells the king "we'll make a MAN of you," he is carelessly handling a sword labeled "argument" in such a way as to threaten him with emasculation. George, with one hand steadying the sword and the other held up in protest, bids him to stop: "A French Crown ... wont pass here." Indeed, he is correct.

A print attributed to Charles Ansell commemorates Sheridan's succumb-ing to the allure of loyalism (fig. 10). In this satire of the royal family's first visit to Sheridan's Drury Lane Theatre, lately cleansed of its Jacobin taint, the politician-playwright is dressed as the ultraloyalist hero of his play *Pizarro*. Brandishing a blazing candle in each hand, he is leading the royal family to their box, and barking orders at the band to play "God Save the King." The arch-Jacobin has been made sensible of the value of royal splendor, popular loyalism, and—more to the point—royal patronage.

Conclusion:
The Metaphor Called a Crown

𝒪𝒻 N a collection of essays on the phenomenon of "invented tradition" that focuses on the modern British monarchy, Eric Hobsbawm begins his introduction with the observation: "Nothing appears more ancient, and linked to an immemorial past, than the pageantry which surrounds the British monarchy in its public ceremonial manifestations. Yet . . . in its modern form it is the product of the late nineteenth and twentieth centuries." Later in the book, David Cannadine's study of the changing significance of royal ritual dates the tendency toward "invented tradition"—the presentation of recent innovation as venerable practice—to the 1870s. During the latter part of Victoria's reign, ritual became a function of royal weakness rather than a show of its potency. Cannadine believes that the waning practical power of the queen, in spite of her unflagging obstreperousness, allowed the development of an aggressive ceremonial grandeur. Because of her fierce moral rectitude, the longevity of her reign, and the perception that she had retired from active politics, Victoria was perceived as a grand matriarch. Her qualities would become important features of modern reigns. Cannadine dates the prototype of the modern British monarch to George V: "By allaying the private probity of his grandmother with the public grandeur of his father, [George V] created a synthesis which both his long-serving successors have emulated."[1]

Cannadine's timeframe requires some modification. As I have demonstrated, George III had already achieved the synthesis that Cannadine attributes to George V. The modern qualities of George's regnal style have been obscured, however, because they were immediately undermined by the fecklessness of his heirs. As Cannadine documents, royal ceremonies under George IV and William IV were inept and, on occasion, even sordid. Victoria's early attempts at ceremonial grandeur were little more successful; she gave up public appearances altogether after the death of her consort in 1861. The revival of republicanism and the importunings of Benjamin Disraeli eventually roused the queen from her melancholic isolation. Yet the resulting jubilees and other displays of what Cannadine considers royal jiggery-pokery had precedents in George III's reign. Elsewhere, Cannadine argues that George III may have anticipated Victoria, but the historical images of the king as lunatic and tyrant precluded his serving as a model for Victorian worship and emulation.[2]

Hobsbawm and Cannadine both argue that the falsehood at the center of invented tradition is the fictitious appearance of continuity. New ideas are given unearned respectability by their association with a tradition of dubious lineage. The fallacy at the center of the contemporary British monarchy is that its rituals represent centuries of unbroken tradition. This fallacy supports both the assumption that ceremony is an integral part of the institution and the inference that the British have a long-cultivated talent for royal ritual, the implication being that upholding this tradition is vital to the national heritage.[3]

My examination of the image and function of monarchy from the Stuart accession to the French Revolution shows that some adjustment of the invention-of-tradition thesis is in order. Seventeenth- and eighteenth-century monarchs refashioned established ideas, images, and institutions in order to give the impression of continuity during times of upheaval and to reinforce the legitimacy of their rule. James I, after all, tacked on the notion of inherited godliness to the venerable ideology of divine right in order to secure his hereditary claim. Anne donned Elizabethan attire to meet her first Parliament and then commandeered the image of the Protestant avenger. George III, with a veritable grab-bag of precedents at his disposal, made good use of Stuart pageantry and paternalism. George revived James I's rigid sense of duty to a particular code of monarchical behavior and Charles I's religiosity, attention to etiquette, artistic patronage, and encouragement of moral propriety at court. At the same time, George catered to the new middle-class interests through hard work, sobriety, and glorified domesticity.

These practices are something more than barefaced manipulation. I believe that it is the nature of monarchy to be constantly reinventing itself in order to adapt to changing political and social mores, while concurrently maintaining an appearance of coherence and consistency. After 1688 the monarch became the embodiment of the nation's history, and the past became an ever-living part of the present. Hence, breaks in the continuity of a royal ritual are superficial; the lessons and practices of the past may not be visible at a particular moment, but they maintain a continuous existence.

The invention of tradition is not a recent innovation, nor is it always done with a willful intent to deceive. Even ceremonial occasions that remain fairly constant in form are imprinted with each ruler's style and personality. Take the sovereign's birthday gala. Aside from minor variations in court dress, decorations, and banquet menu, it follows a fairly standard format: the royal family receives the compliments of the nobility, then they all participate in dinner and dancing. Yet the ritual varies in meaning from reign to reign. William III's discomfort and impatient pacing conveyed a very different impression from George II's calculated snubs and shows of condescension, and both were worlds apart from George III's indomitable efforts to provide confident displays of munificence in wartime. A certain degree of control and manipulation is always at work behind royal ceremonies, but a ritual sometimes takes on a life of its own. Additionally, historical precedent and custom impose constraints on the meanings that a propagandist can affix to a ritual, as chapter 7 demonstrates.

The same is true for the character and image of the monarchy. Every monarch is the product of historical evolution, the temper of the times, and the accident of personality. By the 1790s, George III had weathered a turbulent reign; questions about the right of representation left unanswered by the Revolution Settlement had generated challenges to his authority. His American subjects rejected his control completely, and politicians at home agitated for a more independent Parliament. Republican ideas of the seventeenth century reemerged in political discussions. The French Revolution then gave these ideas new and threatening connotations. In reaction, supporters of the political and social status quo developed their own theories of government to promote order and stability. The resulting debate produced a synthesis that endowed George with the best aspects of reformist and loyalist models of monarchy: an image of paternal authority coupled with republican devotion to the public good.

This synthesis was facilitated by chance events as well as by the king's public persona. During the political confrontations early in George's reign, the opposition christened the king an aspiring despot; this characterization expanded into a portrayal of George as a rapacious tyrant during the War for

American Independence. George's helplessness during his illness of 1788 effaced these earlier images. Moreover, the king had shown himself to be stolid, courageous, and beneficent in 1786, when he was confronted with the knife-brandishing Margaret Nicholson. This incident left a potent and enduring picture of good King George entreating the crowd: "The poor creature is mad! Do not hurt her! She has not hurt me!"[4] The king also provided his subjects with countless affecting images of a devoted patriarch; whenever he appeared in public he always seemed to have children in tow. Moreover, he allowed his subjects access to the royal family's domestic rituals: walks, gardening, visiting, swimming at Weymouth. Court functions became wholesome and family oriented.

This is not to say that George III and his family were above criticism. Until 1793 caricaturists often treated them with shocking disrespect. Artists depicted the king and queen indulging in a miserliness that verged on the pathological. Popular prints conveyed the impression that their Majesties were constantly preoccupied with hoarding riches for shipment to Hanover. Never known for mental dexterity but always famous for his folksy speech, the king commonly appeared in caricatures as a goggle-eyed country simpleton or an infatuated potentate. Whether the artists of these caricatures harbored a malicious intent is questionable. Apparently such satires were considered part of the royal lot: in fact, one of the few prints that offended the royal family was aimed at someone else. James Gillray's *Sin, Death, and the Devil,* which appeared shortly after the king's birthday in 1792, was intended to lampoon Henry Fuseli's illustrations of Milton. William Pitt, Lord Chancellor Edward Thurlow, and Queen Charlotte appeared representing characters from *Paradise Lost.* The queen, as Sin, is a grotesque, bare-breasted, snake-adorned harridan who is protecting Pitt, the figure of Death, from the Devil, Thurlow. It seems ironic that Gillray should produce such an offensive depiction of the queen when he intended pastiche rather than political attack: the idea that Pitt traded on the queen's influence was stale stuff, dating from the Regency Crisis.[5]

Criticism and ridicule ultimately strengthened, rather than undermined, the monarchy's position. The license with which satirists were able to treat the royal person actually helped create an image of a monarch who was endearing in his display of human foibles. George increasingly became identified with the bumbling, well-meaning John Bull. The predominant attitude of the prints shifted from hostility to good-natured amusement. The proliferation of friendly satire undermined the shock value of anti-monarchical attacks, and the wholesale acknowledgment of the king's faults preempted hostile disclosures.

George III responded to attempts at demystification of the monarchy by glorying in his humanity. At the same time he presented a kingly mien through court ritual and through his association with established institutions: the Anglican Church and the courts of law. Churchmen endowed the monarchy with a practical sanctity by stressing the virtue that the institution preserved. In the courts of law, Crown prosecutors gave the monarchy a protective sanctity as they enumerated the dangers that the reform movement posed to the king and hence to the nation.

By the end of the eighteenth century, the royal family was seen as possessing characteristics that are associated with the modern British monarchy. The king coexisted peacefully with the Commons, now considered the democratic, or potentially democratic, branch of the constitution. More important, the monarch's position as moral exemplar and arbiter of fashion and taste eclipsed his political role. The public became increasingly familiar with members of the royal family through prints, pamphlets, and newspapers. Familiarity bred affection. Instead of provoking a widespread republican movement, the gambling, wenching, and extravagant lifestyles of the royal princes increased support for George III. Royal virtues and vices alike provided moral edification. Fathers fed up with their errant sons—a substantial population, one supposes—could identify with the king's tribulations. Mothers concerned with keeping their daughters virtuous could hold up the example of the dutiful princesses. Royal scandals generated spicy newspaper copy and diverting caricatures. The monarchy had become a source of entertainment; it was a family drama with recognizable heroes and villains. Supporters of the French Revolution began the tradition of giving royal misbehavior added piquancy by responding to each incident with predictions that the royal family's scandalous behavior would soon bring down the whole monarchy. Then as now, however, every royal transgression carried with it the possibility of redemption.

It is in such paradoxes as these that the modern British monarchy's mystique and allure lie. The monarchy remains a fascinating conundrum as a firmly rooted, tradition-bound institution continually in flux. Portentous prognoses of the monarchy's imminent decline can spark a fear of loss that stimulates a renewed appreciation of the institution and its members. Resolutions of image-damaging scandals provide the pleasurable tension and release of a dramatic piece and ultimately reaffirm the perception of the royal family's fundamental goodness. The monarchy is contradictory in many senses. As I have demonstrated, George III's monarchy comprised antithetical elements. By the 1790s, the king was sufficiently idealized to allow clergymen to place him next to God and sufficiently earthy for caricaturists to place him on the privy. The monarchy developed a multifaceted character that gave it the potential to appeal to a wide range of groups, interests, and individuals. A neo-Filmerite of the 1790s could look at George III and see a semidivine bastion of church and state, while a member of the London Corresponding Society could see him as a potential ally in the fight for republican reform of the Commons against the corrupt practices of politicians.

The question of whether these qualities made George III different from Continental rulers is linked to the current historical debate on whether British society and government were as distinctive as eighteenth-century Englishmen liked to believe. To date, the answer seems to depend on what aspect of Britain one is examining. Jeremy Black, for instance, derides "the customary cliché of British history in this period—one of peace and stability, liberty and property, politeness and tolerance" in light of the government's brutal repression of the Highlands after the 1745 uprising. Gerald Newman points to a common aristocratic culture that Britain shared with the Continent. On the other hand, Gunther Lottes argues that the upheavals of the seventeenth century gave England a unique democratic tradition. Although English and French radical thought sprang from the same ideological sources, England had a more advanced system of representation and a longer tradition of popular participation in politics than did France. Moreover, Linda Colley's work suggests that eighteenth-century perceptions should not be discounted; a perceived "otherness" was instrumental in the formation of a British national consciousness.[6]

In contrast, J. C. D. Clark believes that eighteenth-century British monarchs behaved much like their Continental counterparts. But how similar were Continental rulers themselves in their power, activities, and ruling style? Scholars are beginning to call into question the convenient traditional categorization of seventeenth- and eighteenth-century monarchs as "absolutists" and "enlightened absolutists." Black, a supporter of the paradigm of Britain as an ancien régime state, concludes his *British Foreign Policy in an Age of Revolutions* by reasoning: "The very variety of *ancien régime* political culture can be emphasised.... It then becomes more pertinent to discuss Britain as an instance of an *ancien régime* political system, while accepting that, as in the other cases of such societies, their common characteristics were matched by distinct individual features."[7]

To determine the relative significance of these similarities and differences would require a detailed and systematic analysis of the various regimes. How was each ruler treated in political propaganda and the popular press? What degree of support did each ruler derive from other institutions, such as the aristocracy, the Church, the legal system, and the deliberative and representative bodies? What was the nature of the monarch's relationship with the ruling elite? Do minutes from cabinet meetings and correspondence with provincial leaders and diplomats indicate deference, contention, or reasoned deliberation?

My study of the early modern British monarchy shows the institution to be a continually changing mixture of tradition and innovation. It is sometimes difficult to separate the permanent institutional features of each regime from temporary idiosyncrasies resulting from the personality of the ruler and the country's economic and diplomatic situation. War and the state of the treasury both create and limit opportunities for the exercise of monarchical power—chance and circumstance probably have as much impact upon regnal style as the state's institutional framework.

An impressionistic comparison of George III with his Continental counterparts leads me to believe that George did, in fact, differ significantly from them. The peculiarities of the king and his position come across in one of the many anecdotes in circulation concerning George's casual encounters with his subjects. The king paid an early-morning visit to a Windsor bookshop he liked to frequent. By the time the proprietor had awakened, dressed, and gone downstairs, he found George engrossed in a book. To the bookseller's horror, that book was Paine's *Rights of Man*. The man bustled about the shop hoping to divert the king's attention, but to no avail. Finally, George put down the book, looked up, and engaged the shopkeeper in one of their usual convivial chats. Afterward, the bookseller picked up the volume to see where the king had stopped reading—it was the passage in which Paine said that the king had not sufficient capacity to make a parish constable.[8] The story is probably apocryphal, but, nonetheless, one has difficulty imagining it being told about Catherine the Great of Russia or even the more libertarian Joseph II of Austria.

Notes

Introduction

1. Thomas Paine, *Rights of Man* (2 vols., London, 1791–92), 1:130, 2:38, 70.

2. Walter Bagehot, *The English Constitution* (New York, 1966), 82–97.

3. John Cannon, "The Survival of the British Monarchy," the Prothero Lecture, read 3 July 1985, *Transactions of the Royal Historical Society* 36 (1986): 143–64.

4. Ernest Kantorowicz, *The King's Two Bodies: A Study in Medieval Political Theology* (Princeton, 1957).

5. Tom Nairn, *The Enchanted Glass: Britain and Its Monarchy* (London, 1988), 27–29, 59–60, 126, 146–47, 294.

6. Ibid., 9–10, 89, 155, 277–78, 361–70.

7. Edward Shils and Michael Young, "The Meaning of the Coronation," *Sociological Review*, n.s. 1 (Dec. 1953): 63–81.

8. J. G. Blumer, J. R. Brown, A. J. Ewbank, and T. J. Nossiter, "Attitudes to the Monarchy: Their Structure and Development During a Ceremonial Occasion," *Political Studies* 29 (June 1971): 149–71.

9. Norman Birnbaum, "Monarchs and Sociologists: A Reply to Professor Shils and Mr. Young," *Sociological Review*, n.s. 3 (July 1955): 1–23.

10. Richard Rose and Dennis Kavanagh, "The Monarchy in Contemporary Political Culture," *Comparative Politics* 8 (July 1976): 548–76.

11. Richard H. Gretton, *The King's Majesty: A Study in the Historical Philosophy of Modern Kingship* (London, 1930), 10–32, 178–91.

12. Ernest Jones, "The Psychology of Constitutional Monarchy," *New Statesman and Nation* 11 (1 Feb. 1936): 141–42.

13. Cannon, loc. cit.

14. John Cannon and Ralph Griffiths, *The Oxford Illustrated History of the British Monarchy* (Oxford, 1988), vii; Nairn, 236; William M. Kuhn, "Ceremony and Politics: The

Management of British Royal Ceremonial 1861–1911" (Ph.D. diss., Johns Hopkins University, 1989); see David Cannadine, "The Context, Performance and Meaning of Ritual: The British Monarchy and the 'Invention of Tradition,' c. 1820–1977," in *The Invention of Tradition,* ed. Eric Hobsbawm and Terrence Ranger (Cambridge, 1983), 101–64.

15. Nairn, 22, 28, 43–59, 79, 198–202.

16. Clifford Geertz, "Centers, Kings, and Charisma: Reflections on the Symbolics of Power," in *Culture and Its Creators. Essays in Honor of Edward Shils,* ed. Joseph Ben-David and Terry Nichols Clark (Chicago, 1977), 150–71.

17. David Cannadine and Simon Price, eds., *Rituals of Royalty: Power and Ceremonial in Traditional Societies* (Cambridge, 1987); William M. Kuhn, "Ceremony and Politics: The British Monarchy, 1871–1872," *Journal of British Studies* 26 (1987): 133–62.

18. Cynthia Herrup, "Beyond Personality and Pomp: Recent Works on Early Modern Monarchies," *Journal of British Studies* 28 (1989): 175.

19. Antonio Gramsci, *Selections from the Prison Notebooks,* ed. and trans. Quintin Hoare and Geoffrey Nowell Smith (London, 1971), 269; see also Joseph V. Femia, *Gramsci's Political Thought: Hegemony, Consciousness and the Revolutionary Process* (Oxford, 1981), 23–29, 35–50; Carl Boggs, *Gramsci's Marxism* (London, 1976), 17–18, 36–40.

20. Steve Lohr, "Getting the Royal Treatment, Tabloid Style," *New York Times,* 5 May 1991, 4:4.

21. Bagehot, loc. cit.

22. Edmund Burke, *Reflections on the Revolution in France* (London, 1790), 114.

Chapter 1: History and Legitimacy

1. Paul Kléber Monod, *Jacobitism and the English People, 1688–1788* (Cambridge, 1989), 44. A journalist who was assigned in 1992 to obtain an official pronouncement on the current monarchy's source of legitimacy and the limitations of its powers came up empty-handed. David Cannadine's comments on this occasion are in keeping with Monod's assessment: Peter Lennon, "Queen by Our Grace and Favour," *Guardian,* 29 June 1992, 21.

2. John Neville Figgis, *The Divine Right of Kings* (Cambridge, 1922), chaps. 1–3.

3. Fritz Kern, *Kingship and Law in the Middle Ages,* trans. S. B. Chrimes (Oxford, 1939), 69–133; J. P. Sommerville, *Politics and Ideology in England, 1603–1640* (London, 1986), chaps. 1–2.

4. Christopher Haigh, "Introduction," in *The Reign of Elizabeth I* (Athens, Ga., 1985), 1–25.

5. Roger Lockyer, *The Early Stuarts: A Political History of England, 1603–1642* (London, 1989), 36–37; Jenny Wormald, "James VI and I, *Basilikon Doron* and the *Trew Law of Free Monarchies:* The Scottish Context and the English Translation," in *The Mental World of the Jacobean Court,* ed. Linda Levy Peck (Cambridge, 1991), 36–37, 43.

6. James H. Burns, "The Idea of Absolutism," in *Absolutism in Seventeenth-Century Europe,* ed. John Miller (New York, 1990), 31; Michael Walzer, *Regicide and Revolution: Speeches at the Trial of Louis XVI,* trans. Marian Rothstein (Cambridge, 1974), 16.

7. Figgis, 81–89; Joel Hurstfield, "The Succession Struggle in Late Elizabethan Eng-

land," in *Freedom, Corruption and Government in Elizabethan England* (Cambridge, Mass., 1973), 104–34.

8. See Wormald; J. P. Sommerville, "James I and the Divine Right of Kings: English Politics and Continental Theory," and Paul Christianson, "Royal and Parliamentary Voices on the Ancient Constitution c. 1604–1621," in Peck, *Mental World, 36*–95.

9. King James I, *The Trew Law of Free Monarchies: Or the Reciprock and Mutuall Dutie Betwixt a Free King, and His Naturall Subjects,* in King James I, *The Workes* (London, 1616), 193–95, 201–8.

10. Barry Coward, *The Stuart Age* (London, 1980), 114–29.

11. J. P. Kenyon, *The Stuart Constitution, 1603–1688,* 2d ed. (Cambridge, 1986), 22–23.

12. J. G. A. Pocock, *The Ancient Constitution and the Feudal Law* (Cambridge, 1987), chap. 2; Sommerville, *Politics and Ideology,* chap. 3.

13. Maurice Lee, Jr., *Great Britain's Solomon: James VI and I in His Three Kingdoms* (Urbana, 1991); Kenneth Fincham and Peter Lake, "The Ecclesiastical Policy of King James I," *Journal of British Studies* 24 (1985): 169–207. In emphasizing the Continental influence on absolutist ideology in England and its clash with traditional English constitutionalism, I fall in with the postrevisionist interpretation of the seventeenth century; see Johann P. Sommerville, "English and European Political Ideas in the Early Seventeenth Century: Revisionism and the Case of Absolutism," *Journal of British Studies* 35 (1996), 168–94.

14. Kevin Sharpe, *The Personal Rule of Charles I* (New Haven, 1992), 56–59, 97–130, chaps. 5–7; Kenyon, 28–29, 51–54, 175–76, quote on p. 175.

15. See Conrad Russell, *The Fall of the British Monarchies, 1637–1642* (Oxford, 1991), chap. 2.

16. Kenyon, 180–83, 222–26.

17. See the excerpt of *His Majesties Answer* printed in Corinne Comstock Weston, *English Constitutional Theory and the House of Lords, 1556–1832* (New York, 1965), 261–65.

18. Pocock, 308–12, quote on 310.

19. Ibid., 310.

20. Michael Mendle, *Dangerous Positions: Mixed Government, the Estates of the Realm, and the Making of the Answer to the XIX Propositions* (University, Ala., 1985), 10, 18, passim; J. G. A. Pocock, *The Machiavellian Moment: Florentine Political Thought and the Atlantic Republican Tradition* (Princeton, 1975), 333–66.

21. See Weston, chaps. 1–3; Weston and Janelle Renfrow Greenberg, *Subjects and Sovereigns: The Grand Controversy over Legal Sovereignty in Stuart England* (Cambridge, 1981).

22. Walzer, 51; see also 2–3, 35–37, 42–47, 53; F. D. Dow, *Radicalism in the English Revolution, 1640–1660* (Oxford, 1985), 14–20.

23. Walzer, 4–5; C. V. Wedgwood, "The Trial of Charles I," in *The English Civil War and After, 1642–1658,* ed. R. H. Parry (Berkeley, 1970), 41–58; Helen W. Randall, "The Rise and Fall of Martyrology: Sermons on Charles I," *Huntington Library Quarterly* 10 (1947): 135–67.

24. See Barry Coward, *Cromwell* (London, 1991).

25. John Miller, "The Later Stuart Monarchy," in *The Restored Monarchy, 1660–1688* ed. J. R. Jones (Totowa, N.J., 1979), 31–32.

26. Kenyon, 331–32.

27. Lawrence Stone, "The Results of the English Revolutions of the Seventeenth Century," in *Three British Revolutions: 1641, 1688, 1776,* ed. J. G. A. Pocock (Princeton, 1980), 50–51.

28. Coward, *Stuart Age,* 242.

29. See Ronald Hutton, *The Restoration: A Political and Religious History of England and Wales, 1658–1667* (Oxford, 1985), 3–126.

30. K. H. D. Haley, *Politics in the Reign of Charles II* (Oxford, 1985), 10–13; J. R. Jones, *Charles II: Royal Politician* (London, 1987), 43–62, 88–91; Paul Seaward, *The Restoration, 1660–1688* (New York, 1991), chaps. 3–4.

31. Seaward, chap. 5; Jones, chaps. 8–9.

32. Robert Filmer, *The Anarchy of a Limited or Mixed Monarchy . . . ,* in *Patriarcha and Other Writings,* ed. Johann P. Sommerville (Cambridge, 1991), 132. In this paragraph I also draw upon Sommerville's introductory analysis, as well as on Perez Zagorin, *A History of Political Thought in the English Revolution* (London, 1954), chap. 12, and James Daly, *Sir Robert Filmer and English Political Thought* (Toronto, 1979).

33. David Ogg, *England in the Reign of Charles II* (2 vols., Oxford, 1934), 2:641–51.

34. John Dunn, "The Politics of Locke in England and America in the Eighteenth Century," in *John Locke: Problems and Perspectives,* ed. John Yolton (Cambridge, 1969), 68.

35. Dunn, 45–80; see also Caroline Robbins, *The Eighteenth Century Commonwealthman* (Cambridge, Mass., 1959), 58–67.

36. Maurice Ashley, *James II* (Minneapolis, 1977), 9–10, 111; Seaward, 123–33; Kenyon, 376–78.

37. W. A. Speck, *Reluctant Revolutionaries: Englishmen and the Revolution of 1688* (Oxford, 1988); John Childs, "1688," *History* 73 (1988): 398–424; Childs, *The Army, James II, and the Glorious Revolution* (New York, 1980), 187–89; John Miller, "Crown, Parliament, and People," in *Liberty Secured? Britain Before and After 1688,* ed. J. R. Jones (Stanford, 1992), 53–87.

38. Lois G. Schwoerer, *The Declaration of Rights, 1689* (Baltimore, 1981), 284 and passim; H. T. Dickinson, "How Revolutionary Was the 'Glorious Revolution' of 1688?" *British Journal for Eighteenth-Century Studies* 11 (1988): 125–42; Dickinson, "The Eighteenth-Century Debate on the Glorious Revolution," *History* 61 (1976): 28–45; Kathleen Wilson, "Inventing Revolution: 1688 and Eighteenth-Century Popular Politics," *Journal of British Studies* 28 (1989): 349–86.

39. Lois Schwoerer, "The Glorious Revolution as Spectacle: A New Perspective," in *England's Rise to Greatness, 1661–1763,* ed. Stephen B. Baxter (Berkeley, 1983), 109–49.

40. J. R. Western, *Monarchy and Revolution: The English State in the 1680s* (Totowa, N.J., 1972), chap. 9; Stephen B. Baxter, *William III* (London, 1966), 333–34; Jennifer Carter, "The Revolution and the Constitution," in Geoffrey Holmes, ed., *Britain After the Glorious Revolution* (London, 1969), 39–58.

41. J. C. D. Clark, *Revolution and Rebellion: State and Society in England in the Seventeenth and Eighteenth Century* (Cambridge, 1986), chap. 5.

42. John Brewer, *The Sinews of Power: War, Money and the English State, 1688–1783* (New York, 1989), chap. 5.

43. See Clayton Roberts, "Party and Patronage in Later Stuart England," in Baxter, *England's Rise,* 185–212; Clayton Roberts, "Political Stability Reconsidered," Stephen B. Baxter, "A Comment on Clayton Roberts' Perspective," and Norma Landau, "Country Matters: The Growth of Political Stability a Quarter Century On," *Albion* 25 (1993): 237–74.

44. E. L. Ellis, "William III and the Politicians," in *Britain after the Glorious Revolution,* ed. Geoffrey Holmes (London, 1969), 118; Vincent Carretta, *George III and the Satirists, from Hogarth to Byron* (Athens, Ga., 1990), 1.

45. Baxter, *William III,* 274, 333, 358–59, 370; Western, 328–29, 342–43, 399–400; Jones, "The Revolution in Context," in *Liberty Secured?* 33–34.

46. Edward Gregg, *Queen Anne* (London, 1980), 135–36, 144, 147–49, 152, 165; Geoffrey Holmes, *British Politics in the Age of Anne,* rev. ed. (London, 1987), 187–93, 200, 210–15, 414.

47. Geoffrey Holmes defends the Whigs' decision to impeach the parson: *The Trial of Doctor Sacheverell* (London, 1973), 78–80. I have based my account of the contents of Sacheverell's sermon and the arguments presented during the trial upon this work and on G. V. Bennett, *The Tory Crisis in Church and State, 1688–1730: The Career of Francis Atterbury, Bishop of Rochester* (Oxford, 1975), chap. 6.

48. Ragnhild Hatton, *George I, Elector and King* (Cambridge, Mass., 1978), 16–23.

49. Nicholas Rogers, "Popular Protest in Early Hanoverian London," *Past and Present* 79 (1978): 83.

50. Nicholas Rogers, *Whigs and Cities: Popular Politics in the Age of Walpole and Pitt* (Oxford, 1989), 5, 25, 166, 366–72; Monod, 43, 173–94; Colin Haydon, *Anti-Catholicism in Eighteenth-Century England: A Political and Social Study* (Manchester, 1993), 101–2.

51. Monod, chaps. 2–3.

52. Ibid., 4–7; Hatton, 174–77; Linda Colley, *Britons: Forging the Nation, 1707–1837* (New Haven, 1992), 73–79; Colley, *In Defiance of Oligarchy: The Tory Party, 1714–60* (Cambridge, 1982), 29–50; Haydon, 130–31.

53. Hatton, 145–56, 183–87; John Beattie, *The English Court in the Reign of George I* (Cambridge, 1967), chap. 4.

54. John B. Owen, "George II Reconsidered," in *Statesmen, Scholars and Merchants: Essays in Eighteenth-Century History Presented to Dame Lucy Sutherland,* ed. Anne Whiteman, J. S. Bromley, and P. G. M. Dickson (Oxford, 1973), 113–34; Jeremy Black, "George II Reconsidered," *Mitteilungen des Österreichischen Staatsarchivs* 35 (1982): 35–56; Eveline Cruickshanks, "The Political Management of Sir Robert Walpole, 1720–42," in *Britain in the Age of Walpole,* ed. Jeremy Black (New York, 1984), 23–43; H. T. Dickinson, *Walpole and the Whig Supremacy* (London, 1973), chap. 5.

55. Carretta, 10–40; Bertrand A. Goldgar, *Walpole and the Wits: A Relation of Politics to Literatures, 1722–1742* (Lincoln, Neb., 1976); Alexander Pettit, "The Francis Hare Controversy of 1732," *British Journal for Eighteenth-Century Studies* 17 (1994): 41–53.

56. Thomas Horne, "Politics in a Corrupt Society: William Arnall's Defense of Robert Walpole," *Journal of the History of Ideas* 41 (1980): 601–14.

57. Colley, *Defiance,* 116; Isaac Kramnick, *Bolingbroke and His Circle: The Politics of Nostalgia in the Age of Walpole* (Cambridge, Mass., 1968), 33–38, 90–110; Simon Varey, *Henry St. John, Viscount Bolingbroke* (Boston, 1984), 98–101; H. T. Dickinson, *Bolingbroke* (London, 1970), 259–67.

58. H. T. Dickinson, *Liberty and Property* (London, 1977), 169 and chaps. 3–5.

59. Kramnick, 99; Kramnick, "Augustan Politics and English Historiography: The Debate on the English Past, 1730–35," *History and Theory* 6 (1967): 33–56.

60. Frank McLynn, *The Jacobites* (London, 1985), 29 and passim; Colley, *Britons,* 202.

61. Gerald Newman, *The Rise of English Nationalism: A Cultural History, 1740–1830* (New York, 1987), chaps. 1–6; Rogers, *Whigs and Cities,* chap. 10.

62. Stanley Ayling, *George the Third* (New York, 1972), 66–70.

63. Newman, 175.

64. I. R. Christie, "George III and the Historians—Thirty Years On," *History* 71 (1986): 205–21; Owen, "George II," passim.

65. G. A. Cranfield, *The Press and Society from Caxton to Northcliffe* (London, 1978), 58–69.

66. John Brooke, *King George III* (London, 1972), 221, 239–40, 250–59; Linda Colley, "The Apotheosis of George III: Loyalty, Royalty and the British Nation, 1760–1820," *Past and Present* 102 (1984): 94–129; Colley, *Britons,* chap. 5.

67. B. W. Hill, "Executive Monarchy and the Challenge of Parties, 1689–1832: Two Concepts of Government and Two Historiographical Interpretations," *Historical Journal* 13 (1970): 379.

68. Henry Horwitz, "Liberty, Law, and Property, 1689–1776," in Jones, *Liberty Secured?* 278.

Chapter 2: The Burke-Paine Controversy

1. Linda Colley, "The Apotheosis of George III: Loyalty, Royalty and the British Nation, 1760–1820," *Past and Present* 102 (1984): 102–6; see also John Brooke, *King George III* (London, 1972), 10–12, 314–17, and chap. 8.

2. Robert Hole, *Pulpits, Politics and Public Order in England, 1760–1832* (Cambridge, 1989), 14–21, 60–62, 125.

3. Albert Goodwin, *The Friends of Liberty: The English Democratic Movement in the Age of the French Revolution* (Cambridge, Mass., 1979), 70–71; Isaac Kramnick, "Religion and Radicalism: English Political Theory in the Age of Revolution," *Political Theory* 5 (1977): 506–34.

4. Goodwin, 41–57; Martin Fitzpatrick, "Heretical Religion and Radical Political Ideas in Late Eighteenth-Century England," in *The Transformation of Political Culture: England and Germany in the Late Eighteenth Century,* ed. Eckhart Hellmuth (Oxford, 1990), 339–72.

5. Goodwin, 72–79.

6. Debate, 2 March 1790, *The Parliamentary History of England, from the Earliest Period to the Year 1803,* ed. William Cobbett (36 vols., London, 1806–20) (hereafter *Parl. Hist.*), 28:392–95, 407–11; Norman Sykes observes that Pitt's view was little different from the classic position presented by William Warburton in *The Alliance Between Church and State* (1736): *Church and State in England in the Eighteenth Century* (Cambridge, 1934), 316–25.

7. Quoted in Richard W. Davis, *Dissent in Politics, 1780–1830: The Political Life of*

William Smith, MP (London, 1971), 38; see also John Brooke, *King George III* (London, 1972), 260–62.

8. George III to John Moore, archbishop of Canterbury. 16? March 1795, *The Later Correspondence of George III*, ed. Arthur Aspinall (5 vols., Cambridge, 1962–70), 2:321.

9. Richard Price, *A Discourse on the Love of Our Country, Delivered on Nov. 4, 1789 at the Meeting-House in the Old Jewry, to the Society for Commemorating the Revolution in Great Britain . . .* (London, 1789), 22–23.

10. Ibid., 23–24.

11. D. O. Thomas, *The Honest Mind: The Thought and Work of Richard Price* (Oxford, 1977), 189–93.

12. Price, 34, 49–51.

13. Frank O'Gorman, *Edmund Burke: His Political Philosophy* (Bloomington, 1973), 11–17, 146–47; Frederick Dreyer, *Burke's Politics: A Study in Whig Orthodoxy* (Waterloo, Ont., 1979), 1–5.

14. F. P. Lock, *Burke's Reflections on the Revolution in France* (London, 1985), 25–26; Michael Freeman, *Edmund Burke and the Critique of Political Radicalism* (Chicago, 1980), 128–29.

15. R. R. Fennessy, *Burke, Paine and the Rights of Man* (The Hague, 1963), 88–91.

16. Edmund Burke, *Reflections on the Revolution in France* (London, 1790), 41–43.

17. Thomas, 311–12; O'Gorman, 64–65; Lock, 43.

18. Debate, 11 May 1792, *Parl. Hist.*, 29:1374. For the relationship between Burke and Fox, see Conor Cruise O'Brien, *The Great Melody: A Thematic Biography and Commended Anthology of Edmund Burke* (Chicago, 1992), 414–31; Loren Reid, *Charles James Fox: A Man for the People* (Columbia, Mo., 1969), 269–71.

19. *Parl. Hist.*, 29:1383–84.

20. Ursula Henriques, *Religious Toleration in England, 1787–1833* (London, 1961), 134.

21. Burke, 112–13.

22. Ibid., 114; James Boulton, *The Language of Politics in the Age of Wilkes and Burke* (London, 1963), 97–132.

23. Dreyer, 33–36.

24. Lock, 13–14; Freeman, 28–29.

25. Burke, 34; see also 21–27, 38–39.

26. Ibid., 184.

27. Ibid., 288–95.

28. Fennessy, 10–11, 19–21, 39, 45–47, 103–4, 160–64.

29. Thomas Paine, *Rights of Man* (2 vols., London, 1791–92), 1:117–18, 152; vol. 2, chap. 3, quotes on 2:23–24.

30. For the Norman-yoke theory, see Christopher Hill, *Puritanism and Revolution: Studies in Interpretation of the English Revolution of the 17th Century* (New York, 1958), chap. 3.

31. Paine, 1:120, 63–66, 80–82.

32. Ibid., 2:52; 1:124–29.

33. Ibid., 2:15–16.

34. Ibid., 1:131; 2:119–20, 101, 54.

35. Ibid., 1:62–64, 153–54; 2:4.

36. Ibid., 1:17-19; 2:66-67n.

37. Thomas Paine, *Reasons for Wishing to Preserve the Life of Louis Capet. As Delivered to the National Convention* (London, n.d.), 5, 9-11, 16.

38. John Jones, *The Reason of Man Against the Rights of Man* (2 vols., Canterbury, 1793), 2:18.

39. Paine, *Rights of Man,* 1:123-24, 133-34; 2:vi, 56.

40. Fennessy, 12-13.

41. Paine, *Rights of Man,* 1:51.

42. See especially O'Brien, 402-3, 436-39, 464-66.

Chapter 3: Recasting the Ideological Foundations of the British Monarchy

1. Donald Ginter, "The Loyalist Association Movement of 1792-93 and British Public Opinion," *Historical Journal* 9 (1966): 179-90; J. C. D. Clark, *English Society 1688-1832* (Cambridge, 1985); J. A. W. Gunn, *Beyond Liberty and Property: The Process of Self-Recognition in Eighteenth-Century Political Thought* (Montreal, 1983), chap. 4; Joanna Innes, "Jonathan Clark, Social History, and England's 'Ancien Regime,'" *Past and Present* 115 (1987): 191.

2. H. T. Dickinson, *Liberty and Property: Political Ideology in Eighteenth-Century Britain* (London, 1977), chap. 8; Gunn, 121; John Dinwiddy, "Interpretations of Anti-Jacobitism," and David Eastwood, "Patriotism and the English State in the 1790s," in *The French Revolution and British Popular Politics,* ed. Mark Philp (Cambridge, 1991), 38-49, 160-61. Dickinson reinforces his view in subsequent publications: *British Radicalism and the French Revolution, 1789-1815* (London, 1985), 25-42; *Britain and the French Revolution* (Basingstoke, 1989), 103-25; "Popular Loyalism in Britain in the 1790s," in *The Transformation of Political Culture: England and Germany in the Late Eighteenth Century,* ed. Eckhart Hellmuth (Oxford, 1990), 503-33.

3. R. R. Fennessy, *Burke, Paine and the Rights of Man* (The Hague, 1963), vii, 213-14, 220; Strother B. Purdy, "A Note on the Burke-Paine Controversy," *American Literature* 39 (1967): 373-75; Albert Goodwin, *The Friends of Liberty: The English Democratic Movement in the Age of the French Revolution* (Cambridge, Mass., 1979), 132-33.

4. Robert Hole, "British Counter-Revolutionary Popular Propaganda in the 1790s," in *Britain and Revolutionary France: Conflict, Subversion and Propaganda,* ed. Colin Jones (Exeter, 1983), 53-69.

5. R. R. Dozier, *For King, Constitution and Country: The English Loyalists and the French Revolution* (Lexington, Ky., 1983), 55-78.

6. Eugene Charleton Black, *The Association: British Extraparliamentary Political Organization, 1769-1793* (Cambridge, Mass., 1963), 234-36; M. J. Quinlan, "Anti-Jacobin Propaganda in England, 1792-94," *Journalism Quarterly* 16 (1939): 14-15; Henry R. Winkler, "The Pamphlet Campaign Against Political Reform in Great Britain, 1790-1795," *Historian* 15 (1952): 32-33; Austin Mitchell, "The Association Movement of 1792-1793," *Historical Journal* 4 (1961): 59; Dickinson, "Popular Loyalism," 517.

7. Thomas Paine, *Rights of Man* (2 vols., London, 1791-92), 1:135; Francis Oldys

[George Chalmers], *The Life of Thomas Pain, with a Review of his Writings, Particularly Rights of Man, Parts First and Second* (10th ed., London, 1793, orig. pub. 1791); A. O. Aldridge, *Man of Reason: The Life of Thomas Paine* (New York, 1959), 9; Moncure Daniel Conway, *The Life of Thomas Paine* (London, 1892), xii; Entry for George Chalmers in Leslie Stephen and Sidney Lee, eds., *Dictionary of National Biography* (21 vols., London, 1882–1900; hereafter *DNB*).

8. For St. John, Hervey, and Hey see *DNB*. Tobias Molloy, *An Appeal from Men in a State of Civil Society to Man in a State of Nature* . . . (Dublin, 1792), 246. For Bowles and Gifford see *DNB* and Emily Lorraine de Montluzin, *The Anti-Jacobins, 1798–1800: The Early Contributors to the Anti-Jacobin Review* (New York, 1988), 67–68, 93–96.

9. For Smith see Fennessy, 213. For Hunt and Elliott see *DNB*. For the Adams pamphlet see Conway, 119–20.

10. For Boothby, see *DNB*; John King, *Mr. King's Speech at Egham, with Thomas Paine's Letter to him on it, and Mr. King's Reply, as they all Appeared in the Morning Herald: . . . Tenth Edition with Addition of Mr King's Second Letter from the Herald, February 22, 1793* (Egham, 1793), and *Third Letter from Mr. King to Mr. Thomas Paine at Paris, as Published in the Morning Herald of April 17, 1793* (Egham, 1793).

11. Winkler, 24.

12. [John St. John], *A Letter from a Magistrate to Mr. William Rose, of Whitehall, on Mr. Paine's Rights of Man* (London, 1791), 68–69. For a detailed analysis of the anti-Paine pamphlets see my "The Monarchy as an Issue in English Political Argument in the Decade of the French Revolution" (Ph.D. diss., University of London, 1988), chap. 2. For a more comprehensive survey of conservative writings of the 1790s, see Gayle Trusdel Pendleton, "English Conservative Propaganda During the French Revolution, 1789–1802" (Ph.D. diss., Emory University, 1976). I am grateful to Dr. Pendleton for furnishing me with information on conservative pamphlets that contained significant material on the issue of monarchy.

13. *The Interests of Man in Opposition to the Rights of Man: Or, an Inquiry into the Consequences of Certain Political Doctrines Lately Disseminated* (Edinburgh, 1793), 20.

14. John Bowles, *A Protest Against T. Paine's Rights of Man Addressed to the Members of a Book Society* . . . (London, 1792), 30; see also Brooke Boothby, *Observations on the Appeal from the New to the Old Whigs and on Mr. Paine's Rights of Man. In Two Parts* (London, 1792), 155; *The Civil and Ecclesiastical Systems of England Defended and Fortified* (London, 1791), 33; *Remarks on Mr. Paine's Pamphlet, Called Rights of Man. In a Letter to a Friend* (Dublin, 1791), 39–43.

15. *Remarks*, 35; Thomas Hardy, *The Patriot. Addressed to the People, on the Present State of Affairs in Britain and in France. With Observations on Republican Government, and Discussion of the Principles Advanced in the Writings of Thomas Paine* (Edinburgh, 1793), 6.

16. *Considerations of Mr. Paine's Pamphlet on the Rights of Man* (Edinburgh, 1791), 46–47.

17. Charles Hawtrey, *Various Opinions of the Philosophical Reformers Considered; Particularly Pain's Rights of Man* (London, 1792), 34; [William Cusac Smith], *Rights of Citizens; Being an Inquiry into some of the Consequences of Social Union, and an Examination of Mr. Paine's Principles Touching Government* (London, 1791), 116.

18. *A Defence of the Rights of Man; Being a Discussion of the Conclusions Drawn from those Rights by Mr. Paine* (London, 1791), 15; see also [Gilbert Francklyn], *A Candid Inquiry into the Nature of Government, and the Right of Representation* (London, 1792), 34; Charles Harrington Elliot, *The Republican Refuted; In a Series of Biographical, Critical, and Political Strictures on Thomas Paine's Rights of Man* (London, 1791), 57; [St. John], 69; "An Oxford Graduate," *A Rod in Brine, or A Tickler for Tom Paine, in Answer to his First Pamphlet, Entitled the Rights of Man* (Canterbury, 1792), 57; Hawtrey, 69; *An Humble Address to the Most High, Most Mighty, and Most Puissant, the Sovereign People* (London, 1793), 7; *A Defence of the Constitution of England against the Libels that have Lately been Published on it; Particularly in Paine's Rights of Man* (London, 1791), 52.

19. "Let every soul be subject unto the higher powers. For there is no power but of God: the powers that be are ordained by God. Whosoever therefore resisteth the power, resisteth the ordinance of God: and they that resist shall receive to themselves damnation" (King James Version); John Riland, *The Rights of God, Occasioned by Mr. Paine's "Rights of Man" and his Other Publications* ... (Birmingham, 1792), 6.

20. "A Chaplain of the Navy," *Letters to a Friend on the Test Laws, Containing Reasons for Not Repealing them, and ... Strictures on Mr. Paine's Rights of Man* (London, 1791), 164-72.

21. See note 12.

22. William Lewelyn, *An Appeal to Man against Paine's Rights of Man* (2 vols., Leominster, 1793), 2:7.

23. James Brown, *The Importance of Preserving Unviolated the Systems of Civil Government in Every State: With the Dreadful Consequences of the Violation of it. To which is Added, an Appendix, Containing some Strictures on the Writings of Mr. Paine* (London, 1793), 7-8.

24. [Chalmers], 120-21.

25. John Gifford, *A Plain Address to the Common Sense of the People of England. Containing an Interesting Abstract of Pain's Life and Writings* (London, 1792), 35.

26. Richard Hey, *Happiness and Rights. A Dissertation upon Several Subjects Relative to the Rights of Man and his Happiness* (York, 1792), 181.

27. Molloy, quote on 172, biblical commentary on 71-72, 153-57, 165-69, 239-43.

28. [St. John], 67-68; see also Boothby, 275-76; Hardy, 61; Isaac Hunt, *Rights of Englishmen. An Antidote to the Poison Now Vending by the Transatlantic Republican Thomas Paine* ... (London, 1791), 30; *An Address to the Inhabitants of Great Britain and Ireland; In Reply to the Principles of the Author of the Rights of Man* (London, 1793), 43.

29. Elliot, 25; Bowles, 18; Lewelyn, 1:25; [Frederick Hervey], *An Answer to the Second Part of Rights of Man. In Two Letters to the Author* (London, 1792), 13; [David Rivers], *Cursory Remarks on Paine's Rights of Man* (London, 1792), 19.

30. *Considerations,* 76; see also Hunt, 44-45; *Interests,* 39-40; [Smith], 116-17. Frederick Hervey, *A New Friend on an Old Subject* (London, 1791), 20.

31. Hardy, 69-71; *Interests of Man,* 50.

32. [St. John], 84-94.

33. *Remarks,* 73-74; for the wider debate on influence, see J. A. W. Gunn, "Influence, Parties and the Constitution: Changing Attitudes, 1783-1832," *Historical Journal* 17 (1974): 301-28.

34. Hawtrey, 27–30, 43–44; Hardy, 63–64; Hunt, 79–80; *Address to the Inhabitants*, 25; *Civil and Ecclesiastical*, 40; *Remarks*, 67–68; *Considerations*, 51–52; "Signor Pasquinello," *Crowns and Sceptres, Useless Baubles; A Political Dialogue* (London, 1792), 38.

35. Hawtrey, 37–38.

36. John Jones, *The Reason of Man: With Strictures on Paine's Rights of Man and Some Other of his Writings* (3d ed., Canterbury, 1793), 24–25; see also Bowles, 16–18; [Hervey], 13–14; *Considerations*, 24; King, *Third Letter*, 11.

37. Elliot, 56; see also Hervey, 18; Molloy, 185; "Oxford Graduate," 89–90; Thomas Hearn, *A Short View of the Rise and Progress of Freedom in Modern Europe, as Connected with the Causes which Led to the French Revolution. To which is added a Refutation of Certain Erroneous and Inflammatory Doctrines Newly Propagated ...* (London, 1793), 78–79.

38. Boothby, 141–42; see also Hawtrey, 39–42; [Smith], 104–5; "An Oxford Graduate," 89–90; "A Member of the University of Cambridge" [Graham Jepson], *Letters to Thomas Payne, in Answer to his Late Publication on the Rights of Man* (London, 1792), 33.

39. *Interests*, 50; "An Oxford Graduate," 58–59, 78; Boothby, 277; Jones, 1:25; Bowles, 17; "Tam Thrum, an Auld Weaver" [William Brown], *Looke Before Ye Loup; Or, a Healin' Sa' for the Crackit Crowns of the Country Politicians* (Edinburgh, 1793), 14; Arthur Young, *The Example of France a Warning to Britain* (2d ed., Bury St. Edmunds, 1793), 21–22.

40. Jones, 1:17; see also Elliot, 68–71; Hardy, 4–20; [Jepson], 33.

41. [Rivers], 19; Hearn, 76–77.

42. *Civil and Ecclesiastical*, 58–59; Boothby, 144.

43. *Address to the Inhabitants*, 34–35; see also Hervey, 29–32; [Smith], 62; Molloy, 20–21; Hardy, 9.

44. King, *Speech*, 6–7; [Jepson], 17.

45. J. G. A. Pocock, *The Machiavellian Moment: Florentine Political Thought and the Atlantic Republican Tradition* (Princeton, 1975), 361–71, quote on 362; Gunn, *Beyond Liberty*, 192.

46. Hunt, 19; see also Lewelyn, 68–74; *Considerations*, 51; *Remarks*, 33–34; "An Oxford Graduate," 57; *Cursory Remarks on Dr. Priestley's Letters to Mr. Burke, and Strictures on Mr. Paine's "Rights of Man"* (2 vols., London, 1791), 1:65–66.

47. Elliot, 64–66; Hawtrey, 167; [Adams], 16–17.

48. Elliot, 58–59; Hearn, 74; see also Molloy, 137–38; Hunt, 87.

49. [Jepson], 33; Bowles, 15; [Hervey], 10–11; see also [Adams], 16–17.

50. [St. John], 47; Hervey, 24–26; [Hervey], 60; see also *A Defence of the Rights of Man*, 15–16; [Francklyn], 90; "An Oxford Graduate," 69.

51. Boothby, 135; see also Lewelyn, 2:75–76; [Chalmers], 124; Hey, 111; Hawtrey, 11–15, 19–21.

52. Hunt, 90–91; "An Oxford Graduate," 76–77, 82; Bowles, 21; Hardy, 20, 75–76; Hearn, 76, 79; [Chalmers], 99; Gifford, 59, iii.

53. Hearn 79; see also "Signor Pasquinello," 49; Hardy, 75–76; King, *Speech*, 6.

54. Bowles, 22–23; see also King, *Speech*, 12; Elliot, 25; Hunt, 48; [St. John], 69; Hardy, 76; Boothby, 137; Molloy, 70; [Brown], 13–14; "An Oxford Graduate," 82; Robert Applegarth, *Rights for Man: or Analytical Strictures on the Constitution of Great Britain and Ireland* (London, 1792), 42.

55. Elliot, 25; see also Hardy, 67–68; Bowles, 16–17, 21; Brown, 77; Jones, 18, 22–24; Young, 150–51; [St. John], 67; Boothby, 278; "An Oxford Graduate," 61, 66–67, 74; *Letters to Thomas Paine; In Answer to his Late Publication on the Rights of Man; Shewing his Errors on that Subject; And Proving the Fallacies of his Principles as Applied to the Government of this Country* (London, 1791), 62.

56. "A Chaplain in the Navy," 160; [St. John], 29–30; King, *Speech* 17–18; King, *Third Letter*, 6; [Chalmers], 157–58.

57. The correspondence can be found in the Reeves Papers in the British Library, Additional Manuscripts 16,919–28. The British Library (hereafter BL) also has a bound volume shelved at 1141.d.6 that contains a full collection of association papers: "Part I. Publications Printed by Special Order of the Society for Preserving Liberty and Property Against Republicans and Levellers, at the Crown and Anchor, in the Strand. Part II. A Collection of Tracts, Printed at the Expence of that Society. To Which are Prefaced A PREFACE, and the Proceedings of that Society, Addressed to all the Loyal Associations" (London, 1793). Subsequent references to APLP tracts come from this volume.

58. *A Word or Two of Truth*, 2:iv:15–16; a similar sentiment is expressed in the tenth stanza of an untitled ballad "To the Tune of Hearts of Oak," 2:i:16; [William Jones of Nayland], *John Bull's Second Answer to his Brother Thomas*, 2:ii:8.

59. Grove Taylor, 13 Feb. 1794, Public Record Office, Home Office Papers 42/28/267–68; Alexander Morris, 15 Dec. 1792, BL, Add. MS. 16,922, fo. 112; William Wilson, 10 Dec. 1792, BL, Add. MS. 16,927, fo. 47.

60. "T. N.," 16 Dec. 1792, BL, Add. MS. 16,920, fo. 139; Joseph Moser of Westminster, 25 Jan. 1793, BL, Add. MS. 16,924, fo. 140.

61. See "Appendix to the Bishop of Llandaff's Sermon, Preached in Charlotte-Street Chapel, April 1785," 1:vii:6–7; M. de Lolme, "The Advantages Peculiar to a Monarchy and the English Constitution," 1:viii:5; "The Earl of Radnor's Charge to the Grand Jury of the County of Berks, Jan. 15, 1793," 1:ix:3–4; "The Englishman and Frenchman," 2:iii:5; "The English Freeholder's Catechism," 2:111:15.

62. John Reeves, *Thoughts on the English Government. Addressed to the Quiet Good Sense of the People of England. In a Series of Letters* (London, 1795), 10–13, 24–25, 45–46, 58–77; Reeves, *Thoughts on the English Government. Letter the Second* (London, 1799), 15–16, 46–50, 83–89, 117, 135, 163–67, 170, 179.

63. See Gunn, *Beyond Liberty*, 181–83; Clark, 263–67; Michael Weinzierl, "John Reeves and the Controversy over the Constitutional Role of Parliament in England During the French Revolution," *Parliaments, Estates and Representations* 5 (1985): 75–76.

64. *A Complete Collection of State Trials from the Earliest Period . . . and Continued from the Year 1783 to the Present Time*, ed. T. B. and T. J. Howell (33 vols., London, 1809–26), 26:529–31, 539, 541–48, 552.

65. *The Anti-Jacobin Review and Magazine, or Monthly Political and Literary Censor* (61 vols., London, 1798–1821), 1:iv.

66. Gordon J. Schochet, *Patriarchalism in Political Thought: The Authoritarian Family and Political Speculation and Attitudes, Especially in Seventeenth-Century England* (Oxford, 1975), 5–6, 268–69, 276–81; see also Robert Hole, *Pulpit Politics and Public Order in England, 1760–1832* (Cambridge, 1989), chap. 4.

Chapter 4: The Republican Tradition, the Reform Movement, and the Monarchy

1. See Caroline Robbins, *The Eighteenth-Century Commonwealthman* (Cambridge, Mass., 1959).

2. E. P. Thompson, *The Making of the English Working Class* (New York: Vintage Books, 1966), 177–83. See Malcolm Thomis and Peter Holt, *Threats of a Revolution in Britain, 1789–1848* (Hamden, Conn., 1977); Albert Goodwin, *The Friends of Liberty: The English Democratic Movement in the Age of the French Revolution* (Cambridge, Mass., 1979); see also James Walvin, "English Democratic Societies and Popular Radicalism, 1791–1800" (Ph.D. diss., University of York, 1969). Marianne Elliott, *Partners in Revolution: The United Englishmen and France* (New Haven, 1982); Roger Wells, *Insurrection: The British Experience, 1795–1803* (Gloucester, 1983); see also J. Ann Hone, *For the Cause of Truth: Radicalism in London 1796–1821* (Oxford, 1982).

3. Roger Wells, "English Society and Revolutionary Politics in the 1790s: The Case for Insurrection," I. R. Christie, "Conservatism and Stability in British Society," and Mark Philp, "The Fragmented Ideology of Reform," in *The French Revolution and British Popular Politics,* ed. Mark Philp (Cambridge, 1991), 50–77, 169–226, quotes on 53, 55; see also Christie, *Stress and Stability in Late Eighteenth-Century Britain* (Oxford, 1984). John Dinwiddy, "Conceptions of Revolution in the English Radicalism of the 1790s," in *The Transformation of Political Culture: England and Germany in the Late Eighteenth Century,* ed. Eckhart Hellmuth (Oxford, 1990), 535–60, quote on 551; Craig Calhoun, *The Question of Class Struggle: Social Foundations of Popular Radicalism During the Industrial Revolution* (Chicago, 1982), chap. 1.

4. John Neville Figgis, *The Divine Right of Kings* (Cambridge, 1922), 143.

5. Perez Zagorin, *A History of Political Thought in the English Revolution* (London, 1954), chap. 11; F. D. Dow, *Radicalism in the English Revolution, 1640–1660* (Oxford, 1985), 25–29; James Harrington, *The Commonwealth of Oceana* (1656), in *The Political Works,* ed. J. G. A. Pocock (Cambridge, 1977).

6. Zagorin, chap. 3; Dow, chap. 3.

7. J. P. Kenyon, *The Stuart Constitution, 1603–1688,* 2d ed. (Cambridge, 1986), 90–91; Peter Karsten, *Patriot Heroes in England and America: Political Symbolism and Changing Values over Three Centuries* (Madison, Wis., 1978), 15, 46–47, 110–15.

8. Karsten, 18–20, 24–27; Robbins, 41–47, 64; John Carswell, *The Porcupine: The Life of Algernon Sidney* (London, 1989), chaps. 14–18; David Ogg, *England in the Reigns of James II and William III* (Oxford, 1955), 149–55.

9. Except where otherwise noted, my account of the reform societies in this and subsequent paragraphs is drawn from Goodwin. I also consulted Edward Royal and James Walvin, *English Radicals and Reformers, 1760–1848* (Brighton, 1982), and H. T. Dickinson, *British Radicalism and the French Revolution, 1789–1815* (London, 1985).

10. See excerpts from *Thomas Hardy's Account of the Origin of the LCS* (1799) in *Selections from the Papers of the London Corresponding Society,* ed. Mary Thale (Cambridge, 1983), 6–7.

11. Mark Wilks, *The Origin and Stability of the French Revolution,* 2d ed. (Norwich,

1791), 6–7; Helio O. Alves, "The Painites: The Influence of Thomas Paine in Four Provincial Towns: 1791–1799" (Ph.D. diss., University of London, 1982), 314.

12. Quoted in trial of Horne Tooke, in *A Complete Collection of State Trials from the Earliest Period . . . and Continued from the Year 1783 to the Present Time,* ed. T. B. Howell and T. J. Howell (33 vols., London, 1809–26), 25:115 (hereafter *State Trials*).

13. Goodwin, 201; see also Alves, 63; *Committee of Secrecy of the House of Commons Respecting Seditious Practices* [hereafter *Committee of Secrecy* and year]: *First Report* (16 May 1794), and *Second Report* (7 June 1794), in *The Parliamentary History of England, from the Earliest Period to the Year 1803* [hereafter *Parl. Hist.*], ed. William Cobbett (36 vols., London, 1806–20), 31:760–61; Thomas Walker, *The Original,* ed. Blanchard Jerrold (2 vols., London. 1874), 1:86.

14. Alves, 64; British Library (hereafter BL), *Place Collection,* set 36, fos. 7–8; Trial of Walker, et al., *State Trials,* 23:1055n–1166n.

15. *Committee of Secrecy* (1794), 31:765–66.

16. Ibid., 767; Joel Barlow, *Advice to the Privileged Orders in the Several States of Europe, Resulting from the Necessity and Propriety of a General Revolution in the Principle of Government* (2 vols., London, 1792), 1:11, 13–14, 16–18, 69.

17. *Committee of Secrecy* (1794), 752–54; Christopher Wyvill, *Political Papers* (5 vols., York, 1804), 5:1–4; Edward Griffiths to SCI, 20 Dec. 1792, Public Record Office [PRO], Treasury Solicitors [TS] 11/960/3506; see also other letters from defecting members in this file and in TS 11/953/3497.

18. *Selections from LCS,* 15–16; trial of Paine, *State Trials,* 22:385–95. This issue will be further explored in chapter 6.

19. *Committee of Secrecy* (1794), 751–52, 764–65; Manchester *Herald,* 2 June 1792, quoted in Thomas Walker, *A Review of Some of the Political Events which have Occurred in Manchester during the Last Five Years: Being a Sequel to the Trial of Thomas Walker and Others, for a Conspiracy to Overthrow the Constitution and Government of this Country, and to Aid and Assist the French, being the King's Enemies* (London, 1794), 41–42.

20. Thomas Cooper, *A Reply to Mr. Burke's Invective against Mr. Cooper, and Mr. Watt, in the House of Commons, on the 30th of April, 1792* (London, 1792), 54, 16–18; Charles Pigott, quoted in Richard Lee, *Rights of Kings* (London, 1795), 13–14.

21. PRO, Home Office [HO] 42/21/467; see also *To the Inhabitants of Wakefield,* PRO, TS 11/1071/5061; addresses against the 1792 Proclamation from Hertfordshire and Northumberland, BL, *Place Collection,* set 36, fo. 10.

22. Manchester *Herald,* copy in PRO, TS 11/688/2141.

23. *Addresses, and Regulations of the LCS* (1792), 1–2, in BL, *Place Collection,* set 36, fo. 16; see also *Addresses of Delegates of Several London Societies for Political Information* (1792) and *Meeting of the Manchester SCI, 15 May 1792,* fo. 9; *The LCS to the Nation at Large, May 24, 1792; Address from the LCS to the Inhabitants of Great Britain, on the Subject of a Parliamentary Reform, August 6, 1792.*

24. LCS address, printed in *Committee of Secrecy* (1794), 768–69 (the SCI produced an equally ambiguous address at the beginning of November, cols. 754–56); convention's reply, quoted in trial of Hardy, *State Trials* 24:530.

25. Copies of letters in PRO, TS 11/965/3510 A (2). Norwich letter reprinted with ac-

count of LCS's deliberations and resulting address in *Committee of Secrecy* (1794), 795–801; see also the spy George Lynam's testimony regarding the LCS's reaction in the trial of Hardy, *State Trials,* 24:767.

26. *Committee of Secrecy* (1794), 718. Debate continued into 1793. At the end of January, the Sheffield corresponding society issued a circular letter to solicit opinions on petitioning Parliament. The LCS issued one of its stock temperate answers on 31 January but on 4 March admitted that such a petition would not produce reform; the petition's rejection, however, would awaken the people: *Selections from LCS,* 47–48; *Committee of Secrecy* (1794), 722–23. In response to a similar query made on 6 March by the Nottingham corresponding society, meanwhile, the SCI on 22 March expressed itself in favor of a convention to settle on the best methods of achieving a fair representation: PRO, TS 11/951/3495. The SCI's letter of 16 April to the United Political Societies of Norwich was more strident: the English constitution had lost its democratic character, the government was too corrupt to reform itself, and it was up to the people to form a convention "for the extensive purpose of reform": *Committee of Secrecy* (1794), 812. The idea of a convention was not new (see John Cartwright, *Take Your Choice!* [London, 1776], 91–92), but now such an assembly appeared to be following the path of the French Revolution: T. M. Parssinen, "Association, Convention and Anti-Parliament in British Radical Politics, 1771–1848," *English Historical Review* 88 (1973): 515.

27. *Minutes of the Proceedings of the First General Convention of the Delegates from the Societies of the Friends of the People throughout Scotland, 11–13 Dec. 1792,* printed in Henry W. Meikle, *Scotland and the French Revolution* (Glasgow, 1912), 251–52; Muir was referring to the case of Morton, Anderson, and Craig who would be tried in January 1793: *State Trials,* 23:7–24.

28. Trial of Muir, *State Trials,* 23:151; Thomas Holcroft, *A Narrative of Facts, Relating to a Prosecution of High Treason; Including the Address to the Jury, which the Court Refused to Hear* (London, 1795), 16–17; fragment of paper in Horne Tooke's writing in PRO, TS 11/951/3495; *Politics for the People: Or, a Salmagundy for Swine,* ed. Daniel Isaac Eaton (2 vols., London 1793–94), vol. 1, no. vii, 98; trial of Yorke, *State Trials* 25: 1006–9, 1111–12; Henry Redhead Yorke, *These are the Times that Try Men's Souls! A Letter to John Frost, a Prisoner in Newgate* (London, 1793), 19–20.

29. Charles Pigott, *Persecution. The Case of Charles Pigott: Containing in the Defence he had Prepared, and which would have been Delivered by Him on His Trial, if the Grand Jury had not Thrown Out the Bill Preferred Against Him* (London, 1793), 20–21; Parkinson in John Smith, *Assassination of the King! The Conspirators Exposed . . .* (London, 1795), 42–43; Cooper, 25–26.

30. Fable in *Politics for the People,* vol. 1, no. viii, 102–7; trial of Eaton, 24 Feb. 1794, *State Trials,* 23:1013–54; Thelwall to Alum, Feb. 1794, PRO, TS 11/960/3506; Taylor's spy reports of 31 Jan., 20, 23 Mar., 9 Apr. 1794, PRO TS 11/955/3499; trial of Hardy, *State Trials* 24:367; *Selections from LCS,* 140. Spy reports of Thelwall's speech to LCS of 2 May 1794 by Metcalf and Taylor, TS 11/955/3500 and TS 11/955/3499.

31. John Thelwall, *The Rights of Nature against the Usurpation of Establishments* (London, 1796), 6–7.

32. *Account of the Proceedings at a General Meeting of the London Corresponding Soci-*

ety . . . , St. George's Fields, . . . Mon., the 29th of June, 1795. Citizen John Gale Jones in the Chair (London, 1795), 8–9; Sheffield address quoted in Goodwin, 383.

33. *Account of the Proceedings of a Meeting of the London Corresponding Society held in a Field near Copenhagen House, Monday, October 26, 1795 . . .* (London, 1795), 9–13.

34. Charles Cestre, *John Thelwall* (London, 1906), 131; reports of Thelwall's lectures in PRO, TS 11/955/3499; excerpts from Godwin's writings are scattered throughout *Politics for the People* and Thomas Spence's *One Pennyworth of Pigs' Meat; or Lessons for the Swinish Multitude* (2 vols., London, 1793–95).

35. William Godwin, *An Enquiry Concerning the Principles of Political Justice,* ed. Isaac Kramnick (Harmondsworth, 1976, orig. pub. 1793), 410–27, 454–56.

36. PRO, HO 42/37/421–26, 429–31.

37. Jones's farewell address at the Assembly Room, Brewer Street, Golden Square, 18 Dec. 1795, PRO, HO 42/37/453.

38. See John Gale Jones, *A Sketch of a Political Tour through Rochester, Chatham, Maidstone, Gravesend &c.* (London, 1796); instructions of LCS for Jones and John Binns on their mission to Birmingham and other towns in *Committee of Secrecy of the House of Commons Relative to the Proceedings of Different Persons and Societies in Great Britain and Ireland Engaged in a Treasonable Conspiracy: Report* (15 Mar. 1799), *Parl. Hist.,* 34:632–5.

39. *A Narrative of the Proceedings at the General Meeting of the LCS, Held on Monday, July 31, 1797, in a Field near the Veterinary College, St. Pancras* (London, 1797), 20, 27–29, copy in PRO, Privy Council [PC] 1 40 A 132; *Times,* 1 Aug. 1797; case documented in PRO, PC 1 40 A 129.

40. See papers confiscated from Wych Street, PRO, PC 1 41 A 138; Richard Hodgson, *Proceedings of the General Committee of the LCS . . . on the 5th, 12th, and 19th April 1798* (Newgate, 1798).

41. Except where otherwise noted, my account of these societies in this and subsequent paragraphs is drawn from Elliot and Goodwin.

42. Handbills, information on their discovery, and Joseph White's advertisement seeking discovery of their authors, 6 Nov. 1793, and Thomas Skeleton's report of 13 Nov. on the failure to find any solid evidence and a plan to institute a night watch: PRO, HO 42/27/182, 187, 190–92.

43. Daniel Shelley to duke of Richmond, 16, 26 June 1795, PRO, HO 42/35/30–31.

44. See *At a Numerous and Respectable Meeting of the Friends of Liberty on Monday, November 6, 1797 at the Red Lyon, Type Street,* and an anonymous declaration in PRO, PC 1 41 A 138; *Address of the LCS to the Irish Nation, 30 Jan. 1798* in *Committee of Secrecy* (1799), 645.

45. For further details, see the examination of Thomas Evans, PRO, HO 42/42/353; spy reports of proceedings by Milner, PRO, PC 1 40 A 132, esp. 17 June, 2, 8, 10, 24 July 1797.

46. Information of: J. Scotson, London cotton weaver, on meetings held by John Wheelwright of LCS; anonymous LCS informer, 12 Mar.; Mr. Pillington, surgeon of Exeter, on William Clark of the LCS, 18 Mar. 1798, PRO, HO 42/42/332–35, 355–57, 349; "Copy of Papers found upon Richard Fuller, for the Seduction of the Soldiery," *Committee of Secrecy* (1799), 640.

47. Extracts from the *Union Star* and *The Press* are printed in a pamphlet catalogued *Report . . . [Seditious Societies]* (1799) at the Institute of Historical Research in London. For the *Northern Star* see BL, *Place Collection,* set 38, vol. 3, fo. 37.

48. Floud (local magistrate) to William Wickham, 12 Apr. 1798, on reliability of the informer, Robert Gray, who had once belonged to the group, PRO, PC 1 41 A 139; information of Gray and Joseph Tankard, sergeant in 11th Lt. Dragoons, 15 Apr. 1798, PC 1 42 A 140; examination of James Hughes, 17 Mar. 1798, PC 1 42 A 143.

49. *Second Report from the Commons Committee of Secrecy on the State of Ireland, and the Proceedings of Certain Disaffected Persons in Both Parts of the United Kingdom* (15 May 1801), *Parl. Hist.,* 35:1307, 1309; Thomas Spence, *The Important Trial of Thomas Spence, for a Political Pamphlet Intitled "The Restorer of Society to its Natural State,"* on May 27th 1801, 2d ed. (London, 1801), 27–28; Spence, *The Constitution of the Perfect Commonwealth* (London, 1798). H. T. Dickinson argues that Spence's plan involved administration by parish corporations and a much reduced, if any, national government: *The Political Works of Thomas Spence* (Newcastle-upon-Tyne, 1982), xii–xiii.

50. Wells, *Insurrection,* 25–26; A. W. Smith, "Irish Rebels and English Radicals 1798–1802," *Past and Present* 7 (1955): 78–85.

51. John Baxter, *Resistance to Oppression; the Constitutional Rights of Britons Asserted in a Lecture Delivered before Section 2 of the Society of the Friends of Liberty, on Monday, November 9th 1795* (London, 1795), 4, 6; Richard Dinmore, Jr., *An Exposition of the Principles of the English Jacobins; With Strictures on the Political Conduct of Charles James Fox, William Pitt, and Edmund Burke; Including Remarks on the Resignation of George Washington,* 3d ed. (Norwich, 1797), 11; Samuel Taylor Coleridge, *The Plot Discovered; Or an Address to the People against Ministerial Treason* (Bristol, 1795), 15.

Chapter 5: Religious Sanctity

1. Richard Watson, *A Charge Delivered to the Clergy of the Diocese of Llandaff in June 1798* (London, 1798), 3–4; John Gascoigne, "Anglican Latitudinarianism and Political Radicalism in the Late Eighteenth Century," *History* 71 (1986): 34–37.

2. B. Reay, "Radicalism and Religion in the English Revolution: An Introduction" in *Radical Religion in the English Revolution,* ed. B. Reay and J. F. McGregor (Oxford, 1984), 1–21; Norman Ravitch, *Sword and Mitre: Government and Episcopate in France and England in the Age of Aristocracy* (The Hague, 1966), 90, chap. 3, passim.

3. G. V. Bennett, *The Tory Crisis in Church and State, 1688–1730: The Career of Francis Atterbury, Bishop of Rochester* (Oxford, 1975).

4. H. T. Dickinson, *Walpole and the Whig Supremacy* (London, 1973), 76–77, 174–75.

5. Stephen Taylor, "Sir Robert Walpole, the Church of England, and the Quakers Tithe Bill of 1736," *Historical Journal* 28 (1985): 51–77, quotes on 75–76.

6. Nancy Uhlar Murray, "The Influence of the French Revolution on the Church of England and Its Rivals, 1789–1802" (D.Phil. diss., Oxford University, 1975), 317, 42.

7. Helen W. Randall, "The Rise and Fall of Martyrology: Sermons on Charles I," *Huntington Library Quarterly* 10 (1947): 165.

8. Samuel Horsley, *A Sermon Preached before the Lords Spiritual and Temporal . . .*

January 30, 1793: Being the Anniversary of the Martyrdom of King Charles the First (London, 1793), 3–21.

9. William Lucas, *A Sermon Preached in the Parish Church of St. Lawrence Jewry, Before the Right Honourable Lord-Mayor, and the Worshipful the Court of Aldermen on the Eighth of January, 1792* (London, 1792), 10–14.

10. George Croft, *The Test Laws Defended* (Birmingham, 1790), 18.

11. John Whitaker, *The Real Origin of Government* (London, 1795), 27, 6–15; Charles Daubeny, *A Sermon Occasioned by a Late Desperate Attempt on the Life of his Majesty* (London, 1800), 20–21; Richard Bullock, *Two Sermons Preached at St. Paul's Covent Garden ...* (London, 1793), 12–13.

12. William Hawkins, *Regal Rights Consistent with National Liberties* (Oxford, 1795), 10–15, 18–19.

13. Robert Nares, *Principles of Government Deduced from Reason, Supported by English Experience, and Opposed to French Errors* (London, 1792), 81–99, 137–43.

14. See Bullock, 4–5; Daubeny, 1–8; William Mavor, *Christian Politics: A Sermon ... for a General Fast* (Oxford, 1793), 5–11; Thomas B. Clarke, *The Benefits of Christianity Contrasted with the Pernicious Influence of Modern Philosophy ... A Sermon, on a Day of Thanksgiving for the Providential Escape of His Majesty ...* (London, 1796), 1, 14, 17; Jonathan Boucher, *A Sermon: Preached at the Assizes ...* (Carlisle, 1798), 1, 5; William Coxe, *A Sermon on the Excellence of British Jurisprudence ...* (Salisbury, 1799), 1–4.

15. Murray, 38–40, 68–70.

16. Nares, 69–70; Thomas Rennell, *The Connection of the Duties of Loving the Brotherhood, Fearing God, and Honouring the King, Considered in a Sermon* (London, 1793), 1–9.

17. John Brooke, *King George III* (London, 1972), 260–62.

18. [John Bowdler], *Reform or Ruin: Take Your Choice!* (2d ed., London, 1797), 14; see also 1–5, 8–9, 28, 32.

19. Charles E. DeCoetlogon, *God and the King: A Sermon Delivered ... Before the Rt. Hon. the Lord Mayor, ... &c. on October 25, 1790, being the Anniversary of His Majesty's Accession to the Throne* (London, 1790), 20.

20. Charles E. DeCoetlogon, *The Patriot King, and Patriot People: A Discourse, Occasioned by the General Fast, and Published for the Benefit of the French Emigrant Clergy* (London, 1797), 6, 7–10.

21. See David Hempton, *Methodism and Politics in British Society, 1750–1850* (Stanford, 1984), chaps. 2–3; W. R. Ward, *Religion and Society in England, 1790–1850* (New York, 1973), 27–40; Frederick Dreyer, "A 'Religious Society Under Heaven': John Wesley and the Identity of Methodism," *Journal of British Studies* 25 (1986): 62–83.

22. Elie Halévy, *England in 1815,* trans. E. Watkin and D. A. Barker (New York, 1949, orig. pub. 1913; first English trans. 1924), 387, 590–91.

23. Bernard Semmel, "Introduction: Elie Halévy, Methodism, and Revolution" in Halévy, *The Birth of Methodism in England,* ed. and trans. Bernard Semmel (Chicago, 1971), 1–29; E. J. Hobsbawm, "Methodism and the Threat of Revolution in Britain," *History Today* 7 (1957): 115–24.

24. E. P. Thompson, *The Making of the English Working Class* (New York, 1966, orig. pub. 1963), 42, 46, 368.

25. Bernard Semmel, *The Methodist Revolution* (New York, 1973), chaps. 1, 3-4.

26. Joseph Benson, *A Defence of the Methodists* ... (London, 1793), 58-59; see also Thomas Taylor, *Britannia's Mercies, and her Duty, Considered in Two Discourses, Delivered in the Methodist Chapel, at Halifax on Thursday, November 29, 1798, being a General Thanksgiving Day* (Leeds, 1799), 28-29; Samuel Bradburn, *Equality: A Sermon on 2 Cor. VIII. 14. Preached at the Methodist-Chapel, Broad-Mead, Bristol, February 28, 1794* (Bristol, 1794), 21-24.

27. Anthony Lincoln, *Some Political and Social Ideas of English Dissent, 1763-1800* (Cambridge, 1938), 17-18; Joseph Priestley, *Familiar Letters, Addressed to the Inhabitants of the Town of Birmingham, in Refutation of Several Charges, Advanced Against the Dissenters by the Rev, Mr. Madan* ... (Birmingham, 1790), 9-16; Robert Hall, *Christianity Consistent with a Love of Freedom: Being an Answer to a Sermon* ... *by the Rev. John Clayton* (London, 1791), 17; George Walker, *The Dissenters' Plea* ... *against the Test Laws* (Birmingham, 1790), 7-8, 14, 25.

28. Priestley, 12, 42; Samuel Heywood, *High Church Politics* ... (London, 1792), 74-78, 113-14, 171, 186.

29. Hall, 29; William Frend, *Peace and Unity Recommended to the Associated Bodies of Republicans and Anti-Republicans* (St. Ives, 1793), 26-27; Gilbert Wakefield, *The Spirit of Christianity, Compared with the Spirit of the Times in Great Britain* (London, 1794), 7-8.

30. Daniel Stuart, *Peace and Reform Against War and Corruption* (London, 1794), 14; J. E. Cookson, *The Friends of Peace: Anti-War Liberalism in England, 1793-1815* (Cambridge, 1982), 14-20, 119-20, 134-36; Roland Bartel, "The Story of Public Fast Days in England," *Anglican Theological Review* 37 (1955): 190-200.

31. "A Volunteer" [Anna Laetitia Barbauld], *Sins of Government, Sins of the Nation; Or a Discourse for the Fast, Appointed on April 19, 1793* (London, 1793), 3-5, 36.

32. William Fox, *A Discourse on National Fasts, Particularly in Reference to that of April 19, 1793, on Occasion of the War Against France* (London, 1793), 16, 3-5, 10-11; Fox, *A Discourse, Occasioned by the National Fast, February 28, 1794* (London, 1794), 7-8.

33. See Thomas Broadhurst, *Obedience to God, Rather than Men, Recommended* ... (Taunton, 1795), 20-23; John Edwards, *Inattention of Christians to Set Days of Public Fasting Justifiable* ... (Birmingham, 1796), 6-17.

34. William Winterbotham and Gilbert Wakefield were convicted of sedition for sermons they preached in 1792 and 1798, respectively: *A Complete Collection of State Trials from the Earliest Period* ... *and Continued from the Year 1783 to the Present Time,* ed. T. B. Howell and T. J. Howell (33 vols., London, 1809-26), 22:823-908, 27:679-760.

35. Susan Pedersen, "Hannah More Meets Simple Simon: Tracts, Chapbooks, and Popular Culture in Late Eighteenth-Century England," *Journal of British Studies* 25 (1986): 84-113; Ward, chap. 2. For the spiritual revival of the 1690s see Bennett, 20-22.

36. F. C. Mather, *High Church Prophet: Bishop Samuel Horsley (1733-1806) and the Caroline Tradition in the Later Georgian Church* (Oxford, 1992), 25-55, 74-76, 228-49, quotes on 228, 309.

37. J. C. D. Clark, *The Language of Liberty, 1660-1832: Political Discourse and Social Dynamics in the Anglo-American World* (Cambridge, 1994), 99; Clark, *English Society, 1688-1832:*

Ideology, Social Structure and Political Practice During the Ancien Regime (Cambridge, 1985), 234.

Chapter 6: Legal Sanctity

1. Douglas Hay, "Property, Authority and the Criminal Law," in *Albion's Fatal Tree,* ed. Hay (London, 1975), 28.

2. Howard Nenner, *By Colour of Law: Legal Culture and Constitutional Politics in England, 1660–1689* (Chicago, 1977), intro. and chap. 1.

3. I have based my account of the history of seditious libel prosecutions on Philip Hamburger, "The Development of the Law of Seditious Libel and the Control of the Press," *Stanford Law Review* 37 (1985): 661–765; Thomas Andrew Green, *Verdict According to Conscience: Perspective on the English Criminal Trial Jury, 1200–1800* (Chicago, 1985), chap. 8; and William Holdsworth, *A History of the English Law* (16 vols., London, 1937), 8:333–46.

4. John Barrell, "Imaginary Treason, Imaginary Law: The State Trials of 1794," in *The Birth of Pandora and the Division of Knowledge* (Philadelphia, 1992), 119–43, quote on 142.

5. Clive Emsley, "An Aspect of Pitt's 'Terror': Prosecutions for Sedition During the 1790s," *Social History* 6 (1981): 173–74.

6. On the use of special juries see F. K. Prochaska, "English State Trials in the 1790s: A Case Study," *Journal of British Studies* 13 (1973): 68–69.

7. *A Complete Collection of State Trials from the Earliest Period . . . and Continued from the Year 1783 to the Present Time* [hereafter *State Trials*], ed. T. B. Howell and T. J. Howell (33 vols., London, 1809–26), 22:477n., 480–81.

8. Ibid., 507–8, 521–22.

9. Ibid., 22:823–27, 869–76, quotes on 825, 846, 870; for the jury, see Emsley, 170.

10. *State Trials,* 23:618–19.

11. Ibid., 841–42, 844–46, 866.

12. Perceval to Scott, 2 March 1794, Public Record Office [PRO], Treasury Solicitors' Papers [TS], 11/959/3505 iii; Alan Wharam, *The Treason Trials, 1794* (Leicester, 1992), 132; L. J. Lincoln and R. McEwan, eds., *Lord Eldon's Anecdote Book* (London, 1960), 55.

13. Albert Goodwin, *The Friends of Liberty: The English Democratic Movement in the Age of the French Revolution* (Cambridge, Mass., 1979), 367.

14. *State Trials,* 23:1171, 1175–76.

15. Ibid., 1332–37, 1345.

16. Ibid., 1394–1403; 24:963.

17. *Morning Chronicle,* 26 Sept. 1794; Trial of Robert Thomas Crossfield, 12 May 1796, *State Trials,* 26:1–224; PRO, Privy Council Papers [PC], 1 22A 37; John Smith, *Assassination of the King!* (London, 1795).

18. *State Trials,* 24:201, 1190, 952.

19. Ibid., 878, 906; the *Place Collection* in the British Library, set 36, fo. 235, contains pertinent selections from the *Morning Chronicle* of Nov. 1794 regarding the treason charge; see also William Godwin's anonymous "Cursory Strictures on the Charge Delivered by Lord Chief Justice Eyre to the Grand Jury," 21 Oct. 1794, fo. 181.

20. *House of Commons Sessional Papers of the Eighteenth Century,* ed. Sheila Lambert (147 vols., Wilmington, Del., 1975), 97:35.

21. Clive Emsley, "Repression, 'Terror' and the Rule of Law in England During the Decade of the French Revolution," *English Historical Review* 100 (1985): 801–25.

22. *The Parliamentary History of England, from the Earliest Period to the Year 1803,* ed. William Cobbett (36 vols., London, 1806–20), 30:582; bill also cited in Justice Buller's Charge to the Grand Jury, 11 April 1798 in trial of James Coigley et al., 21–22 May 1798, *State Trials,* 26:1196–97; see also trials of William Jackson and of the Defenders, 25:783–890, 26:225–462.

23. *State Trials,* 27:331–34, 381; 26:721–826.

24. Emsley, "An Aspect of Pitt's 'Terror,'" 160–66.

25. *State Trials,* 25:1005, 1014; 22:1035, 1033.

26. PRO, TS 11/927/3275; *Sun,* 22 and 26 May 1796.

27. *State Trials,* 22:385–95.

28. Ibid., 23:117–24, 138–46, 173–74, 205–14, 229–30.

29. Daniel Holt, *A Vindication of the Conduct and Principles of the Printer of the Newark Herald* . . . (Newark, 1794), 14–15; *State Trials,* 22:1189–1238.

30. Brief for the prosecution of William Holland, Feb. 1793, PRO, TS 11/175/702.

31. D. Hamilton to Home office, 14 Dec. 1792, PRO, HO 42/23 384B; Trial of Walker et al., 2 Apr. 1794, *State Trials* 23:1055–1166; A. Herbert to John Bone, 28 Apr., 4 June 1797, PRO, PC 1 41 A 138.

32. Eaton's trials took place on 3 June and 10 July 1793; see *State Trials,* 22:765, 780–84, 822.

33. Ibid., 26:12; 27:676.

34. Ibid., 23:131–32, 1152–53, 1148.

35. Trial of Yorke, 23 July 1795, ibid., 25:1149.

36. Ibid., 23:12, 1366.

37. Ibid., 25:258; 26:326.

38. Trial of Hardy, ibid., 24:1127; Trial of Watt, ibid., 23:1329; see also Trial of Rowan, ibid., 22:1069, 1083; Trial of Muir, ibid., 23:208–9.

39. Trial of Winterbotham, ibid., 22:434, 826.

40. J. C. D. Clark, *English Society, 1688–1832: Ideology, Social Structure and Political Practice During the Ancien Régime* (Cambridge, 1985), 348, chaps. 6–7.

41. *State Trials,* 23:231.

Chapter 7: Court Culture, Royalist Ritual, and Popular Loyalism

1. Linda Colley, "The Apotheosis of George III: Loyalty, Royalty and the British Nation," *Past and Present* 102 (1984): 94–129. I consulted newspapers that had relatively high circulations; these provide a representative display of the main political interests in England during the 1790s. On the government's side, the *Times* supported the Pitt administration. The *Sun* and *True Briton* were less the champions of Pitt and his ministers than of government in general. These newspapers were established in October 1792, at the instigation of George Rose, secretary of the Treasury, to counteract reformist pro-

paganda. On the opposition's side, the *Morning Chronicle* was the main supporter of Charles James Fox and his party. Another whiggish paper, the *Morning Post,* was edited by Daniel Stuart who, although an associate of the Whig Friends of the People, supported principles closer to those of the more radical corresponding societies. Before Stuart gained control of the paper in 1793, it was under the Prince of Wales's influence. I also examined surviving issues of the *Courier* and the *Telegraph,* two reformist papers. See Karl Schweizer and Richard Klein, "The French Revolution and the Developments in the London Daily Press to 1793," *Publishing History* 18 (1985): 85-97; Lucyle Werkmeister, *The London Daily Press, 1772-1792* (Lincoln, Neb., 1963); Arthur Aspinall, *Politics and the Press* (London, 1949); Martin J. Smith, "English Radical Newspapers in the French Revolutionary Era, 1790-1803" (Ph.D. diss., University of London, 1979); Wilfred Hindle, *The Morning Post, 1772-1937* (London, 1937); Ivon Asquith, "James Perry and the Morning Chronicle, 1790-1821" (Ph.D. diss., University of London, 1973).

2. Malcolm Smuts, *Court Culture and the Origins of a Royalist Tradition in England* (Philadelphia, 1987), 15-37.

3. Gordon J. Schochet, *Patriarchalism in Political Thought: The Authoritarian Family and Political Speculation and Attitudes, Especially in Seventeenth-Century England* (Oxford, 1975), 18-19, 86-88, passim.

4. Linda Levy Peck, *The Mental World of the Jacobean Court* (Cambridge, 1991), 6-7.

5. Kevin Sharpe, *The Personal Rule of Charles I* (New Haven, 1992), 209-16; Simon Schama, "The Domestication of Majesty: Royal Family Portraiture, 1500-1850," *Journal of Interdisciplinary History* 12 (1986): 169-74.

6. Sharpe, 209-16.

7. Barry Coward, *Cromwell* (London, 1991), 99-101; Roy Sherwood, *The Court of Oliver Cromwell* (London, 1977), 155.

8. See K. H. D. Haley, *Charles II,* Historical Association Pamphlets, no. 63 (London, 1966); Rachel Weil, "Sometimes a Scepter Is Only a Scepter: Pornography and Politics in Restoration England," in *The Invention of Pornography: Obscenity and the Origins of Modernity,* ed. Lynn Hunt (New York, 1993), 124-53.

9. Stephen B. Baxter, *William III* (London, 1966), 248-49, 278-80, 307-8.

10. Marc Bloch, *The Royal Touch: Monarchy and Miracles in France and England,* trans. J. E. Anderson (New York, 1989), bk. 1, chap. 1; bk. 2, chap. 6; R. O. Bucholz, "'Nothing but Ceremony': Queen Anne and the Limitations of Royal Ritual," *Journal of British Studies* 30 (1991): 293-99; see also *The Augustan Court: Queen Anne and the Decline of Court Culture* (Stanford, 1993).

11. Edward Gregg, *Queen Anne* (London, 1980), 51-56, 72-73, 99-100, 120, 137-38, 154-55; Geoffrey Holmes, *British Politics in the Age of Anne,* rev. ed. (London, 1987), 194-98, 346; Bucholz, "Nothing but Ceremony," 299-314.

12. Ragnhild Hatton, *George I, Elector and King* (Cambridge, Mass., 1978), 132-34, 170-73, 292; John Beattie, *The English Court in the Reign of George I* (Cambridge, 1967), 2-3, 11-15; Linda Colley, *Britons: Forging the Nation, 1707-1837* (New Haven, 1992), 198-200.

13. Hatton, 48-68, 99-100, 128-40, 158-63; J. H. Plumb, *The First Four Georges* (New York, 1957), 39-41; Joyce Marlow, *The Life and Times of George I* (London, 1973), 69-70.

14. Beattie, 14, 55; Hatton, 132; Jeremy Black, "George II Reconsidered," *Mitteilungen des Österreichischen Staatsarchivs* 35 (1982): 37–39.

15. John Brooke, *King George III* (London, 1972), chap. 7; Morris Marples, *Six Royal Sisters, Daughters of George III* (London, 1969).

16. Marples, 35, 41–42, 74; Ingram Cobbin, *Georgiana, or Anecdotes of George III* (London, 1820), 7–8, 26, 42; *Sun*, 30 Apr. 1795.

17. *Times*, 7 and 29 June 1792; see clippings from *Morning Chronicle* on debate regarding voluntary subscriptions in British Library [BL], *Place Collection*, set 36, fos. 100–109.

18. *Times*, 18 Jan., 6 June, 19 Jan., 19 Nov. 1791; *Morning Post*, 6 Sept. 1791.

19. *Times*, 5 June 1793; *Sun*, 4 June 1794; *Morning Chronicle*, 17 Jan. 1792, 5 June 1793, 5 June 1794.

20. *Morning Post* and *Morning Chronicle*, 20 Jan. 1795; *Times* and *True Briton*, 6 June 1797.

21. *Times*, 17 Apr. 1795.

22. *Morning Chronicle*, 9 Apr. 1795, 19 Feb. 1796 (in BL, *Place Collection*, set 37, fos. 202–3); *Morning Post*, 16 March 1795; see also 21 Jan. and 17 Apr. for further complaints about royal expenditure.

23. *Times*, 15, 18 Apr. 1797; *Morning Chronicle*, 17 Apr. 1797; *Morning Post*, 20, 26, 29 Apr. 1797. Naval mutinies took place at Spithead and the Nore in April and May 1797.

24. See the "Alphabetical List of the Addresses Presented to his Majesty, with the Dates of their Presentation, and the Passage in which the Addressers Deviated from the Accustomed Forms of Congratulation, to Give their Opinion on the Measures Pending in Parliament, or on the General State of Public Affairs" in *A History of Two Acts . . . ; Including the Proceedings of the British Parliament, and of the Various Popular Meetings, Societies and Clubs, etc.* (London, 1796), 791–822, quote on 797.

25. *Times, True Briton,* and *Morning Chronicle,* 20 Dec. 1797; Hindle, 71; J. E. Cookson, *The Friends of Peace: Anti-War Liberalism in England, 1793–1815* (Cambridge, 1982), 100, 137, 152.

26. *Times*, 5 June 1799, 28 July, 4, 6, 8, 9 Aug. 1792, 19 Jan. 1796; *Sun*, 5 June 1799, 19 Jan. 1796.

27. Marples, 46, 75–77, 79–81; *Times*, 2 July 1794, 25 Sept. 1798; *Morning Chronicle*, 28 Aug. 1794, 15 Aug. 1796.

28. George, Prince of Wales, to George III, 9 Mar. 1795 and undated, *The Later Correspondence of George III*, ed. Arthur Aspinall (5 vols., London, 1962–70), 2:312–16; *Sun*, 17 May 1796; Marples, 46, 77; see also *Times*, 15 Aug., 13 Nov. 1794, 15 Aug. 1798; *True Briton*, 1 July 1795.

29. C. B. Jewson, *The Jacobin City: A Portrait of Norwich in Its Reaction to the French Revolution, 1788–1802* (Glasgow, 1975), 78–80, 85–87; *Telegraph*, 13 Aug. 1795.

30. *Sun*, 21 Jan. 1795; *Telegraph*, 2 Aug. 1795; *Times*, 30 Nov. 1795; *True Briton*, 7 July 1795.

31. Letter from John Carter, Mayor of Portsmouth, 17 June 1794, Public Record Office [PRO], Home Office [HO] 42/31/190; *Times*, 28 June 1794.

32. *True Briton*, 16 Oct. 1797; see also coverage of story in the *Times*, 17, 21, 24, 30, 31 Oct., 2, 3, Nov. 1797.

33. Jewson, 41, 48–49, 91–92; James Thompson, *The History of Leicester in the Eighteenth Century* (Leicester, 1871), 213–14; *Times,* 25 Sept. 1798 (celebration of coronation anniversary).

34. Quoted in John Alfred Langford, *A Century of Birmingham Life* (2 vols., Birmingham, 1868), 2:35; for accounts of other provincial celebrations see *Sun,* 4, 7 June, 16 Aug. 1793, 5 June 1794, 5 June 1799.

35. Langford, 42–43, 82, 88; Jewson, 41, 48–49, 67, 91–92, 95; Brown, 243, 246; *The History of the City of Norwich* (Norwich, 1869), 299; J. A. Picton, *Memorials of Liverpool* (2 vols., London, 1873), 1:270–71; James Wheeler, *Manchester: Its Political, Social and Commercial History, Ancient and Modern* (Manchester, 1836), 94; *Sun,* 8 June 1795; see also 26 Oct. 1794.

36. Woodward, *The Birth of a Princess,* 29 Jan. 1796, *Catalogue of Political and Personal Satires Preserved in the Department of Prints and Drawings in the British Museum,* ed. M. D. George (vols. 5–11, London, 1935–54), 8781.

37. John Money, *Experience and Identity in Birmingham and the West Midlands, 1760–1800* (Manchester, 1977), 261–62; petition printed in Birmingham *Gazette,* quoted by Langford, 2:14–15.

38. Langford 2:42; *Times* and *Morning Chronicle,* 20 Jan. 1794; see also impact of George III's patronage of a newly developed pure English wool fabric, *Morning Chronicle,* 6 June 1799; *Sun,* 20 Jan. 1798.

39. G. M. Ditchfield, "The Priestley Riots in Historical Perspective," and David L. Wykes, "'The Spirit of Persecutors Exemplified': The Priestley Riots and the Victims of the Church and King Mobs," *Transactions of the Unitarian Historical Society* 20 (1991): 3–16, 17–39; Martin H. Smith, "Conflict and Society in Late Eighteenth-Century Birmingham" (D.Phil. diss., Cambridge University, 1978), 2–41; Money, 259–67; R. B. Rose, "The Priestley Riots of 1791," *Past and Present* 18 (1960): 68–85.

40. Oliver DeLancy to Sir William Fawcett, 21 July 1791, George III to Henry Dundas, 16 July 1791, *Later Correspondence of George III,* 1:554, 551; *Times,* 18–19 July 1791.

41. Published in the weekly *London Gazette* for five consecutive editions from 22 May to 21 June.

42. See selection of opposition newspapers of Oct. 1792 in BL, *Place Collection,* set 36, fos. 10–12; Joseph Barratt, "Brief History," 23 Sept. 1861 in Alexander Gordon, *Historical Account of Dob Lane Chapel, Failsworth* (Manchester, 1904), 48; William Patterson to John Reeves, 27 Dec. 1792, BL, Add. MS. 16,923, fo. 67.

43. Alan Booth, "Reform, Repression and Revolution: Radicalism and Loyalism in the North-West of England, 1789–1803" (Ph.D. diss., University of Lancaster, 1979), 111; R. B. Rose, "The Jacobins of Liverpool, 1789–1793," *Liverpool Bulletin* 9 (1960–61): 35–37, 46–48; Thomas Harpley to John Reeves, 25 Dec. 1792, BL, Add. MS. 16,923, fo. 85; Austin V. Mitchell, "The Association Movement of 1792–1793," *Historical Journal* 4 (1961): 61–64.

44. Henry Bateson, *A Centenary History of Oldham* (Oldham, 1949), 96; John Foster, *Class Struggle and the Industrial Revolution* (1974), 35; William Brimlow, *Political and Parliamentary History of Bolton* (2 vols., Bolton, 1882), 1:9–10; Langford, 2:29; Francis Hill, *Georgian Lincoln* (Cambridge, 1966), 166; William Gardiner, *Music and Friends; or, Pleasant Recollections of a Dilettante* (2 vols., Leicester, 1838), 2:221; Money, 233; Samuel Bam-

ford, *Autobiography*, ed. W. H. Chaloner (2 vols., London, 1967), 1:44; J. Hall of Grimsby to John Reeves, 5 Jan. 1793, BL, Add. MS. 16,928, fo. 7.

45. Alan Booth, "Popular Loyalism and Public Violence in the North-West of England, 1790–1800," *Social History* 8 (1983): 298–99.

46. *Sun,* 18 Jan. 1793; T. Horner of Frome to John Reeves, 15 Dec. 1792, BL, Add. MS. 16,922, fo. 121; W. Patterson of Wakefield to John Reeves, 27 Dec. 1792, BL, Add. MS. 16,923, fo. 67.

47. PRO, Treasury Solicitors' Papers [TS] 11/954/3498.

48. R. Savage, 4 July 1794, PRO, HO 42/32/224; "A Friend to the Constitution" to John Reeves, 26 Nov. 1792, BL, Add. MS. 16,919, fo. 45.

49. "A Lover of My Country," 14 May 1794, PRO, HO 42/30/88–89; "A Royalist," 9 Aug. 1794, HO 42/33/1; Information collected against Hardy, PRO, TS 11/966/3510 B (4); Declaration by H. Eyles, Master of Freemasons Lodge, New Brentford, and Brethren, 2 Jan. 1795, HO 42/34/2–3.

50. Thomas Walker, *A Review of Some of the Political Events which have Occurred in Manchester during the Last Five Years* . . . (London, 1794), 39–40; W. Roberts of Liverpool, 11 June 1794, PRO, HO 42/31/118–19.

51. *Times,* 26 Oct., 29 Nov. 1792.

52. Tate Wilkinson, *The Wandering Patentee; Or, a History of the Yorkshire Theatres, from 1770 to the Present Time* (4 vols., York, 1795), 4:109–10, 117–18, 210–12.

53. Police shorthand writer's report of Panton Street debates, 3 Nov. 1795, PRO, HO 42/37/411.

54. *Morning Chronicle,* 14, 18 Apr. 1794; *Times* and *Sun,* 19 Apr. 1794.

55. *Times,* 18 Oct. 1797.

56. John Binns, *Recollections* (Philadelphia, 1854), 42–43.

57. *True Briton,* 26–27 Aug. 1796; "To the Inhabitants of Great Yarmouth," PRO, HO 42/39/93–94; J. L. Hammond and Barbara Hammond, *The Village Labourer, 1760–1832* (London, 1911), 121; John Bohstedt, *Riots and Community Politics in England and Wales, 1790–1810* (Cambridge, Mass., 1983), 181–89; Hill, 196.

58. Malcolm Thomis, *Politics and Society in Nottingham, 1785–1835* (Oxford, 1969), 180–81; Cornelius Brown, *The Annals of Newark-upon-Trent* (Newark, 1879), 246; W. H. G. Armytage, "The Editorial Experience of Joseph Gales, 1786–1794," *North Carolina Historical Review* 28 (1951): 351–52.

59. Gayle Trusdel Pendleton, "Radicalism and the English 'Reign of Terror': The Evidence of the Pamphlet Literature," in *The Consortium on Revolutionary Europe, 1750–1850: Proceedings 1979,* ed. Owen Connelly (Athens, Ga., 1980), 195–205, quote on 198.

Chapter 8: The Public Image of George III

1. Linda Colley, "The Apotheosis of George III: Loyalty, Royalty, and the British Nation, 1760–1821," *Past and Present* 102 (1984): 94–129; Colley, "Whose Nation? Class and National Consciousness in Britain, 1750–1830," *Past and Present* 113 (1986): 97–117; Colley, *Britons: Forging the Nation, 1707–1837* (New Haven, 1992), chap. 5; James J. Sack, *From Ja-*

cobite to Conservative: Reaction and Orthodoxy in Britain, c. 1760–1832 (Cambridge, 1993), chap. 5, quotes on 131, 135.

2. Vincent Carretta, *George III and the Satirists from Hogarth to Byron* (Athens, Ga., 1990), 297–312 and passim.

3. Richard Newton, *Their New Majesties,* 12 Sept. 1797, *Catalogue of Political and Personal Satires Preserved in the Department of Prints and Drawings in the British Museum* [*BMC*], ed. M. D. George (vols. 5–11, London 1935–54), 9032.

4. James Gillray, *Fatigues of the Campaign in Flanders,* 20 May 1793, *BMC* 8327; Isaac Cruikshank, *Preparing for Action or an English Man of War Engaging Two Dutch Doggers,* 9 June 1793, *BMC* 8329; Cruikshank, *The Wet Party or the Bogs of Flanders,* 7 December 1793, *BMC* 8351.

5. Henry James Pye in *Sun,* 2 Jan. 1795; see also 22, 24 Oct. 1794, 6–8 Apr. 1795; *Times,* 28 July, 10 Dec. 1794, 4 Mar., 6 Apr. 1795; *Morning Post,* 6, 13 Apr. 1795; *Morning Chronicle,* 6, 11 Apr. 1795.

6. *Sun, Times, Morning Chronicle,* 9 Apr. 1795.

7. For press coverage of the scandal, see *A Review . . . of the Astonishing Misrepresentations and Gross Contradictions . . . Circulated in all the Daily Presses Relative to a Late Domestic Fracas, in a Family of the First Rank . . .* (London, 1796) and *Observations on the Various Accounts of a Late Family Difference in High Life, Now Happily Adjusted . . .* (London, 1796). For details of the prince's marriage see Christopher Hibbert, *George IV, Prince of Wales, 1762–1811* (London, 1972), chaps. 13–14.

8. *Sun,* 12 Feb. 1796; see also 14 Jan.; *True Briton,* 8 Feb. 1796; *Morning Chronicle,* 14, 19 Jan., 13 Feb. 1796; *Morning Post,* 22 Jan., 6 June 1799.

9. *Times,* 19 May 1797; *Morning Post,* 3 June 1797; *True Briton,* 19 May, 5 June 1797.

10. *True Briton,* 22 Aug. 1793.

11. *Sun,* 23 Jan. 1795, 1 Feb. 1796.

12. *Times,* 20 Jan. 1794.

13. Thomas Paine, *A Letter to Mr. Secretary Dundas in Answer to his Speech on the Late Proclamation* (London, 1792), 7–8, 14, 17.

14. Charles Pigott, *The Jockey Club, or A Sketch of the Manners of the Age* (3 vols., London, 1792), 3:13–16, 1:13–14.

15. *The Pernicious Principles of Thomas Paine Exposed in an Address to Labourers and Mechanics by a Gentleman,* 6th ed. (London, 1800?), 5–7; also published as *The Principles of Modern Reformers Exposed* (Sheffield, 1792), copy in Public Record Office [PRO], Home Office Papers [HO] 42/23/632.

16. Carretta, 11–40.

17. *BMC* 8080.

18. 6 June 1791, *BMC* 7873.

19. Carretta, 26, 28–29.

20. Lynn Hunt, *The Family Romance of the French Revolution* (Berkeley, 1992); Hunt, ed., *Eroticism and the Body Politic* (Baltimore, 1991).

21. Ida Macalpine and Richard Hunter, *George III and the Mad Business* (New York, 1969), 75–76.

22. See Jeffrey Merrick, *The Desacralization of the French Monarchy in the Eighteenth*

Century (Baton Rouge, La., 1990); Dale Van Kley, *The Damiens Affair and the Unraveling of the Ancien Régime* (Princeton, 1984).

23. 5 Nov. 1793, *BMC* 8346; Ronald Paulson, "Gillray: the Ambivalence of the Political Cartoonist," in *Satire in the Eighteenth Century,* ed. J. D. Browning (New York, 1983), 164; Colley, *Britons,* 210.

24. *BMC* 8515.

25. *A Complete Collection of State Trials from the Earliest Period . . . and Continued from the Year 1783 to the Present Time* [hereafter *State Trials*], ed. T. B. Howell and T. J. Howell (33 vols., London, 1809–26), 24:682–83; see Privy Council's examination of the printers, 9 Oct. 1794, PRO, PC 1 22 A 37.

26. David Bindman, *The Shadow of the Guillotine: Britain and the French Revolution* (London, 1989), 58.

27. "The Pop-Gun Plot Found Out, or Ministers in the Dumps," broadside (n.d.), British Library [BL] 806.k.16 (fo. 120).

28. John Binns, *Recollections* (Philadelphia, 1854), 59.

29. E. P. Thompson, "The Moral Economy of the English Crowd in the Eighteenth Century," *Past and Present* 50 (1971), 76–136; William Eyre of Sheffield to Henry Dundas, 31 July 1791, PRO, HO 42/19/354–55; William Wilson to John Reeves, 10 Dec. 1792, BL, Add. MS. 16,927, fo. 47.

30. Information from William Brooke, 21 Nov. 1792, PRO, HO 42/22/85–86.

31. See, for example, Joseph Arthur of Macclesfield, 22 Dec. 1792: Arthur at various times admired Paine, declared himself a republican, and said England did not need a king, PRO, Treasury Solicitors' Papers [TS] 11/954/3498; Daniel Crichton, convicted 8 Jan. 1793 for damning the king during a visit to the Tower of London, PRO, TS 11/1024/4227; Anthony Saunderson, vagrant, jailed 12 Dec. 1792 for damning the king and wishing the army would turn: he had been provoked by the company's singing "God Save the King" at a Halifax public house, PRO, TS 11/1071/5062.

32. Information against Stephen Murphy, 25 Jan. 1794, PRO, TS 11/1071/5059; Information against Ebenezer Hollich sent 1 July 1794, TS 11/957/3502–the husbandman was afraid to report his master until he was approached by an attorney who had been told of Hollich's use of seditious expressions, PRO, HO 42/32/415–17.

33. See also the case of William Francis, victualler of Essex, who damned the king and spoke favorably of joining the French. He had been drinking heavily after news of the bankruptcy of a man in his debt. His neighbors sent in a petition attesting to his good character: indicted 31 July 1794, PRO, TS 11/924/3238. Murphy, the London baker, also received an avowal of his loyalty from his former master.

34. Information against William Powis, 6 Oct. 1793, PRO, TS 11/897/3055.

35. See John Gifford, *An Account of the Attack Made upon the King* (London, 1809); and newspaper excerpts in *The History of Two Acts . . .* (London, 1796), 4–7.

36. *The Autobiography of Francis Place,* ed. Mary Thale (Cambridge, 1972), 145–47.

37. Binns, 54–58.

38. *Truth and Treason! or A Narrative of the Royal Procession to the House of Peers, October the 29th, 1795. To which is Added, an Account of the Martial Procession to Covent-Garden Theatre, on the Evening of the 30th* (London, 1795), 4–8.

39. Information against Louis Boyer, 29 Oct. 1795, TS 11/1046/4536; see also information against George Eliot of Birmingham, 31 Oct. 1795, TS 11/1045/4505, and William Unwin of Newark, 31 Oct. 1795, TS 11/1045/4504.

40. *The Senator; or Clarendon's Parliamentary Chronicle,* first series (28 vols., London, 1791–1801), 13:306–7, 363; Richard Lee, *The Happy Reign of George the Last* (n.d.); Lee, *The Death of Despotism and the Doom of Tyrants* (London, 1796); Lee, ed., *Rights of Kings* (London, 1795); *The LCS to the British People,* 18 Nov. 1795, printed in *History of Two Acts,* 350–51.

41. Binns, 63; see accounts in the *Morning Chronicle* and *London Gazette* of 6 Feb. 1796 in BL, *Place Collection,* set 37, fos. 200–201; *Times,* 6 Feb. 1796.

42. BL, 1872.a.1, fo. 50; copy also in *Place Collection,* set 38, vol. 3, fo. 61.

Conclusion

1. Eric Hobsbawm, "Introduction: Inventing Traditions," and David Cannadine, "The Context, Performance and Meaning of Ritual: The British Monarchy and the 'Invention of Tradition,' c. 1820–1977," in *The Invention of Tradition,* ed. Eric Hobsbawm and Terrance Ranger (Cambridge, 1983), 1 (Hobsbawm), 139–40 (Cannadine).

2. David Cannadine, "The Last Hanoverian Sovereign? The Victorian Monarchy in Historical Perspective, 1688–1988," in *The First Modern Society: Essays in English History in Honour of Lawrence Stone,* ed. A. L. Beier, David Cannadine, and James M. Rosenheim (Cambridge, 1989), 162.

3. *Invention of Tradition,* 1–9, 160–62.

4. Quoted in John Brooke, *King George III* (New York, 1972), 314.

5. James Gillray, *Sin, Death, and the Devil. Vide Milton,* 9 June 1792, *Catalogue of Political and Personal Satires Preserved in the Department of Prints and Drawings in the British Museum,* ed. M. D. George (vols. 5–11, London, 1935–54), 8105.

6. Jeremy Black, *Culloden and the 45* (New York, 1990), 188; Gerald Newman, *The Rise of Nationalism: A Cultural History, 1740–1830* (New York, 1987), chap. 1; Gunther Lottes, "Radicalism, Revolution and Political Culture: An Anglo-French Comparison," in *The French Revolution and British Popular Politics,* ed. Mark Philp (Cambridge, 1991), 78–98; Linda Colley, "Britishness and Otherness: An Argument," *Journal of British Studies* 31 (1992): 309–29; Colley, *Britons: Forging the Nation, 1707–1837* (New Haven, 1992).

7. J. C. D. Clark, *Revolution and Rebellion: State and Society in England in the Seventeenth and Eighteenth Century* (Cambridge, 1986), chap. 5; Jeremy Black, *British Foreign Policy in an Age of Revolutions, 1783–1793* (Cambridge, 1994), 513; see also H. M. Scott, ed., *Enlightened Absolutism: Reform and Reformers in Later Eighteenth-Century Europe* (Basingstoke, Eng., 1990); John Miller, ed., *Absolutism in Seventeenth-Century Europe* (New York, 1990); Nicholas Henshall, *The Myth of Absolutism: Change and Continuity in Early Modern European Monarchy* (London, 1992).

8. Ingram Cobbin, *Georgiana, or, Anecdotes of George the Third* (London, 1820), 11–12.

Index